The Jesuit Missions Peru, 1570–1610

The rulers of the overseas empires summoned the Society of Jesus to evangelize their new subjects in the 'New World' which Spain and Portugal shared; this book is about how two different missions, in China and Peru, evolved in the early modern world. From a European perspective, this book is about the way Christianity expanded in the early modern period, craving universalism.

In China, Matteo Ricci was so impressed by the influence that the scholar-officials were able to exert on the Ming Emperor himself that he likened them to the philosopher-kings of Plato's *Republic*. The Jesuits in China were in the hands of the scholar-officials, with the Emperor at the apex, who had the power to decide whether they could stay or not. Meanwhile, in Peru, the Society of Jesus was required to impose Tridentine Catholicism by Philip II, independently of Rome, a task that entailed compliance with the colonial authorities' demands.

This book explores how two leading Jesuits, Matteo Ricci (1552–1610) in China and José de Acosta (1540–1600) in Peru, envisioned mission projects and reflected them on the catechisms they both composed, with a remarkable power of endurance. It offers a reflection on how the Jesuits conceived and assessed these mission spaces, in which their keen political acumen and a certain taste for power unfolded, playing key roles in envisioning new doctrinal directions and reflecting them in their doctrinal texts.

Ana Carolina Hosne is a Marie Curie Fellow of the Gerda Henkel Foundation at Heidelberg University.

Routledge studies in the modern history of Asia

The Jesuit Missions to China and Peru, 1570–1610

Expectations and appraisals of expansionism

Ana Carolina Hosne

Routledge
Taylor & Francis Group

LONDON AND NEW YORK

First published 2013
by Routledge
2 Park Square, Milton Park, Abingdon, Oxfordshire, OX14 4RN
Simultaneously published in the USA and Canada
by Routledge
711 Third Avenue, New York, NY 10017

Routledge is an imprint of the Taylor and Francis Group, an informa business

First issued in paperback 2015

British Library Cataloguing in Publication Data
A catalogue record for this book is available from the British Library

Library of Congress Cataloging in Publication Data
Hosne, Ana Carolina.
The Jesuit missions to China and Peru, 1570-1610 : expectations and appraisals of expansionism / Ana Carolina Hosne.
pages cm -- (Routledge studies in the modern history of Asia ; 85)
Includes bibliographical references and index.
1. Jesuits--Missions--China--History. 2. Jesuits--Missions--Peru--History. 3. Ricci, Matteo, 1552-1610. 4. Acosta, José de, 1540-1600. I. Title.
BV2750.H67 2013
266'.251--dc23
2012051114

ISBN 978-0-415-52982-2 (hbk)
ISBN 978-1-138-18179-3 (pbk)
ISBN 978-0-203-76065-9 (ebk)
Typeset in Times New Roman
by Taylor & Francis Books

Contents

Figures

China

Peru

Acknowledgments

The successful completion of this book would not have been possible without the help of many people and institutions along the winding road towards it, and I take this opportunity to thank them all. The work on this project began as a doctoral dissertation and the early steps were guided in countless constructive ways by my advisor Ana Maria Presta at the Universidad de Buenos Aires, who has offered invaluable assistance, support and guidance ever since I was a graduate student. Special thanks go to the National Council for Scientific and Technological Research in Argentina (CONICET) for its financial support during my doctoral and postdoctoral studies. Outside my home country, a great debt of gratitude goes to my mentor at the European University Institute, Antonella Romano, for her enlightened critiques and suggestions and for keeping me intellectually stimulated, as well as for providing her unwavering support in all my academic endeavours, this book included. I want to express my warmest thanks to the professors, colleagues and friends who kindly read parts of the book manuscript in its various stages: Jan Szeminski, Michela Catto and Cecilia Tossounian. Special thanks also go to Nicolas Standaert, Jan Szeminski, Juan Carlos Estenssoro, Pablo Blitstein and John K. Nelson for helping me clarify some key aspects in the process of writing this book.

A number of institutions have made this project possible with their material support. From the moment I gathered the very first primary sources for my doctoral dissertation until today I have always found enthusiastic support at the Ricci Institute for Chinese-Western Cultural History at the University of San Francisco. I express my enormous gratitude to its director, Wu Xiaoxin, to the Dean of the USF School of Humanities, Marcelo Camperi, to Melissa Dale who was Assistant Director of Research during my stay at the Ricci Institute, and the programme assistant May Lee. The library of the Ricci Institute and its wonderful collection benefit from the generosity and expertise of Mark Mir, to whom I am immensely grateful for the crucial assistance with which he always provided me when I needed it the most.

My special thanks go to the Center for Chinese Studies in Taipei, Taiwan and its friendly staff who kindly hosted me during my research stay in Taipei when I was working on my doctoral thesis.

I was a Max Weber Fellow at the European University Institute when this project turned into a book manuscript. Special debts of gratitude are owed to the Max Weber Programme, and to its director, Ramon Marimon, for his help and support during those lovely and inspiring days in Fiesole at the beautiful Villa La Fonte. My thanks also go to the wonderful Susan Garvin. Last but not least, I am indebted to David Barnes, not only the best editor ever but also a smart reader, for his assistance with this project.

My thanks are also owed to the Lilly Library at Indiana University in Bloomington for the material support it provided during the final stages of my work on the manuscript. Breon Mitchell, David Frasier and Zachary Downey assisted me during my stay in Bloomington and procured many of the images for this book. I want to thank the Archivum Romanum Societatis Iesu, especially Mauro Brunello, who also very generously helped me during the last stages.

My deepest thanks go to my Routledge editor, Peter Sowden, and to Jillian Morrison for their kind support throughout the publishing process. My appreciation is also owed to Steve Smith, who offered invaluable and generous advice, and to friends and colleagues who provided precious help and suggestions at various points: Claudio Ingerflom, Paz Estevez, Ruy Farias and Nadja Aksamija.

Finally, I do not have enough words to express my gratitude to my family, especially my parents, Carol and Roberto, for their wholehearted support. This book is dedicated to them.

Notes on translations, orthography and citation norms

This book is based on archival and published sources and secondary literature, including Chinese, Italian, Spanish, Portuguese, French, Latin and Chinese. Unless specified, all translations of quotations into English have been made by the author, who alone accepts responsibility for any inaccuracy. Citations of primary documents from archives are provided in endnotes.

I have adopted the modern pinyin system of romanization for the transcription of Chinese names and terms. There are a few exceptions, for example 'Canton' rather than Guangzhou, the former being more familiar to the reader; and 'Peking' instead of the modern Beijing.

Regarding Quechua terms, spelling is represented with Hispanicized Quechua; variations in orthography in the Spanish sources of the sixteenth and early seventeenth centuries have been respected.

Abbreviations

AUG	*Archivio Università Gregoriana, Roma*
AHSI	*Archivum Historicum Societatis Iesu*
ARSI (manuscript collections)	Archivio Romano Societatis Iesu (Roman Archives of the Society of Jesus):
	Fondo Gesuitico
	Prov. Japonica-Sinica
	Prov. Toletana
	Assistentia Hispaniae
Cartas de Japão & China	Cartas que os Padres e Irmãos da Companhia de Iesus Escreverão dos Reynos de Iapão & China, Evora,1598
Catechismus	Alessandro Valignano [1586] (1972) *Catechismus Christianae Fidei*
DCC	Luciano Pereña (ed.) [1584] (1985) *Doctrina Christiana y Catecismo*
De Proc	José de Acosta. [1588] (1954a), *De Procuranda Indorum Salute*
EM	José de Acosta (1954c) *Escritos Menores*
FLC	First Lima Council (1551–1552)
FR	P. D'Elia (1942–49) *Fonti Ricciane*, Vols I–III
Handbook	N. Standaert (ed.) (2001a) *Handbook of Christianity in China*, Vol. I, 635–1800
HNyM	José de Acosta [1590] (1954b). *Historia Natural y Moral de las Indias.*
JRSP	Matteo Ricci [1608] (1965), *Jiren Shipian Tianxhue chuhan*, Vol. I
LL	Lilly Library, Bloomington, Indiana University
MM	Félix Zubillaga (ed.) *Monumenta Mexicana*, Vols I. (1956), II (1959).

MP	Antonio Egaña (ed.) *Monumenta Peruana*, Vols. VII (1954), XIII (1958) and XVIII (1961).
MS	John Witek and Joseph Sebes (eds) (2002) *Monumenta Sinica*, Vol. I (1546–62).
OS	P. Tacchi Venturi SJ (1911–1913) *Opere Storiche,* Vols I–II
Sumario	Alessandro Valignano [1583] (1954), *Sumario de las Cosas de Japón*
SCL	Second Lima Council (1567–68)
SJ	Societas Jesu (Society of Jesus: Jesuits)
TLC	Third Lima Council (1582–83)
TZJY	Anonymous [1605] (2002), *Tianzhu Jiaoyao*, Vol. I
TZSL	Michele Ruggieri [1584] (2002), *Tianzhu Shilu*, Vol. I
TZSY	Matteo Ricci [1603] (1965), *Tianzhu Shiyi, Tianxue chuhan*, Vol. I

Introduction

The Society of Jesus dreamt of both its own universalism and that of Christianity. Wherever the mission, it inevitably shared and mingled with local religions, accommodating itself to the specific context. That is what this book is about: how this process unfolded in Peru and China in the late sixteenth and early seventeenth centuries.

The first question to pose and answer is: why Peru and China? Obviously, the choice of specific cases and settings often contains an element of arbitrariness. The arbitrary element lies in the selection of two learned Jesuits who composed vast works: José de Acosta (1540–1600) and Matteo Ricci (1552–1610). However, the selection is far from random, for these two Jesuits have many things in common. Both José de Acosta and Matteo Ricci were not just 'vineyard labourers' – as the Jesuits liked to define themselves. They were savants who, apart from being prolific authors, also composed catechisms in their respective missions in Peru and China. Acosta was the main author of the Spanish text of the Third Lima Council catechetical corpus – also translated into Quechua and Aymara – entitled *Doctrina Christiana y Catecismo para Instrucción de Indios* (1584–85) – Christian Doctrine and Catechism for the Instruction of Indians (Pereña 1985) (hereafter cited as DCC).[1] Ricci, in China, produced the *Tianzhu Shiyi* (1603), usually translated into English as True Meaning of the Lord of Heaven. In this respect, both Acosta and Ricci offer a perfect balance between the excessive intellectualism attributed to the Jesuits, which was genuine, and the true missionary and devotional goals that oriented their actions (Curto 2005: 9). The time frame of this book spans the arrival of José de Acosta in Peru in 1571 to Ricci's death in Ming China, in 1610.

Even though catechisms might at first glance appear dry, this is hardly the case when it comes to Acosta and Ricci. The richness of their output lies in the way their texts reflect the projects they envisioned for their new missions, laying the foundations for the missionaries to come. Together with Jesuit correspondence and other works by Acosta and Ricci, this book explores the way in which these catechisms reflect their mission projects, shaped over time, with a remarkable power of endurance. However, the catechisms composed by Acosta and Ricci were not the first ones in those mission spaces, so both of them embraced the task of undoing a previous doctrine to redirect it in the mission context. Of course, they did not make their decisions regarding doctrinal texts single-handedly, but worked within the context of the guidance and instructions they received from both their superiors and local authorities.

The rulers of the overseas empires summoned the Society of Jesus to evangelize their new subjects in the 'New World' which Spain and Portugal shared. The crowns of Castile and Aragon and John II of Portugal were given responsibility for missionary work, which was called the right of royal patronage, i.e. the Spanish *Patronato* and the Portuguese *Padroado*.[2] This meant that, from the outset, the Jesuits were dependent upon the whims of secular authorities and compelled to rely upon the support and protection of the rulers of those lands in which their Order served and to yield to the constraints they imposed (Alden 1996: 656). The Jesuit missions in Peru and in China will provide us with different and telling examples of how this relationship evolved over time.

Expanding missions

From a European perspective, this book is about the way Christianity expanded in the early modern period, craving universalism. The Society of Jesus was founded by Ignacio de Loyola in 1534 and recognized by Pope Paul III in 1540 through the bull *Regimini Militantis Ecclesiae*. In Part Seven of its Constitutions, the Society established that, apart from the three vows of religious life – obedience, poverty and chastity, the Jesuits must make a fourth vow to the Pope, *circa missiones*, to allow themselves to be sent wherever they were needed. In effect, the Jesuits' fourth vow, by which the professed members of the Society oblige themselves to 'special obedience to the sovereign pontiff regarding missions', is a vow about 'missions'. It was with the European overseas expansion and the conquest of the 'New World' that the modern concept of 'mission' was born; and it evolved over time. In the Society's first decades, the term 'mission' was interchangeable in meaning with 'journey' or 'pilgrimage' – always referring to an apostolic endeavour (Corsi 2008b: 27). According to the Jesuit technical glossary, it involves at least two missionaries in a mission space (Glossario Gesuitico 1992: 35–36). Throughout the history of the Society of Jesus, missions have always played a prominent role; in fact – as mentioned above – the universal apostolate *circa missiones* was part of the Society's Constitutions. However, beyond definitions, the term 'mission' presented much greater flexibility in Europe or overseas, being defined by neither distance nor geographical boundaries. Moreover, as will be shown in this book, the activities carried out in a mission could involve different endeavours, far beyond preaching, confessing and converting (Colombo 2010: 38). Taking these observations a little further, the missions overseas started with the voyage itself. The time on board ship provided a transition between the European college environment and the mission space, a place where the missionaries would be trained in pastoral care under the supervision of older, more experienced, fathers. Young missionaries were plunged into an extreme physical and emotional trial, being called upon to be the moral support to others (Brockey 2000: 64–70). However, there is one core aspect that the notion and meaning of mission retained: the sense of 'sending out' (Clossey 2008: 15). As for the 'where', Jerome Nadal, one of the first Jesuits, did not leave room for doubt: *totus mundus nostra fit habitatio* – our place is the world.[3]

Most of the period that this book analyses, 1570–1610, corresponds to the first decades of the Superior General Claudio Acquaviva (1581–1615). This is a period in which the group identity, inspired to a great extent by the universalism sought by the Jesuits, coalesced (Corsi 2008d: 552; Broggio, Cantù, Fabre and Romano 2007: 11). Indeed, the Society came to a solid view and definition of its apostolic activities both in and beyond Europe, in multiple and diverse spaces.[4] The Iberian Peninsula, which contained two assistancies of the Society of Jesus, became the springboard for all the Jesuits' endeavours outside Europe.[5]

The Portugal province was the first to engage in the missions overseas – to the Portuguese Indies with Francis Xavier in the East in 1542, and then in 1549 with Manoel da Nóbrega in Brazil. Later, the Spanish crown commanded the evangelization of the *Indias Occidentales*. The strength of the idea of Europe as Christian and occidental was crucial in the sixteenth century, in such a way that '*Indias Occidentales*' would not only refer to a specific geographical area – although from 1565 it also comprised the Philippines – but would also become that part of the world in which the *republica christiana* would continue to grow (Mignolo 1995: 325–26).

The Portuguese *Indias* were the most requested, for Francis Xavier's experience in the East served as an inspiration for many future missionaries. Indeed, Francis Xavier (1506–52) arrived in Goa, India in 1542 and left for Japan in 1549, where he marvelled at the erudition of the Japanese, men of 'letters and reason'. But his admiration for Japan was soon eclipsed by that for China when he learned that the Japanese refered to the Chinese as 'wiser and extremely learned' (*Monumenta Sinica*, hereafter cited as MS – Witek and Sebes 2002: 125). China thus became one of the most desirable places in the East for the Jesuits and was immortalized as such when Francis Xavier died on the island of Shangchuan, immediately in front of the southern coast of China, while awaiting a Chinese interpreter. However, these preferences for the Portuguese *Indias* were not to Ignatius of Loyola's liking. In a letter of March 26 1553, addressed to the Fathers and Brothers of the Society of Jesus, General Loyola explains that, before the foundation of the Society, 'when our first fathers lost hope of going to Jerusalem', Father Diego Lainez – who was to be the second Superior General of the Society – said to him that he was inclined to go the *Indias* – the Portuguese *Indias*, we gather – to convert the gentiles, because they lacked labourers. And the Saint – Loyola – answered:

> I do not have that inclination as, having made a vow of obedience to the Pope, to be ruled by his will, and to be sent anywhere on earth to serve

the Lord, we must be indifferent and do what we are told, without being more inclined to one part than another. And if I were, like you are, more inclined to go to the Indies, I would try to incline myself to the opposite side, to reach that perfect indifference, which is necessary to reach the perfection of obedience.

(Lilly Library – hereafter referred to as LL, Loyola 1753[1553]: 25–26)

However, 'perfect indifference' did not always win the battle when it came to requests by potential missionaries to be sent to the *Indias*. This book approaches how and why these preferences were expressed in the Jesuit missions in Peru and in China.

José de Acosta in Peru

Previous to the arrival of the Society of Jesus in Peru, there had been a 'first evangelization', which commenced with the conquest in 1532, supported by a blossoming-yet-fragile pastoral and ecclesiastical jurisdiction. At that time, the Dominicans, Franciscans, Augustines and Mercedarians were in charge of evangelizing the Indies. By and large, they were receptive to local pre-Hispanic religions and believed that the Indians had to embrace Christianity gradually, saving complex dogma like the mysteries of faith for later. That receptivity was also noticeable in the use of doctrinal texts in Quechua, such as the *Plática para todos los Indios* by the Dominican Domingo de Santo Tomás (1560). This text, however, along with others, was to be removed from circulation when Tridentine Catholicism found its way to Peru in the Third Lima Council (TLC; 1582–83).

Sent by Philip II, the Spanish admiral Pedro Menéndez de Avilés (1519–74) organized an expedition to La Florida; he wanted to take members of the young Order, the Society of Jesus. On March 20, 1565, Menéndez obtained permission from Philip II for the entry of the Society of Jesus into America. However, the Jesuits never boarded the ships for, when General Borja (1565–72) sent his instructions from Rome to Spain, Menéndez and his expedition had already left. But the experience served the purpose of positioning Spanish America as a vast open land for the Jesuits to settle. Indeed, soon after, in 1568, the Jesuits established a mission in Peru. A few years later, in 1572, they arrived in New Spain – modern Mexico.

Summoned by Philip II, the Society of Jesus arrived in Peru in 1568 to form part of the colonial enterprise in a harsh Counter-Reformation context. Previously in that same year, Philip II had decided to carry out an entire political, economic and religious reorganization in the Indies, which resulted in the arrival in Peru of Viceroy Toledo (1515–82), the Society of Jesus and the Inquisition. The Society thus became involved in the colonial enterprise, and José de Acosta played a key role in accommodating the mission to the requirements imposed by the royal authorities, empowered in Peru through the *Patronato real* – royal patronage. It is no longer a matter of debate that

José de Acosta, the main theologian in Peru, authored the Spanish text of the *Doctrina Christiana y Cathecismo* (hereafter cited as DCC; 1584–85) (Pereña 1985), which to a great extent fed on his *De Procuranda Indorum Salute* [1588] (1954a) (hereafter cited as De Proc).[6] The present book proposes a systematic analysis of the influence of his works – mainly *De Procuranda* – on the DCC. The DCC had a double purpose: to erase, on the one hand, the first evangelization receptive to pre-Hispanic elements based on minimal content for salvation and, on the other hand, to establish Tridentine orthodoxy as a final direction, incompatible with the indigenous 'idolatrous' religions. The DCC reflects the purposes, intentions and goals of the Jesuits in Peru, all of whom found in Acosta a spokesman who, more than once, overshadowed other Jesuits who had envisioned things differently in that mission. The permanence of the DCC in Andean lands is remarkable; it continued to be used until 1944, when replacing it was proposed. That, however, had to wait until the Second Vatican Council (1962–65).[7]

Matteo Ricci in China

In China, the Jesuits discovered that the culture they encountered was similar to that of Europe in the complexity of many of its aspects: cultural, economic, intellectual, material, etc. Their apostolate inspired the so-called *accommodation* or adaptation, which goes back to the origins of the Society and its founder, Ignatius of Loyola. It refers to the capacity of adapting to diversity, to accommodate to the culture that the missionary addresses in order to make the Gospel – and the Spiritual Exercises – more accessible to the hearer. The will to accommodate is exemplified by Loyola's famous expression 'Enter through the door of the other so as to make them leave through our door' (Standaert 2003: 52). Much has been said, from more or less critical perspectives, about Jesuit accommodation in the missions to the East, especially in those spaces distant from Portuguese colonial administration hubs like Goa. Without abandoning their core Ignatian spirit, accommodation became a realistic approach in those missions in which the Jesuits did not have political and/or coercive power on their side. Alessandro Valignano (1539–1606), Visitor of the Order in the missions to the East, in his *Sumario de las Cosas de Japón* (1583) (hereafter cited as Sumario) – Japan Summary – clearly expresses the improbability of the Japanese accommodating to the Jesuits, so accommodation had to work the other way around. Based on this sensible and realistic view, Valignano set the guidelines for the Jesuit missionaries in China, who as a very first requirement had to learn the local language. Over time, the missions to the East were conceived by Jesuit historiography as the realm of accommodation and cultural adaptation promoted by the Society and, more specifically, by the Italian Jesuits. Eventually, Matteo Ricci and his 'accommodation method' became a paradigmatic example for the China mission. It was not difficult to idealize the missions to the East when compared to those to the overseas possessions of the Spanish empire, which were very different from the Portuguese. It was an empire of actual conquest, occupation and forced Hispanicization. In Spanish America, Christianization was one of the cogs in the colonial and colonizing machine, only made possible through political and coercive power.

In China, Matteo Ricci was so impressed by the influence that the scholar-officials were able to exert on the Ming emperor himself that he likened them to the philosopher-kings of Plato's *Republic*. In Ricci's view, China became the place where the consummation of Plato's *Republic* took place, while the West had only speculated about it (FR I: 51–56). Many of these 'philosophers' were the Chinese scholar-officials who participated – not all of them succeeded – in the civil service examination to obtain official posts within the empire. The Confucian canon was an essential part of the curriculum tested by the government examinations required of nearly all candidates for the Chinese imperial bureaucracy.[8] Over time, in Ricci's eyes, these scholar-officials, also portrayed as literati, were regarded by the Jesuits as exclusively 'Confucian'. The term 'Confucianism' as such does not exist in Chinese. Ricci translated the term *rujia* as 'Confucianism'; but *rujia* indicated not a precise moral orientation or body of doctrines, but a professional training with the general goal of state service (Nylan 2001: 1–71; 366–67). Moreover, Ricci also interpreted Confucianism as a single orthodox synthesis. He was convinced that the core Confucian books contained evidence of primordial monotheism. What is more, Confucianism, as conceived by Ricci, was opposed to 'idolatrous' and 'heterodox' Buddhism and Daoism. He always named and presented the three as watertight categories.

In 1603, two years after establishing a fourth Jesuit residence in Peking, Ricci published his *Tianzhu Shiyi*, usually translated as True Meaning of the Lord of Heaven (TZSY; [1603] 1965), to be followed by other editions in different cities. With the full support of Valignano, Ricci's TZSY aimed to replace a first catechism, the *Tianzhu Shilu* or True Record of the Lord of Heaven (1584; TZSL), composed by the first Jesuit to enter China, his companion Michele Ruggieri. Ruggieri's TZSL was a first step towards creating a Christian terminology in Chinese. More than the allegedly Buddhist terminology that Ruggieri used in the TZSL, the watershed dividing the two catechisms is Confucianism as shaped by Ricci permeating the entire teachings of the Lord of Heaven. Ricci's TZSL also fed on Valignano's own catechism, the *Catechismus Christianae Fidei*, printed in Lisbon in 1586 (1972). During the remainder of the seventeenth century, many works appeared that treated some of the topics included in the TZSY in great detail, but none of these writings had the same success.[9] Not only was the TZSY reprinted several times, but it was also translated into several other languages – including Japanese and Korean – right up to modern times (Standaert 2001a: 621 onward, *Handbook of Christianity in China* –hereafter cited as Handbook).

What Ricci shaped – and this remained practically unaltered in the China mission – was the view of Confucianism as a system of social and political morality. Ricci's notion of Confucianism as the cornerstone of Chinese culture would grow stronger in seventeenth-century Europe. These are all elements that merged in the teachings of the Lord of Heaven, as conceived by Ricci. The period analysed in this book witnesses the inception of these notions as forged by the first Jesuits in China, starting with Ricci. However, as some scholars have argued in recent years, 'Confucian Christianity' did not occupy as central a role in certain Christian communities as local norms, social practices, religious cults or ancestral rituals (Brockey 2007: 47 onward; Menegon 2009: 7 onward). Moreover, it is a well-known fact that the Jesuits and their missionary policies in China did not exclusively aim at conversion from the top down. In the last years of Ricci's sojourn in Beijing, he himself noticed how, with a few more missionaries, it was possible to visit the surrounding villages and work actively among other social strata.

Focusing on two Jesuits, Acosta and Ricci, makes it inevitable to wonder whether they ever met. They did not, at least not in person. But Acosta heard about the first Jesuits in China, thanks to a missionary in the Philippines, Alonso Sánchez. He provided Acosta with information about the mission to China and, specifically, Michele Ruggieri and Matteo Ricci's endeavours at that moment in Zhaoqing, in Canton Province. Acosta and Sánchez met in New Spain – present-day Mexico – in 1587, when Acosta had left Peru for good and was spending a year in New Spain before returning to Europe. However, before that encounter, which provided Acosta with fresh information regarding the progress of the China mission, China had already served as inspiration for the Spanish Jesuit in many ways, as will be shown in this book.

Within, outside and beyond Jesuit missions; methodological questions

Inevitably, the analysis of such distant missions as to Peru and China involves methodological quandaries regarding scale, connections and intersections. In terms of general methodological trends, various alternatives 'beyond comparison' have come to light in recent years (Subramanyan 1997; Gruzinski 2001; Werner and Zimmerman 2006). Connecting histories presents challenges different to those of the specialist, as Sanjay Subramanyan suggests when posing the provoking question about a realistic methodological alternative that does not require one to become a specialist in everything (Subramanyan 1997: 744–45). The literature on connecting histories has become more abundant since the globalization process inevitably changed our frameworks for reflection and, therefore, our ways of revisiting the past (Gruzinski 2001: 89). In this regard, the universalism characteristic of the Society of Jesus has been recently treated as 'global'. Indeed, the Jesuit missions themselves became challenging spaces for connections between 'global' and 'local', inspiring scholars to reflect on the methodological problems they involve (Catto *et al.* 2010). However, Jesuit expansionism still needs further analysis of the connections among and throughout the missions and, in turn, of the interaction with the historical and local contexts within the missions. Regarding this last aspect, one of the major risks when envisioning the Jesuit missions in a 'global' dimension is that of overlooking the historic and local contexts wherever they were established. This book is about the Society of Jesus and its missions in Peru and in China, not merely considered *in relation to* each other, but also *through* the lens of one another; it attempts to shed light on their intersections, in this case marked by the ever present 'colonial difference'. Indeed, in Peru, the Jesuits contributed to the configuration of a modern colonial world, coloniality being a constituent of modernity (Mignolo 2000: 13–50).

The book is divided into two parts; the first comprises three chapters. Chapter One presents 'selective' biographies of Acosta and Ricci. A first focus is on their education in Jesuit colleges and the cultural baggage they took with them to their missions, which is also reflected in their various works. But the stress is mostly placed on Acosta's and Ricci's lives in the missions, in which their keen political acumen and a certain taste for power unfolded. In turn, an analysis of their ability to adapt to the political circumstances of their missions reveals the more or less conflictive relationship with their confreres in those spaces. Last but not least, these selective life histories underscore the individual dimension as well as the personal imprint of these two Jesuits in their respective missions in Peru and China within the Ignatian legacy.

The second chapter focuses on the expansion of the Society of Jesus outside Europe, when summoned by both the Spanish and Portuguese crowns to evangelize their possessions; that relationship profoundly shaped the nature of the missions in Peru and China. In Peru, the Society of Jesus was required to impose Tridentine Catholicism by Philip II, independently of Rome, a task that entailed compliance with the colonial authorities' demands, and specifically those of Viceroy Toledo during the early years. In the missions to the East, the Portuguese *Padroado* had a much less oppressive presence than its Spanish counterpart in Peru. Instead, the Jesuits in China were in the hands of the scholar-officials, with the Emperor at the apex, who had the power to decide whether they could stay or not. Michele Ruggieri and Matteo Ricci's entry into mainland China in 1583 is here contextualized against the backdrop of the previous Jesuit experience in Japan, as they were led by Visitor Alessandro Valignano's policies in that mission. Last but not least, the Philippines gained a prominent role as a strategic point that the Spanish, especially from New Spain, used for entering – or attempting to enter – China, in a Jesuit geopolitical scenario.

The third chapter focuses on the concepts and processes of 'Hispanicization' in Peru and 'accommodation' in China. In the missions to the East, Visitor Valignano was the planner and promoter of accommodation in the second half of the sixteenth century; time and experience would give concrete meaning to the Visitor's general directive of accommodation when carried out in China. Ruggieri and Ricci were the first to implement it, each in their own way. This chapter is about their different approaches in the interpretation and implementation of Valignano's command of accommodation. Meanwhile, in

Peru, Hispanicization was supported and promoted by the colonial state, which was able to exert coercion whenever necessary. However, the main focus here is the analysis of Hispanicization as envisioned by Acosta. Finally, this chapter examines a point of intersection between Hispanicization and accommodation. As two religious men of the sixteenth century, Acosta and Ricci were both concerned – at times obsessed – about idolatry, 'finding' its specific manifestations in their respective missions.

The second part of the book focuses on texts. José de Acosta and Matteo Ricci were both involved in composing catechisms that, for different reasons, were conceived to redirect a previous doctrinal path by replacing catechetical texts they found no longer suitable for the missions. Both Acosta and Ricci played key roles in envisioning this new doctrinal direction and reflecting it in their texts. To comprehend this change, Chapter Four first focuses on the doctrinal texts previous to the arrival of Acosta in the Peru mission, on the one hand, and on the first catechism that Michele Ruggieri composed in China, on the other. In the case of Peru, there was an early set of doctrinal texts predating the Jesuits; but in the China mission the issue was a catechism that the first Jesuit in China, Michele Ruggieri, did not find, but created. This is the one that Matteo Ricci – and Alessandro Valignano above him – considered needed to be redirected. The purpose of this chapter is to witness the craftsmanship applied to doctrinal texts along the respective paths leading to the authoritative catechisms by Acosta and Ricci.

Chapter Five examines three doctrinal themes that the DCC and TZSY share: one God as the creator of all things, the immortality of the soul, and rewards and punishments in the hereafter. The purpose is to analyse how these core Christian principles are interwoven according to the specificity of the mission space in which they were introduced. In both spaces the missionaries had to make complex belief systems comprehensible by resorting to a familiar – and limited – canon of European concepts. Unlike in Peru, in the China mission the Jesuits soon found opponents who objected to their views and interpretation of Chinese thought. In sum, apart from exploring the interweaving of the Christian tenets, this chapter also approaches the obstructed dialogues and miscommunications in the mission spaces. The conclusions move briefly forward to the early seventeenth century, putting the Peru and China missions in perspective, beyond Acosta and Ricci, for a last reflection on how the Jesuits conceived and assessed these spaces.

Notes

1 The term 'corpus' in this book refers to the entire set of different doctrinal texts composed within the Third Lima Council, which comprised three catechisms, a *platica* and *cartilla* (types of doctrinal texts), a vocabulary list for Quechua and Aymara, and annotations regarding these translations. There were also, in a more 'penitent' vein, 'Instructions against the Indian rites and ceremonies', a report on Indian rites and superstition, a confession manual (*confesionario*), exhortations to die in peace and some sections on the obstacles to validating marriage.

2 The rights of royal patronage granted to Portugal and Spain involved the exclusive right of navigation, conquest and commerce in their overseas possessions. Royal patronage also meant controlling major appointments of Churchmen and the management of Church revenues. In turn, the kings were given charge of evangelization of the 'gentiles' in their overseas possessions.

3 AHSI (1962) Hieronymi Nadal, *Comentarii de Instituto Societatis Iesu (Epistolae et Monumenta P. Hieronymi Nadal, tomus V)*, edidit Michael Nicolau SI, Romae Monumenta Historica Societatis Iesu: 90.

4 Acquaviva was a great promoter of rural missions in Europe, which formed part of the universal vision of the promotion of Christian faith (Prosperi 1999). This universalism during Acquaviva's tenure expressed itself in several ways. One of the most impressive was the consolidation of an extremely important normative and pedagogical work of the Society of Jesus: the *Ratio Studiorum* – Plan of Studies – a brief text published in 1599, embodying the Society of Jesus' massive commitment to education, which extended to the various mission spaces and people involved in its apostolate.

5 The basic unit of the Society of Jesus was the *province*. Provinces were in turn grouped into larger administrative divisions, according to a geographical criterion, called *assistancies*. The four original assistancies comprised the Italian, Spanish, Portuguese and German provinces. Each province had its missions, but their geographical location could be in another province.

6 Among the authors who have claimed Acosta's authorship of the Spanish text of the TLC corpus, see León Lopetegui (1942: chapter XVII); Mateos (1954: XVI); José de Acosta ([1590] 1940: LXXXII); Enrique Bartra (1967); J. G. Durán (1982: 240); Francesco Lisi (1990: 65–68); Alan Durston (2007: 90–92).

7 The canonical character of the Third Lima Council corpus was kept alive for decades and materialized in a series of partial editions. The Spanish and Quechua texts of the *Doctrina Christiana y Catecismo* were reprinted in Rome in 1603, and that same year the *Confessionario* was printed in Seville – all, apparently, under the auspices of the Jesuit Diego de Torres Bollo, the province's representative in Spain. A further edition of the Spanish-Quechua *cartilla* and catechisms appeared in several compilations of pastoral texts, like those composed by the Creole Franciscan Luis Gerónimo de Oré between 1598 and 1607 and Jesuit Pablo de Prado in 1645, as well as dozens of works from the eighteenth, nineteenth and twentieth centuries. A proof of the enduring status of the TLC is the Sixth Lima Council's decision to reprint the entire Third catechism by sermons in 1771. The TLC corpus's Quechua translations of the common prayers are still in use in the Andes, with some dialectal adaptations (Durston 2007: 103–04).

8 These books include, first, the Four Books or *Si Shu*: the Analects, the Invariable Mean, the Great Learning and the Mencius. The Analects and the Invariable Mean are attributed to Confucius; the Great Learning has been attributed to Confucius' disciple Zeng zi (505?–436? BC); while the Mencius comprises the dialogues of Mencius, disciple of Confucius. They were so grouped by the thinker Zhu Xi (1130–1200) during the Song dynasty in the eleventh century. Second are the Five Classics: the Book of Odes, Book of Documents, Book of Rites (originally one text to which two others were eventually added), the Book of Changes, and the Spring and Autumn Annals. Tradition speaks of a Music classic, but if it ever existed it has been lost or incorporated into one of the three Rites classics (Nylan 2001: 8).

9 The only comparable works are Jesuit Giulio Aleni's *Wanwu Zhenyuan* (*c.*1628) and *Sanshan lunxue ji* (*c.*1629) (Standaert 2001a: 621 onward, *Handbook of Christianity in China* – hereafter cited as Handbook).

Part I
The men and the missions

1 The men

Selective biographies of José de Acosta and Matteo Ricci

Besides being the main figures in this book, José de Acosta (1540–1600) and Matteo Ricci (1552–1610) were two exemplary representatives of the Jesuit intellectual apostolate. In fact, their versatility makes it impossible to encompass all the different facets of their personalities and their works. This chapter is not limited to merely providing facts about their lives, but will attempt to provide 'selective' life histories of the two Jesuits. Basically, Acosta and Ricci have three things in common: their education in Jesuit colleges, which they both put to good use in their missions and expressed in the works composed in those spaces; their melancholic moods; and, most important, their taste for power. Much has been said about the closeness to power, typical of the Jesuit Order. However, there are always new angles to discover in particular contexts, especially when contrasting different mission spaces, such as Peru and China. Even though Acosta and Ricci are the main figures in these pages, this chapter also features other less known, sometimes self-effacing, Jesuits in Peru and in China, who also contributed to shaping these missions.

Given that Acosta was twelve years senior to the Italian Jesuit, and merely for chronological purposes, his selective life history is the first to follow this brief introduction.

José de Acosta: Jesuit, theologian and politician

Life in Spain and arrival in Peru

José de Acosta was born in 1540 in Medina del Campo, at the time a prosperous city in Castile. His father was a merchant; four of the five brothers joined the novitiate of the Society of Jesus, José among them. All did their basic studies at the Jesuit College in Medina del Campo. José also had three sisters, two of whom became nuns. This devout family was later claimed to have Jewish blood, to be new Christian – *cristianos nuevos* – both the information and accusation being spread by another member of the Society, Alonso Sánchez (1547–93), a missionary in the Philippines, when José de Acosta was already an elderly man.

In 1551, Acosta joined the Jesuit College in Medina del Campo, where he took his first three religious vows in 1554. Besides his studies in the field of humanities, he also wrote comedies and religious plays on biblical themes. Already a man of frail health, in 1559 Acosta settled in the Jesuit college at Alcalá de Henares, where he followed regular philosophy and theology courses from 1559 to 1567.[1] It was during this period that Acosta demonstrated his interest in scholastic matters together with an in-depth study of Thomism. The Thomism he was taught was deeply influenced by the great Dominican theologian in Salamanca, Francisco de Vitoria. Through both public and private disputes, Acosta had the chance to display his public-speaking skills.

Acosta made a brilliant career at the University of Alcalá, becoming an expert not only in theology but also in other disciplines – ecclesiastical and civil law, natural sciences and history, among others (Mateos 1954: IX). He showed a particular interest in the events and problems related to the conquest of America, especially the points of view of the Spanish professors in the School of Salamanca: Francisco de Vitoria, Diego de Covarrubias and Melchor Cano, among others. In 1566, towards the end of his theology studies and at the age of twenty-six, Acosta was ordained priest and taught theology at the newly inaugurated Ocaña College, something he was very good at, according to the first catalogue – *primus* – included in the triennial catalogue.[2]

But the most important fact in those years was his decided inclination towards a 'vocation for the Indies' (Lopetegui 1942: 39–42). The Jesuit colleges in Spain sought to channel missionary enthusiasm towards the Spanish Indies. In 1561, Acosta expressed his desire to become a missionary to Jerome Nadal (1507–80), one of the first members of the Society, but apparently he did not have in mind the *Indias Occidentales*. This can be inferred from an ambiguous statement of Acosta's: 'I long to go to the Indies, despite having to live among the blacks, and I feel the calling to work for the love of Our Lord, with whatever my capacities allow me until the very end'.[3] León Lopetegui, who wrote an extensive biography of Acosta, surmises from the contents of the letter and the date of his missionary vocation that Acosta initially wished to be sent to the Portuguese Indies, as indicated in his remark about the 'blacks' under Portuguese jurisdiction (Lopetegui 1942: 43). Eventually, Acosta's explicit acceptance of being sent to Spanish America seems to be weakened by his need to make clear that this destination is not of inferior quality to the Portuguese Indies:

> I have no preference for going to any place in particular, but I think I would feel better among people with certain abilities and not too thick-headed … . Also, now that there is a route to Spain's Western Indies, I thought that if I were among those, Your Paternity would send me there. I could do my part if I were ordered to do what I do here, like reading theology or preaching or any other ministry. And if obedience sent me to

those other Indies and I had to stay in Goa or nearby, I feel a certain disgust to think that what is over there is more than what is over here.[4]

In sum, beyond preferences, Acosta always expressed his missionary fervour, and so he wrote to the General of the Society, Francisco de Borja (1510–72), mentioning his desire to be 'a soldier of Christ' in the *Indias* in a letter of 1568, repeated in April 1569 (Acosta 1954c: 251–52, *Escritos Menores* – hereafter cited as EM). It was precisely in 1568 that Phillip II authorized the Society of Jesus for missions in Spanish America, a destination previously restricted to the four mendicant orders: Dominicans, Franciscans, Augustinians and Mercedarians. General Borja had nurtured plans for Acosta in the Roman College, but the authorities of the Viceroyalty of Peru had repeatedly requested virtuous and learned men and that made him change his mind. Towards the end of 1570 Borja wrote to the Provincial of Peru, Jerónimo Ruiz de Portillo, in these terms:

> Send Father Fonseca, who is currently Vice-chancellor in Cordoba, to establish the novices, and F. José de Acosta to teach and preach – they are among the best we have in Spain – and two or three other good men.
> (Egaña 1954, *Monumenta Peruana I*: 390 –
> hereafter cited as MP I, etc.)

In 1570 in Alcalá, Acosta pronounced the fourth vow and in 1571 Borja finally sent him to Peru to teach theology, a subject in demand because of the increasing number of students in Lima.[5] Before landing in Peru, Acosta stayed in the Antilles and Central America – Santo Domingo, Puerto Rico, South Cuba and, seemingly, Jamaica – for approximately one year. Here Acosta gathered information that he later reported in his main works, i.e. *De Procuranda Indorum Salute* (1588) and the *Historia Natural y Moral de las Indias* (1590) (hereafter cited as HNyM). A few days after his arrival in Lima in 1572, Acosta inaugurated the studies of moral theology at the Jesuit College in that city, the first of the Society in the province of Peru. Soon after, in mid-1573, the provincial, Jerónimo Ruiz de Portillo, sent him on a lengthy mission through the interior of Peru and the main cities of the Viceroyalty. The information Acosta gathered in this journey of a year and a half was included in his work *De Procuranda Indorum Salute*, which he finished in 1577 and published in Spain in 1588. His travels took him to regions inhabited solely by natives and a few Spanish settlements in the burgeoning cities of this widespread territory. Acosta made this trip in the company of the Jesuit Antonio González de Ocampo, but mostly he travelled with the Jesuit Luis López and with Brother Gonzalo Ruiz, a *mestizo* – mixed-race – with 'sound knowledge of the Indian language' (Mateos 1954: XI). Besides Cuzco, Acosta visited Arequipa, La Paz, Potosí and Chuquisaca, cities that would host future Jesuit colleges. It was then that Acosta acquired the rudiments of the Quechua language. In those visits he also became familiar with the *reducciones*, i.e. Spanish-style towns and villages into which Indians were resettled, under the orders of Viceroy Toledo (1515–84), to 'more efficiently' organize mining labour and the Indians' conversion to Christianity. Toledo wanted to meet Acosta and therefore invited him to Chuquisaca. There he met important dignitaries in the viceroy's entourage, who counselled him in matters concerning the basic organization being carried out in Peru. One of these was the Licenciado Polo de Ondegardo, whose work *Informaciones acerca de la Religión y Gobierno de los Incas* – Information about the Religion and Government of the Incas – proved to be of great value to Acosta, becoming one of the main sources of *De Procuranda*.

In late October 1574, Acosta returned to Lima, the capital city of the Viceroyalty. He had been summoned by Provincial Portillo to a prosecution by the Inquisition against the Dominican Francisco de la Cruz, who had arrived in Peru in 1561. Acosta was appointed qualifier of the Holy Office of the Inquisition in a case that ended with an *auto de fe* celebrated in Lima in April 1578, when Francisco de la Cruz was burned at the stake after six years in prison. It was a long process with political connotations that went far beyond the theological and doctrinal aspects: there was suspicion of a conspiracy of Lascasian tone during the Viceroyalty of Toledo (Abril Castelló 1992: 79 onward). Acosta accused Francisco de la Cruz of being 'a devilish cunning Heresiarch'; indeed, the reason for condemning de la Cruz was his Erasmian tone, which was questioned in this trial. As we shall see in Chapter Four, these are matters that Acosta would analyse in the fourth and fifth book of his *De Procuranda Indorum salute*. The issue in question was de la Cruz's stand regarding the knowledge needed for the salvation of the Indians. The charge of Lutheran heresy in the case of de la Cruz is linked to the Protestant doctrine of Justification solely by faith (Bataillon 1977: 173; Estenssoro 2003: 191).[6] But accusations by the Inquisition were not exclusively made against the Dominicans. A Jesuit, Luis López, was imprisoned in 1578 as well; but, unlike de la Cruz, López did not go through an *auto de fe* and was not burned at the stake (Abril Castelló 1992). Very critical of Toledo's regime, López was accused by Toledo himself of being one of de la Cruz's collaborators and of introducing 'false sects' in Peru (MP II: 734). As a result of his good relationship with the Inquisition, Acosta gradually drew apart from some of the Jesuits in Peru. Moreover, his close ties with Viceroy Toledo aroused suspicion. Beyond these internal disagreements, the Society of Jesus was given a pre-eminent role by the royal authorities regarding the evangelization and indoctrination of the Indians in Peru, while the Dominicans were pushed into the background. The royal representatives expelled them in 1572 from the Chucuito Province.

José de Acosta's provincialate in Peru (1576–81)

In 1576, aged thirty-five at the time, Acosta was appointed provincial, in replacement of Jerónimo Ruiz del Portillo. Being provincial entailed a yearly visit around the province and keeping detailed records of all the activities carried out in each of the residences by each of the individuals, meaning that Acosta was unable to continue teaching theology at the University of Lima. He had started teaching at the university at Toledo's request, interrupting his lessons at the Jesuit college in Lima.

In 1576 the Provincial Congregation of the Society was held. It consisted of two stages: the first in Lima, in January 1576, and the second in Cuzco, in October of the same year. The constitutions of the Congregation, signed by the secretary Luis López, contain an outline of several points later developed by Acosta in *De Procuranda* (MP II: 54–87; 201–05). Acosta had prepared a draft of this work for this first provincial congregation to set the basis for the Society's evangelization project. The most outstanding Jesuit *lenguas* – a Spanish term referring to those who mastered the vernaculars – in Peru, Alonso de Barzana, Bartolomé de Santiago and the *mestizo* Jesuit Blas Valera, worked very intensively in Cuzco those days. But it was Barzana who mainly wrote the catechisms in Quechua and Aymara, the same ones that the Society used until the approval of the *Doctrina y Catecismo para Instrucción de Indios*, the Third Lima Council corpus. In a letter that General Mercurian sent to Alonso de Barzana on November 19 1576, Mercurian congratulates the latter for the Quechua lexicon he had composed – the *Bocabulario* – that would enable the fathers to learn the language. And the general also mentions how he found consolation in Barzana's catechisms, both the brief and the greater. In that same letter, we find out that Barzana originally wanted to go to the China mission. However, in order to prove that Barzana belonged to the mission in Peru, Mercurian told him: 'The vow you made to go to China, you have it well commuted in those lands – Peru – where there is more predisposition to preach the Gospel than in China' (MP II: 37). At that time, there had been a succession of missionaries from different orders who had failed to enter China, until Michele Ruggieri succeeded in the early 1580s. Jesuit Barzana was one of Luis López's fellows. They were together in the Cuzco, Potosí and Arequipa colleges, and López was his confessor as well. López had a difficult personality and was a nonconformist who had written some very critical 'Chapters' against Viceroy Toledo and the titles of Spanish domain in the *Indias Occidentales* (Mateos 1954: XV). As mentioned above, López was arrested by the Lima Inquisition and accused together with the Dominican Francisco de la Cruz in the same process, in 1573–76 (Mateos 1949: 150 onward).

Apart from the catechisms in Quechua and Aymara, and the lexicon – the *Arte and Bocabulario* – Barzana also wrote a confession manual in those languages – *Confessionario*. Unlike Mexico, where a printing press already existed, it was not possible to print these works in Peru, so it was agreed that Baltasar Piñas would take all the texts to Rome. They had to be reviewed by *lenguas* and theologians to then obtain a confirmation papal bull and a licence from Philip II. Piñas embarked in 1577 and must have arrived in Rome in 1578, where he met with Mercurian, who agreed on the printing of all the texts, recommending that permission be asked of the *Consejo Real* – the royal council – first. However, in the end, Mercurian warned that Piñas had not brought the texts to be printed, and claimed that it was not convenient to request the papal bull as previously agreed (Vargas Ugarte 1953: XII–XIII).

In his capacity as provincial, Acosta visited Cuzco in 1578 when he toured the new foundations; the *doctrina de indios* – Indian parish – of Juli, in Chucuito, for Indians only; and the colleges of Potosí, Arequipa and La Paz. The *doctrinas de indios* were Indian parishes in which the priests – *curas doctrineros* – were in charge of the religious instruction of the Indians. In Acosta's times, each *doctrina* had 400 Indians. The main problem that the Society of Jesus had to deal with was Toledo's imposition of the *doctrinas de indios* as the preferred evangelization method in the province of Peru, for this represented a harsh attack on the Jesuit vocation of mobility. As mentioned in the introduction, the Jesuits' fourth vow – in Part Seven of the Constitutions – by which the professed members of the Society oblige themselves to 'special obedience to the sovereign pontiff regarding missions', was a vow about 'missions' – *circa missiones*. In short, mobility lay at the core of Jesuit missions. But the *doctrinas de indios* required a commitment to spiritual care – *cura de almas* – in the long term, so Jesuits had to settle there. Moreover, in the *doctrinas* the parish priests received a stipend, which was also against the Formula of the Institute – the fundamental rules of the Society. In this regard, José de Acosta played a key role by adopting a conciliatory approach regarding the *doctrinas*; in fact the Society did not have much of a choice if the Jesuits wanted to stay in Peru after Toledo's threatening tone. However, Acosta's good relationship with Viceroy Toledo would eventually divide the Society in Peru. As a result, a group of Jesuits was formed against Toledo's policies, headed by the Visitor of the Society in Peru, Juan de la Plaza and Luis López (Lisi 1990: 70 onward). Moreover, Acosta's good relationship with the Inquisition caused even greater problems within the Society in Peru. In his capacity as qualifier and personal friend of the inquisitors, Acosta was fully aware of the accusations against Luis López, imprisoned in 1578.

Actually, four months later another Jesuit, Miguel de Fuentes, was also taken prisoner, but it went no further than that. Unlike the other Jesuits, Acosta had access to this information and these procedures. Juan de la Plaza embarked from Sanlúcar de Barrameda to Peru in 1574 and arrived in Lima in 1575, to start office as visitor. He finished his duties in Peru in 1577 and went to Mexico three years later, in February 1580, to continue with the visits in the Mexican province. Acosta's provincialate in Peru coincided with Visitor Plaza's last period of service; and the coexistence of two superiors often caused frictions. In summary, the questions regarding the rapport between the Inquisition and the Jesuits made all the Jesuits in Peru grow mistrustful of Acosta and suspect him of having betrayed the Society in these Inquisition trials.

Before focusing on Acosta's performance at the Third Lima Council (TLC) (1582–83), it is important to first make reference to the two previous councils.

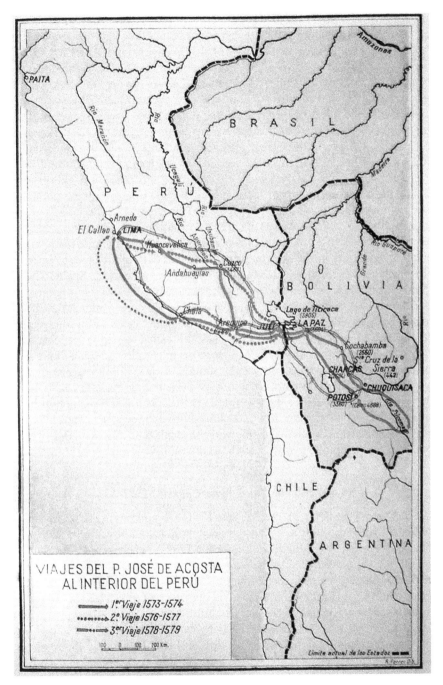

Figure 1.1 José de Acosta's journeys in the interior of the Peru province, León Lopetegui SJ, *El Padre José de Acosta S.I. y las misiones*, Madrid (1942)

This will help us understand the Spanish crown's purpose in overtly organizing these councils. In a nutshell, their purpose was none other than the subjection of the colonial church to the authority of the Spanish crown. The First Lima Council (FLC), held in 1551–52, was organized by the Archbishop of Lima, Jerónimo de Loayza, at Philip II's request. Loayza invited the bishops of Cuzco and Quito and all the representatives of the suffragan churches to a council with the idea of organizing the Church in Peru. However, the initiative was resisted by the suffragan bishops and the meeting was called off. An analysis of these problems and misunderstandings reveals two underlying trends in the Church in Peru in the second half of the sixteenth century: one to refuse to recognize the *Patronato regio* and its attributes and another to uphold the crown's authority and its intent to rule over the colonial church, independently of papal authority. This conflict is essential to an understanding of José de Acosta's actions during the TLC, and the steps he subsequently took in Rome advocating aggressive policies against the secular clergy, as expressed in the constitutions of the TLC (Lisi 1990: 40). Viceroy Toledo was unable to attend the council as he had to go back to Spain, where he returned in 1581; his trip was one of the reasons for the delay in organizing the council. His successor was Viceroy Martín Enríquez, and Alfonso de Mogrovejo succeeded Loayza as archbishop. Both Viceroy Enríquez and Archbishop Mogrovejo reinforced a steadfast alliance with the Spanish crown, which caused problems with the bishops of certain suffragan churches. One event that involved José de Acosta shows his close relationship with the royal authorities. In an attempt to neutralize Sebastián de Lartaún, Bishop of Cuzco, who was opposed to the royal policies, the viceroy and the archbishop requested Acosta to write a report against him. However, Provincial Piñas firmly prevented the Jesuit from following through with this demand, while Acquaviva grew indignant with the whole situation.

Acosta's last years in Peru: the Third Lima Council (1582–83)

The TLC was finally held on August 15 1582, and many scholars have highlighted the important role that the Society of Jesus played in it, as it was officially represented by Provincial Baltasar Piñas – successor to Acosta in that office – and Juan de Atienza, rector of the college in Lima. José de Acosta unquestionably played a leading role in the council, and his authorship of the council constitutions and the Spanish text of the TLC catechetical corpus is no longer under discussion (see Introduction, note seven).

Acosta himself assessed the work that he carried out in the council as his most important undertaking in his last years in Peru. This is what he wrote in a letter to Acquaviva in April 1584:

> During all these years I have dedicated my efforts to the provincial Council here celebrated, and which entailed many difficulties and hard work, and it was done in God's best service and was fruitful. Because,

even if it were no more than the Christian doctrine and catechism written and translated into the language of these Indies by the work of the Society and now printed in our house, it has been very useful.

(MP III: 401)

The more Acosta cultivated a solid relationship with the leading personalities of the council – especially Mogrovejo and Enríquez – the more distant he became from the Order in Peru. He focused on the synod and hardly participated in the Society's provincial congregation in 1582. Besides, he had already requested his return to Spain in 1580.

José de Acosta stands out not only because of his authorship of the council constitutions and his performance during the council, but also because of his defence of the council decrees in Lima, Madrid and Rome (Lopetegui 1942: 75–79). In 1584, from Lima, Acosta wrote to Acquaviva asking him to intercede before the Pope in favour of the council, to counteract its rejection by important groups in Rome motivated by his harshness towards the secular clergy (Lisi 1990: 82). Making good use of his writing skills, Acosta addressed the matter very cleverly, mentioning the behaviour of the clergy in the *Indias Occidentales* and its negative impact on the salvation of the natives. He claimed that

> each land has its own ailments and the same cure does not apply to all equally. The main concern here is the welfare and salvation of these natives and everything depends on the good example given by the priests and their zeal.
>
> (EM: 322)

Acosta repeatedly stressed the negative influence of the Spaniards' behaviour on the Indians, responding to the appeals by the chapters with lists of examples from the council acts, almost like a conclusion. The Jesuit regarded the Indians as – first –

> the object of scandalous behaviour and bad examples and [they] see in the law of Christ only greed and think that is the only reason for their indoctrination. Second, the Indians are insulted and cheated, because the priest makes them work at what he wants and pays them what he wants … . Third … keeping them busy in their farms and trade leaves no time for doctrine.
>
> (EM: 324–25)

Acosta finally set sail for Mexico at the end of May 1586, after claiming that he had done everything in his power to delay his departure because the Society in Peru needed his influence in the provincial council. However, interpretations aside, some scholars agree that the reason for leaving Peru was his particular situation in the Order (Lopetegui 1942: 577; Lisi 1990: 77–78). In a memo to Pope Clement VIII he claims that the reasons for returning were disease – a 'grieving heart' – and sadness, in view of which the general had ordered him to go back to Spain. According to Mateos, this 'disease of the heart' that Acosta attributed to moral suffering was the effect of the Andean heights. However, those who knew him often commented on his melancholic personality. As Acquaviva wrote in a letter to Piñas in 1583, it was that 'melancholic mood that gets hold of him' (Mateos 1954: XVI–XVII).

On his trip to New Spain Acosta took with him the TLC documents, at the request of Archbishop Mogrovejo, to present them to the pope and obtain his approval. In Mexico, Acosta met the Jesuit Alonso Sánchez, missionary in the Philippines, who had travelled twice to Macao – the Portuguese port near Canton, in the South China Sea. On his first voyage in 1582, Sánchez sailed from the Philippines to China to carry out two tasks assigned to him by the governor of the Philippines: to have Philip II recognized as King of Portugal and to establish commercial relationships between the islands and China (Astrain 1913: chapter three). Sánchez was successful in the first mission and failed in the second. In fact, failure in carrying out this second assignment aroused in him the desire to make war against China, as became apparent a few years later. This episode involving Sánchez will be analyzed at greater length in the next chapter, so let us now focus on the motives that drove Acosta to write the two memos against Sánchez's war plans.

In 1586, Sánchez left Mexico, arriving in Seville that same year, to negotiate in Madrid and Rome some issues regarding the Philippines. On his previous trips to Macao he had been informed of the problems that the Jesuits Ruggieri and Ricci and other Portuguese priests had come up against when trying to enter the Ming empire. The unbending Ming attitude toward foreigners and the obstacles the Jesuits had had to overcome drove Sánchez to state that the Christian word should be introduced in China in the same way as in Spanish America: first, by force of arms and, in a second stage, by preaching the Gospel. From Mexico, Acosta wrote two memos addressed to General Acquaviva confuting Sánchez's arguments. The first, 'Remarks on the War against China', of March 15 1587, listed four reasons why it was unlawful to make war against the Middle Kingdom and the second, 'Response to the Grounds for a War against China', of March 23 1587, was a complement to the first.[7] Acosta rebuts each of the statements in each of the chapters of Sánchez's memo about war against China, which Acosta considers unlawful. At the same time, Acosta is full of praise for the Jesuits who were in China, attempting to bring the word of Christ by peaceful means. This contrast between spreading the word by peaceful means in China, and doing otherwise in Peru and Mexico, apart from the – justified – submission by force of the 'barbarians' in the Caribbean, is a core aspect of Acosta's *De Procuranda*, to which I will return later.

When the two memos reached Acquaviva in July 1587, the general appointed Acosta as Sánchez's superior, with the order that any matters to be discussed in Madrid should be supervised and approved by him. Acosta remained in Mexico around a year and in March 1587 he left for Spain, carrying with him the works he had written in America: *De Procuranda Indorum Salute* and the first two books of *Historia Natural y Moral de las Indias*. In Madrid, at the end of 1587, Acosta had an interview with Phillip II and began procedures to have the TLC decrees approved: not an easy task as the council had imposed severe restrictions on the *curas doctrineros* – parish priests – regarding certain matters, like gambling, generating bitter complaints from the secular clergy. However, Acosta managed to keep the main decrees in force, especially those referring to the reform of the clergy, and obtained final approval of the council text, with some changes introduced by the Roman Curia aimed at softening the strict measures against the secular clergy.[8] The decree of approval was issued on the last day of October 1588, and Phillip II issued a *cédula real* – royal charter – for execution in September 1591. In short, Acosta accomplished his mission in Rome.

While Acosta was carrying out these negotiations in Rome, his first work, *De Procuranda Indorum Salute*, preceded by the treatise *De Natura Novi Orbis*, was published in Salamanca. *De Procuranda* was the first work written by a Jesuit in Spanish America; its full title is *De Natura Novi Orbis Libri Duo, et De Promulgatione Evangelio apud Barbaros, sive De Procuranda Indorum Salute Libri Sex*. It included a dedication to Phillip II in Latin, dated Madrid 1588, replacing a previous dedication to General Mercurian. This work will be further analysed in the second part of the book.

Acosta's literary activity in Spain was very intense. The Jesuit undertook the translation from Latin of the two books of *De Natura Novi Orbis*, which, with the five books that were originally written in Spanish, together make up his best-known work: *Historia Natural y Moral de las Indias*, published in Seville in 1590. One of the most original and outstanding features of this work is Acosta's idea of the interrelation between the 'natural world' and the 'moral world' as a rational continuity between the natural and moral. Acosta adjusted certain Aristotelian notions with regard to physics and cosmology in order to adapt them to the *Indias Occidentales*; in sum, he applied and updated Aristotelian thought in the 'natural history' part to explain the 'New World', and this is one of the reasons why Acosta's was undoubtedly a remarkable contribution to scientific thought in the sixteenth century (Acosta [1590] 1940: XXXII–XXXIII).

That same year – 1590 – the Third Lima Council constitutions, in Latin, were printed in Madrid. This had been ordered by Phillip II and approved by Pope Sixtus V. Finally, two more books composed by Acosta in Latin were published in Rome in 1590: *De Christo Revelato Libri Novem* and *De Temporibus Novissimis Libri Quatuor*.

Back to Spain: Acosta's political intrigues

Once in Spain, Acosta found out that a group of Spanish Jesuits – known as *memorialistas* – wanted to subject the Society of Jesus in the Iberian

Peninsula to the authority of the Inquisition and detach it from Rome. This was their solution to the spiritual and religious slackness ascribed to the Order, as well as to the authoritarian government of Acquaviva. The *memorialistas* were new Christians or *conversos*. During Claudio Acquaviva's tenure, a discriminatory legislation in 1593, officially barring the *conversos*, took place. However, the anti-*converso* policy started with Mercurian. The *conversos* participated in the revolt of some Spanish Jesuits against their central government in Rome (Maryks 2010: 117 onward). We must not forget that Acosta was a new Christian, as denounced by Alonso Sánchez.

The Spanish 'faction' devised a plan in 1595 which aimed at getting rid of Acquaviva by having him appointed Archbishop of Naples in the Capua see (Santos Hernández 1999: 131 onward). Phillip II suggested carrying out visits to the Order's different residences to satisfy the complaints of the *memorialistas* about alleged abuse and irregularities (Pinta Llorente 1952: chapter two). For that reason Claudio Acquaviva, well aware of Acosta's exceptional qualities – besides considering his good relationship with Phillip II and his services in Lima as qualifier of the Inquisition – picked him as his emissary before Philip II, who was at the time under the influence of this group of Spanish Jesuits. Meeting Acquaviva's expectations, in 1589 Acosta succeeded in negotiating with Philip II to appoint Jesuits in charge of the visits, instead of Bishop Manrique. Philip II authorized the Jesuits to carry out the visits; he claimed that he 'truly loved the Society, but they had better not get in his way'. José de Acosta was appointed Visitor of Andalucía and Aragón and Jesuit Gil González Dávila Visitor of Toledo and Castile. However, after this achievement in favour of the Society, Acosta's behaviour became unpredictable and ambiguous, especially regarding the organizing of the Fifth General Congregation of the Society.

From being Acquaviva's emissary against this group of Spanish Jesuits initially supported by Phillip II, Acosta switched to their side. There is proof of this in two documents of the time: the *Diario* – diary – of 1592 and the *Memorial a Clemente VIII* (EM: 353–68; Astrain 1909: 524) – Memorandum to Clement VIII. The *Diario* is a gripping document, in which Acosta himself narrates what became a game of intrigue in the alternating interviews with the Pope and General Acquaviva discussing the appeal to the Fifth General Congregation of the Order. Acosta points out one of the reasons for his change of attitude, regarding the double visit to Andalucía and Aragón. He claims that, even though the general had 'heartily approved' his visit he 'did not see that the right cure was conceived for all the other matters' (Mateos 1954: XXVI). A second reason had to do with Acosta's demotion by Acquaviva. After informing Philip II about the visit to Aragón in September 1591, the Jesuit stayed at the college in Madrid awaiting Acquaviva's orders, expecting an appointment as provincial in some Spanish see. But this appointment never arrived and Acosta received instead the order to preside over the professed house of Valladolid at the beginning of 1592. His spokesman, the Visitor Gil González Dávila wrote to Acquaviva:

Father José has spoken to me clearly and I see him so overburdened with melancholy that it fills me with concern … . The truth is that, Your Paternity not being able to grant him a position in these provinces, … he [Acosta] is still given a suitable position, so this does not become a reason for certain people being always eager to talk and ready to give their opinion.

(Astrain 1909: 520)

Acosta went to Rome as an agent of Phillip II and behind the backs of his superiors, with the idea of convincing Pope Clement VIII to impose on the Society – especially on Acquaviva – an extraordinary General Congregation to examine matters in Spain, with the powerful influence of Philip II on all the matters addressed. This idea was conceived by Acosta himself and he mentioned it to Phillip II in September 1591, expecting to be appointed to carry it out. In Rome he presented himself before Pope Clement VIII informing him about the condition of the Society of Jesus in Spain and the need for an extraordinary General Congregation. He blamed Acquaviva's government, 'absolute and excessively tyrannical in his ways' – for all the major evils (Mateos 1954: XXVI–XXVII). In short, Acosta begged the Pope to put a stop to this situation by imposing a General Congregation. Despite the Pope's decision to wait for Acquaviva's approval, Acosta chose to side with the Inquisition 'because the King is with the Inquisition and the Pope is with the King. If in Rome they believe we should not be advisors of the Holy Office, in Spain they feel just the opposite' (Astrain 1909: 527).

Acosta met with Acquaviva to warn him about a possible visit of a bishop or an Inquisitor to the Society in Spain – a very awkward situation – and to suggest that a General Congregation was a solution that Phillip II would find satisfactory. While Acquaviva was considering it, Acosta met with both the Pope and a personage who played an important role in this event: the Jesuit Francisco de Toledo, who would shortly afterwards be named Cardinal and who was not on friendly terms with Acquaviva. Acquaviva obeyed Pope Clement VIII's orders but complained that Acosta had carried out the negotiations behind his back; actions that the general regarded as an attempt to discredit him just before the General Congregation. Acquaviva's vexation towards Acosta became evident when the general ordered him to move his living quarters from the residence of the general – where Acosta had been staying – to the Penitentiary, without attributing him a position or title of any kind (Pinta Llorente 1952: 53).

The Fifth General Congregation of the Society of Jesus opened in Rome on November 3 1593. The litigating Spaniards – the *memorialistas* – were cornered, as the other Jesuits who had been summoned defended Acquaviva and the integrity of the Society's Institute. From the Spanish point of view, the *memorialistas* tried hard to obtain the independence of a group of Jesuits from the Italian General Acquaviva, who disagreed on Spanish methods and projects.

Once again, the Jesuit Alonso Sánchez appeared in Acosta's life. In 1592, even before knowing about Acosta's disloyalty, Acquaviva decided to send Alonso Sánchez to Madrid to defend the Society's Institute before Phillip II and the Inquisition. This time, it was Sánchez who was supposed to keep watch on Acosta. The problem was that Sánchez was a very sick man at that time, unable to carry out his mission until mid-1593, when Acosta was in the thick of negotiations in Rome. As already mentioned, it was Sánchez who informed Philip II that Acosta was a new Christian and 'none of these men, sooner or later, would conceal who they are'. Besides 'he has been driven by ambition, giving honourable sermons and desiring the allegiance of princes and celebrities. Indirectly he has sought to be praised and exalted' (Astrain 1909: 543). Correspondence of the time between Italian and Spanish Jesuits reveals an extreme rejection of the *conversos*. They were very close to the government of Phillip II and Rome feared them precisely because of their 'exaggerated hispanicization' within the Society of Jesus (Fabre 2008: 93–94).

Thanks to the important services rendered to Spain in the Philippines and Macao, Sánchez had no difficulty in approaching Phillip II and the royal counsellors. The only obstacles were his ailments. By and large, the main reason for Sánchez's aggressive actions against Acosta was his condition as *converso*, a disqualifying description for the Spaniards of the sixteenth century. Similar opinions against Acosta were voiced in Rome, describing him as a covert agent of the 'rebels'. Some memos against him reached the Pope. Acosta heard about this from Cardinal Toledo, and it drove him to write a disclaimer, *Memorial de Descargo o Apologia*, addressed to Clement VIII himself (Mateos 1954: XXIX).

To conclude, the Fifth General Congregation had a positive effect on the Society of Jesus, in the sense that it helped to downplay the dispute generated by the Spanish *memorialistas*. As already mentioned, the General Congregation turned out to be the opposite of what was expected, strengthening even more the authority of Acquaviva. At the same time, Phillip II was satisfied with Acosta and the results of the Congregation. Like the Pope, the King never left Acosta to his fate in Rome. As for Acosta, he did not hesitate to swear allegiance, loyalty and obedience to Acquaviva, who apparently harboured no hard feelings against him. After completing his period as superior of the professed house of Valladolid in 1595, Acquaviva encouraged Acosta to publish his works, i.e. his sermonaries and theological works. However, distrust was always present in their relationship. At first, the general was opposed to Acosta's appointment – suggested by several Jesuits – as rector of the college in Salamanca.

Acosta dedicated his last years mostly to literary activity, which he combined with his duties as rector of the college in Salamanca. Between 1596 and 1599, he published in that city three volumes of sermons in Latin: *Quadragesimam* (1596), *Conciones de Adventu* (1597) and *Tomus Tertius Concionum Iosephi Acostae* (1599). He died in Salamanca in 1600, at the age of fifty-nine, leaving several works unfinished.

Matteo Ricci in China: Jesuit and versatile politician

From Italy to China

Matteo Ricci was born in Macerata – capital of the province of Macerata in the Marche region – in central Italy, on October 6 1552, to a family of noble origin. Matteo was the eldest of thirteen children. The Society of Jesus opened a college in Ricci's home town in 1561, counting Matteo as one of its first students. Ricci spent seven years at the Macerata College, where his initial efforts were focused on mastering Latin grammar and acquiring the rudiments of Greek syntax. He graduated into the class of humanities, having spent two or three years reciting the letters of Cicero and other Roman poets while learning Greek grammar. Heavy doses of Latin – Cicero, Caesar, Sallust, Livy, Curtius for prosody, Virgil and Horace for poetry – and more difficult Greek prose prepared the students for the rhetoric class. In this discipline, memory was of foremost importance, as students were expected to recite long passages from Cicero and other authors. The heart of Greek learning was Aristotle: just as Cicero dominated the Latin curriculum (Fois 1982:216; Po-chia Hsia 2010: 4). Ricci would make very good use of this educational background once in China. Seven years later, in 1568, his father Giovanni Battista Ricci sent him to study law at *La Sapienza* in Rome. But Ricci's mind was not set on becoming a lawyer; he first joined the Sodality of the Annunciation at the Roman College of the Jesuits and on August 15 1571, Ricci asked to be admitted to the Society. His father went to Rome to dissuade him, but all attempts proved fruitless. In October 1573, after professing religious vows, Ricci joined the Roman College, where he began to study philosophy, physics, mathematics, rhetoric and other disciplines. One of Ricci's eminent professors was the famous mathematician Cristophorus Clavius (1537–1612), who undertook the reform of the Gregorian calendar. Fascinated by stories of Martino Da Silva, a Portuguese missionary who had travelled from India to Rome in 1576, Ricci requested he be sent to the East. Unlike Acosta, it remains unknown what motivated Ricci to make a formal request for the Indies. Whatever the reasons, Ricci was a successful candidate. In May 1577 Ricci left Rome for good and set out towards Portugal. The Portugal province was the first to engage in the missions overseas, ahead of the Spanish provinces with Francis Xavier, who arrived in India in 1542 and then with Manoel da Nóbrega in Brazil, in 1549. The distant missions became a 'natural' vocation of the Jesuit province in Portugal for both historical and geographical reasons; and that vocation also became a massive phenomenon (Castelnau 2007: 22–24). When Ricci arrived in Lisbon, the ships sailing to Goa, India, had already departed, so he stayed at Coimbra until March 1578. During his stay, Ricci learned the Portuguese language. At the time, the School of Philosophy of the University of Coimbra, the most prestigious university in Portugal, had undertaken the writing of commentaries on Aristotle, later known under the name *Conimbricenses*. Ricci began the study of theology at this university, but completed the first year in Goa, where he arrived in September 1578, together with the Portuguese Duarte de Sande and the Italian Michele Ruggieri. Ricci was ordained priest in Cocin, in July 1580.

In 1581, Visitor Valignano gave the order to send Francesco Pasio and other Jesuits to Japan, and Ricci to Macao, to join forces with Ruggieri in the attempt to enter China, which had closed its doors to Western foreigners, after a considerable number of years of Portuguese presence in the south. It was Ruggieri who had requested Ricci as companion for the China mission in 1581. Ruggieri had been learning Chinese in Macao, but he hardly practised it until he visited the Canton Province in April 1580, when the Portuguese trade fair took place. He went back to the city of Zhaoqing, in that province, a couple of times, before he returned to Macao in 1582 to meet Pasio and Ricci. In 1583, Pasio left for Japan, where he was assigned, and Ricci joined Ruggieri in Zhaoqing that same year. In this city the Jesuits built a first house and the first church, which they finished constructing in 1585. By then Ricci had adopted the Chinese version of his name, *Li Madou*.

In Zhaoqing, in 1584, the Jesuits launched their first publication in Chinese: the Ten Commandments. At the end of that year, the Jesuits sent a version to Rome, together with a translation of the main prayers into Chinese, i.e. the Pater Noster, the Hail Mary and the Creed. The printing press had been invented in Europe barely a hundred and fifty years before, whereas in China it had played a major role since the eighth century. Ricci always marvelled at the power of the written word in China, and he and his successors relied on the widely available printing press for the circulation of all their works. On his arrival, Ricci gave the local scholar-officials some objects he had brought over from Italy, such as glass triangles from Venice, clocks, prisms and holy paintings, all of which made a profound impression on the Chinese, who were unaware of the concept of perspective in painting. But Ricci's scientific knowledge, demonstrated in the design of his *Mappamondo*, printed for the first time in Zhaoqing in 1584, also impressed the Chinese. According to Ricci, the vast distances and seas separating their land from the Jesuits' calmed the Chinese and dispelled their fear of any plan of conquest, 'one of the major obstacles – said Ricci – to converting these people' (D'Elia 1942: 211, *Fonti Ricciane* – hereafter cited as FR I, etc.).

In those first years in the province of Canton – when they lived in Zhaoqing – the two Jesuits used to dress and look like bonzes – Buddhist monks – with shaven heads and wearing Buddhist habits. They announced that they served the Lord of Heaven – *Tiandi* – and came from India – *Tian zhuguo* – a place that for the Chinese represented all the nations west of China. At the time, the Jesuits referred to the Lord of Heaven using the word *Tiandi*, later replaced by *Tianzhu*. As Ricci explained, both *di* and *zhu* refer to 'lord' or 'master', and they are joined to *tian*, which means heaven (FR I: 180). It was one of the first baptized, a Chinese called Cheng, who came up with the name *Tianzhu*, which to date has remained the term for referring to the Catholic religion in China, as *Tianzhu jiao*. The Jesuits were unaware that it was the name of a Buddhist deity. Feeling the urgent need to transmit their doctrine, Michele Ruggieri soon started to write the *Tianzhu Shilu* or True Record of the Lord of Heaven (TZSL) of 1584. In his TZSL Ruggieri summarizes core aspects of the Christian doctrine with an apologetic tone in the form of a dialogue, a literary style shared between Europe and China. Chapter Four analyzes this doctrinal text; it suffices here to say that Ruggieri's TZSL translated Christian terminology for the first time. The manuscript circulated in the intellectual circles in the capital city, Canton, and Zhaoqing, in the same province of Guandong. There was a first edition of twelve hundred copies, soon followed by another one to total three thousand copies. Beyond the circulation of these manuscripts among the literati, the population of Zhaoqing was bewildered by the missionaries. Rumour had it that the Jesuits were alchemists who could turn mercury into silver, which was baffling as everybody knew they lived modestly. However, the Chinese did not know that the Jesuits received help from Macao. Ricci referred to the Daoist belief – or 'superstition' – of turning mercury into silver as 'pure madness' (FR I: 104).

In the first years of his mission, in his correspondence with Europe, and later in his account of the introduction of Christianity into China addressed to a European audience, Ricci would always describe the three 'sects' in China, i.e. Confucianism, Buddhism and Daoism, as three watertight categories.[9] This never did justice to the much more complex Chinese intellectual life in Ming China that Ricci grew familiar with, as shown in Chapter Three. Ricci especially stressed that Confucianism was the belief system of the ruling classes. Since all the scholar-officials had to go through an examination system to be granted positions in the imperial administration, and since the examination system was based on the Four 'Confucian' Books as its cornerstone, the *letterati* – Ricci explained – grounded their knowledge on Confucian doctrine (FR I: 44). And he said so in so many words to a distant European audience:

> That sect of literati is the oldest in China; that explains why it has always had control of the government, why it flourishes, why it has the most books and is the most esteemed. In this sect nobody is appointed by choice but by the study of the arts and no graduate or magistrate ever ceases to profess it. Its author or … authority has no idols. It only venerates heaven and the earth or the King of heaven.

> (FR I: 115)

Just as important as the element of political power, Ricci regarded Confucianism as the only non-idolatrous 'sect' in China.

As mentioned above, Ruggieri and Ricci wore the habits of Buddhist monks, as a first attempt to appear as religious persons. Some time before, Alessandro Valignano had observed that, in Japan, Zen Buddhist monks enjoyed great prestige. However, in China, Buddhism was a popular religion, something Ricci noted later somewhat disparagingly. Furthermore, the omnipresence of Buddhist idols led to his rejection of this 'sect', which in Ricci's view was no other than the incarnation of idolatry on Chinese soil; 'the devil is after them', as he said in a letter to Acquaviva in October 1585 (Tacchi Venturi 1911–1913: 57, *Opere Storiche* – hereafter cited as OS II, etc.). In a letter to the Vice Provincial of the Order in the East, Francesco Pasio, in the last years of his life, Ricci maintains this distinction of Confucianism with respect to the rest of the idolatrous 'sects'. He tells Pasio that 'even though the sect of the learned people does not talk about super-natural things, in moral issues it coincides with us' (OS II: 386–87). In sum, the non-idolatrous gentility that Ricci implicitly ascribed to the 'Confucians' also responded to his idea of Confucianism as a moral system that served to govern the empire wisely but was lacking in metaphysical or supernatural foundations. Compatible with Christianity at a moral and ethical level, the latter could provide Confucianism with a supernatural base.

Ruggieri had adapted to the new environment, apparently with no real contradictions towards the Buddhist persona. But he would be eventually sent back to Rome. In the autumn of 1588 Valignano requested the papacy to send an embassy to Beijing – an idea first suggested by Ruggieri in 1581 – and the visitor picked the latter for the mission. Nothing indicates that Valignano chose Ruggieri because he was a favourite in the China mission. Actually, in early 1584, Valignano had selected Duarte de Sande to be the superior of the mission and not Ruggieri. Ricci narrates how Ruggieri was willing to go back to Europe, for 'he was old, and could not learn the language' (FR I: 250). But Ruggieri was certainly not so old, at least not as to be sent back. Moreover, criticism and the absence of any kind of appreciation toward Ruggieri were also expressed in Europe. Indeed, once in Europe, Ruggieri produced a Latin translation of the Four 'Confucian' Books (see Introduction, note eight).[10] But he was not allowed to publish it because of the opposition of Valignano. In a letter to Acquaviva of December 16 1596 Valignano claimed that, through Father Gil de la Mata, he had heard that Ruggieri wanted to print a book of sentences cherished by the Chinese. Adapting Ruggieri's and Ricci's names to an awkward Spanish, Valignano continued undermining Ruggieri's work, for the Jesuit did not master the Chinese language and letters, so it seemed reasonable to Valignano

> to advise Your Paternity not to print it, for it cannot be well done, since father Miguel Rogerio [Ruggieri] knows little about Chinese language and letters, but father Mateus Ricio [Ricci], who learned it very well ... showed a good deal of that book that he had just composed and he told me he would sent it to Your Paternity ... as it is still left to curiosity to show the Europeans a moral doctrine that the Chinese have, be it father Mateus Ricio's and not Rogerio's .... And the same applies to the catechism, for Mateo Ricio, who understands the letters better now, is making another one, that it will be much better than Rogerio's.[11]

It is not hard to see Ricci's influence on the contents of this letter, since the visitor did not know Chinese. As for the mention of both catechisms, Ruggieri's TZSL and Ricci's TZSY, they will be analysed in the second part of the book.

After Ruggieri's departure, Ricci remained alone in Zhaoqing for several months, until Valignano sent Antonio de Almeida (1557–91) to meet Ricci in Zhaoqing. In 1589, the new governor in that city, who replaced Wang Pan – friend of the Jesuits – expelled the missionaries. That same year, the Jesuits arrived in Shaozhou, also in Guandong province, where they founded a second residence. Life in Shaozhou was far from easy. The people were aggressive with the Jesuits, and the air laden with impurities caused the death by malaria of Almeida in 1591 and of another father, Francesco de Petris in 1593, leaving Ricci very 'melancholic' (FR I: 331). But it was in this moment that Ricci started his friendship with Qu Taisu (1549–1611), a prominent literatus very fond of alchemy, a Daoist practice. For this reason he approached the Jesuits, who were suspected of producing silver. Ricci tells how he gradually introduced him to the world of mathematics, especially arithmetic and geometry. Qu wished to be baptized, but certain life habits he – along with other Chinese – normally practised became a serious obstacle to conversion: polygamy and concubines.

In 1591 Ricci began to study the Four Books or *Si Shu*: the Analects, the Great Learning, the Invariable Mean and the Mencius (see note 12). Then he started to translate them into Latin. This translation entailed a painstaking search for the right terms to express Christian names and concepts in Chinese, which enabled Ricci to write the TZSY, i.e. the catechism that would replace Ruggieri's TZSL. Ricci also set to the task of studying the digest of works known as the Five Classics, which are the Book of Changes, Book of Odes, Book of Documents, Book of Rites and the Annals of Spring and Autumn. Along with the Four Books, this compendium was the cornerstone of Confucian education.[12] And it became the same for the Jesuits: the learning of the Four Books and the Classics was part of their training in China, with a Chinese master who would go to their residence every day to read these works out loud. Ricci emphasized the value of the Four Books as moral philosophical works comparable to Seneca's or 'another of our famous authors among the gentiles', as he said to Acquaviva in a letter of December 10, 1593 (OS II: 117–18).

In 1596 Ricci finished the TZSY, which to a great extent fed on the Confucian canon, and was already fully dedicated to its revision. Apart from the copies that Ricci made for the closer literati, he sent a Latin version to the Bishop of Japan, in Macao, Luis Cerqueira. The visitor, Alessandro Valignano and the superior of the mission, Duarte de Sande, examined the text and highlighted all those points that needed to be corrected on the contents but not on the Chinese terminology. For different reasons, such as the death of Duarte de Sande, Ricci received the first corrected draft in 1601, the same year that the permission from the Inquisition in Goa arrived, which was imperative for printing 'all the books necessary for this Christianity' (FR II: 289).

In 1595 Ricci met a powerful mandarin who was passing through Shaozhou on the way to Peking to take his sick child to be cured. Ricci tells that he befriended the man with the excuse that he could cure the boy and asked to accompany him on his trip. They arrived together in Nanjing that same year. The city was hostile towards Ricci; an officer accused him of disrupting social order and expelled him. Yet this brief stay in the city was very significant, since Ricci left the bonze attire for good, changing to that of a Chinese scholar. Ricci narrates this experience in the third person:

> With Father Valignano's new trip to Macao – in October 1592 – F. Mateo Ricci tried to make the necessary changes in this enterprise so that the Fathers would have the authority to spread the Holy Gospel. And so they had already removed from the house the name of Buddhist monks that everybody used to address them … . With beards shaved … and short hair, as is customary in our land, the Chinese could only think of Buddhist monks, because they [the Jesuits] had no wife and recited the office and spent their time in church, all things similar to Buddhist monks. For that reason, F. Valignano warned of the need for us to let our hair and beards grow, because wearing them this way … led to thinking we were idolaters; because in China, shaving one's beard and hair is typical of idol worshipper sects.
>
> (FR I: 335–37)

Ricci took the initiative also at the suggestion of Qu Taisu, probably between the years 1589 and 1590. Even so, these measures required Valignano's approval, which he granted in 1594 – in a memo written in Portuguese – grounded on his understanding that bonzes in China did not have the same prestige as in Japan:

> Given that bonzes in China are snubbed and ignored by the mandarins, in using this bonze name we lose in credit and reputation. For a time, it suits to have the name of a scholar [*letrado*] rather than of a bonze. It is therefore advisable to refrain from wearing shaven heads, like the bonzes … to let beards and hair grow ear-length, like the Portuguese in the olden days … . Likewise, to wear the clothes that guests wear … or something appropriate for this, according to the custom … of the Chinese.[13]

Thus the fathers adopted a purple silk dress with blue edging and a square black hat, just like the mandarins. Ricci's study and translation of the Four Books and the adoption of Mandarin-style clothes in Nanjing helped open a network of relationships between the Jesuit and the literati and scholar-officials of different ranks, also including members of the imperial family (FR I: 380, note 4). Shortly afterwards, Ricci settled in Nanchang.

Ricci's intellectual experience in Ming China

Life in Nanchang was the starting point of an intense intellectual life for Ricci, in which he mingled and interacted with famous scholars in the academies, in a much more flexible milieu than that implied in his rigid idea of 'sects' conveyed to Europe. In Jiangxi province, where Nanchang is located, there were more private academies than in any other province, a total of 294 out of 1,946 academies in the Ming dynasty; it supplied one of the highest numbers of *jinshi* degree holders – the highest degree in the civil service examination system (Po-chia Hsia 2010: 149). But in Nanchang, Ricci was also introduced to the less official aspects of Confucianism, the world of academies and discussion circles. Ricci was beginning to appreciate that Confucianism was not a monolithic orthodoxy but a living doctrine with a variety of conflicting tendencies (Rule 1986: 22). As Ricci himself narrated in his *storia*, he also established relationships with controversial figures of the time, such as the thinker Li Zhi (1527–1602), who abandoned his wife to pursue enlightenment as a Buddhist monk, and flouted social norms by accepting unmarried young women as disciples. In Nanchang, Ricci also met one of the most outstanding scholars in that city at the time, Zhang Huang (1527–1608), an old man in his seventies, who used to teach many disciples in the city of Donghu, currently Hebei. In 1592, Zhang Huang was elected president of the famous Academy of the White Dear – *Bailudong Shuyuan*. He was impressed by Ricci's virtue and earnestness. Indeed, even though Ricci was always exhausted by the continual flow of guests he received at the residence, with no time left for study, he did not take up Zhang Huang's suggestion to order his servants to say that he was not at home – when he actually was. Ricci rejected lying as 'not virtuous' and 'forbidden for men of God' (Huang 1998: 131). Ricci actually made reference to a habit of the Chinese of telling lies, which he conceived as an obstacle against true friendship:

> There is no doubt of ... how blossoming insincerity and lies are in this kingdom, even among learned and noble men, as well as literati. It is because of this that nobody trusts anyone here, being the realm of suspicion, not only among friends but also among close relatives, between brothers, father and son, and nobody can be trusted. And everything among them is about an external politeness, and beautiful words, without true friendship and love coming from inside.
>
> (FR I: 101)

Ricci's friendship with the princes of *Le an* and *Jian'an* commanderies was the opportunity for the Jesuit to offer them the most valued gift: a treatise, usually translated as On Friendship or *Jiaoyou Lun*, of 1595, which was his first work in Chinese. The humanistic hue of Ricci's treatise is undebatable. One of the – many – works that influenced this writing is Cicero's *Laelius*, which places great stress on the bond between friendship and virtue. Ricci feigns the reason that drove him to write it, i.e. the princes' curiosity about how Europeans felt about friendship, so – always in the third person – 'the Father answered with all the material he could gather from our philosophers, saints and all the ancient and modern authors' (FR I: 368). The Latin humanism and stoicism of authors like Cicero, Quintilian and Seneca, which formed part of Ricci's cultural baggage, embodied attributes that the Chinese themselves held in high regard, such as the concept of virtue, and Ricci perceptively recognized this common ground (Spence 1985: 156–57). In doing so, Ricci started a 'spontaneous' transmission of Renaissance and humanistic culture in China, furthered with other works that succeeded this treatise (Standaert 2003: 368–75). Li Zhi had made some copies of Ricci's *Jiaoyou Lun* for his disciples; in fact, he himself had composed a piece on friendship. Ricci and Li Zhi were personal friends and both wrote on the subject, each of them establishing different models of it. But, despite their divergent perspectives, Li Zhi's Treatise on friends and Matteo Ricci's *Jiaoyou Lun*, shared common features (Huang 1995). Li Zhi also composed a poem for Ricci, included in his A Book to Burn or *Fen Shu*, in which he characterizes Ricci as a 'mountain recluse', a *shanren* (Li Zhi [1590] 1975).

In Nanchang, Ricci solemnly professed the fourth vow on January 1, 1596. That same year he composed his treatise, the *Xiguo Jifa* or Occidental Method of Memory, for the children of the Jianxi Province governor, also intended to circulate among the literati. Many of the literati whom Ricci met in the course of his life were those who participated and succeeded in the civil service examinations to obtain official posts within the empire. The learning process involved in this examination would begin with rote memorization during childhood. When learning about this training, Matteo Ricci composed his *Xiguo Jifa*. Partly inspired by Cicero and Quintilian, the most usual mnemonic system according to Western tradition was the architectural type, which Ricci showed to the Chinese as a memory palace (Spence 1985: 5). Over its six chapters, the *Xiguo Jifa* provides clear directions about how to build a memory palace, taking as a starting point the idea that human memory is like a storehouse in which men can store what they remember, ready to be used whenever they want. This is presented 'as a matter widely discussed by scholars in the West' (Ricci [1596] 1965: 9–10). Pleased with this and other gifts, the governor promised to start procedures to obtain a licence – an indispensable requirement – for the Jesuits to buy a house.

In 1597, Valignano disassociated himself from his responsibilities in India and dedicated himself exclusively to the supervision of the Japan and China missions; that same year he appointed Ricci as superior of the China mission. On his visit to Macao, Valignano had suggested that the Jesuits in the Ming empire try to penetrate the court in Peking and approach the emperor. Otherwise, the mission would face an uncertain future (FR II: 4). Ultimately, it took Ricci almost twenty years to found a residence in Peking. In October 1596, in a letter to Father Giulio Fuligatti in Rome, Ricci explained the great difficulties his mission had to face while attempting to spread the Christian faith. More than ever, the mission's success depended on the Jesuits being able to approach the emperor to then reach other layers of society:

> Now we are hoping to reach the king and, with his grace, obtain the licence to preach the faith. With his approval I guarantee that soon millions of souls will be converted. From what I can see, when I discuss with them, things about their laws disavow their sects and confirm our law. But, as I say, right now we do not want to force their conversion and are content to lay the foundations of an important work.
>
> (OS II: 216)

Due to the suspicions that Western foreigners aroused in the empire, obtaining a licence to preach the 'holy law' was of fundamental importance to the Jesuits. That is why in a letter to Acquaviva in 1596 Ricci told him that the fathers were required to 'tread with great caution'. In the same letter Ricci also boasts of the influential personalities whose friendship he had gained, like the sons of the Governor of Peking (OS II: 225). Like every foreign religion, the teachings of the Lord of Heaven had to be recognized by the emperor and they had to be officially allowed to remain in the empire with freedom to worship. All foreign religions had to be in line with the Confucian state orthodoxy at the ritual, religious, social and political levels, expressed in the concept of 'orthodoxy' – *zheng*. Any religious belief and activity divergent from the state orthodoxy of Confucianism could be regarded as 'heterodox' – *xie* – by the government if it was perceived as a threat to harmony and public order. It is important to notice that the Confucian concept of *zheng* is of another order than the monopolistic, all-inclusive, Mediterranean type of orthodoxy, of which Christianity – in its seventeenth-century, Roman Catholic, post-Tridentine form – was an outstanding example. Confucian orthodoxy is most explicit and demanding when dealing with beliefs, norms and rituals that are directly related to the social and political order and with individual self-perfection. Advised by his friends and interlocutors, the literati and scholar-officials, Ricci would always try to prove that the Christian teachings of the Lord of Heaven were on the side of orthodoxy – *zheng* – while he placed Buddhism and Daoism on the side of heterodoxy – *xie* – a recurring claim and distinction in Ricci's TZSY. Such claims had never been made by any other alien religion in China – in that respect it was a new phenomenon in the history of Chinese thought (Zürcher 1997: 615–21).

In 1598, Ricci left Nanchang and stopped at Nanjing; he arrived in Peking, the capital city of the empire, that same year. However, he found a hostile atmosphere, the same he had encountered before in Nanjing, and so prudently went on his way. On his return to Nanjing in 1599 Ricci was warmly greeted by the literati, whereupon he decided to found a residence. During the first years in Guandong, both Ruggieri and Ricci

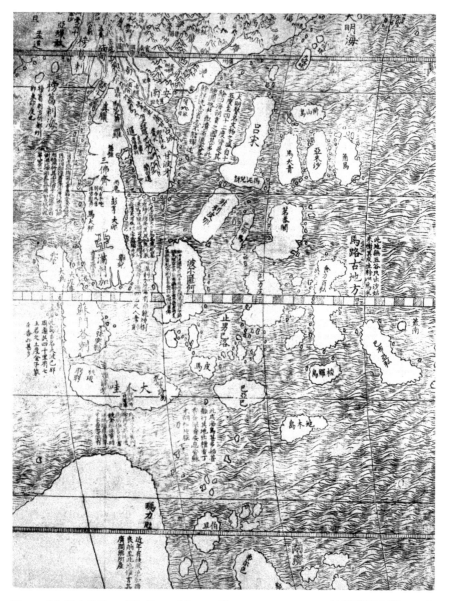

Figure 1.2 Detail from Ricci's world map *Kunyu wanguo quantu* 坤輿萬國全圖 (1602)
Source: Courtesy of USF Ricci Institute for Chinese-Western Cultural History

witnessed the great appeal that Western science held for the Chinese. Again, aiming to arouse the interest of the Chinese literati, Ricci set about spreading his scientific knowledge. In his view, none of the literati could object to the precision and accuracy of his scientific information and thus they no longer dared refer to the Jesuit's homeland – Europe – as 'barbarian', as they usually did with all lands outside the Middle Kingdom – one of the Chinese names for China (FR II: 51). Ricci's first scientific revelation to the Chinese was his vision of the rest of the world, which he did through his world map or *mappamondo*. It was not that the Chinese ignored the existence of distant lands, but compared to the precise information they had about countries in Asia, their knowledge of Europe could be hazy. In turn, Ricci's *mappamondo* fed on Chinese sources to correct his knowledge of Asia. Ricci reproduced some world maps he had brought from Europe and 'translated' their orientation into the Chinese convention, placing the Euro-Asian continent to the left and America to the right in order to put China in the central position. This was in keeping with the Chinese style, with China, the Middle Kingdom, in the centre described in detail and the surrounding countries described sketchily. Ricci's *mappamondo* was reprinted several times in the empire – sometimes in unauthorized versions – and reached the hands of the Wanli Emperor himself (Foss 1982: 179–182).

Another group of Ricci's scientific works was in the field of astronomy, referring to calculations related to the calendar, based on Arabic calculations introduced at the time of the Mongol Yuan dynasty (1271–1368) and of fundamental importance in China. These needed adjustments in relation to the seasons. A similar problem had arisen in Europe when the Gregorian calendar was adopted in replacement of the Julian one. In that case, the calculations had been made by Cristophorus Clavius, Ricci's teacher at the Roman College. But Ricci was aware of his limits for this task. He was not an astronomer, so he wrote to Rome requesting that one be sent to China. Ricci's contribution to mathematics was considerable. He brought Euclidean geometry commented by Clavius to China, as well as his arithmetical treatises and the *Astrolabium*. Together with his friend Xu Guangqi (1562–1633), a convert literatus, he translated into Chinese and published the *Elements* of Euclid, along with brief arithmetical treatises. These works involved a significant burden of translation of countless mathematical concepts (Martzloff 1995: 309–22). Joseph Needham pointed out that, after the arrival of the Jesuits in China, Chinese science blended with universal science. But, even though there was an exchange, it never affected the characteristics of Chinese scientific knowledge (Needham 1965: I, 148–49). In fact, the literati converts like Xu Guangqi and Li Zhizao (1565–1630), who worked in collaboration with Ricci, viewed Western science – especially in the fields of geometry and arithmetic – as a continuation of and complement to the Chinese mathematical tradition (Jami 1991: 157).

In 1600, Ricci set out for Peking in the company of Diego de Pantoja (1571–1618), the only Spaniard in the China mission before Ricci's death, who had arrived in the Middle Kingdom in 1597. In April 1596, Pantoja and eighteen other Jesuits embarked from Lisbon to Goa. He went together with Niccolò Longobardo (1559–1654), the future superior of the China mission who succeeded Ricci. In April 1597, led by Valignano and the Portuguese Jesuit Emanuel Dias, they all left from Goa, arriving in Macao that same year in July. When Ricci and Pantoja headed to Peking, they were taken prisoners in Tianjin by the eunuch Ma Tang; six months later they were released by a written order from Emperor Wanli (1573–1619) and entered Peking on January 24 1601.

Securing the mission in the imperial capital

In Peking, Ricci and Pantoja received the treatment given to ambassadors and the state paid for their accommodation and other expenses; the Jesuits were lodged in a house outside the city walls. On the second day, they entered the imperial palace. However, according to protocol, Emperor Wanli only appeared before his concubines and the eunuchs, and so Ricci never met him in person. The privilege of being allowed to enter the imperial palace served Pantoja as an opportunity to observe and describe the Chinese political system. Pantoja grew disgusted with the eunuchs, whom he viewed as the vilest group in Chinese society. He described them in a long account from Beijing to Luis de Guzmán, Archbishop of Toledo, entitled Account of the Entry of some Fathers of the Society of Jesus in China, of the Singular Events that Occurred and the Remarkable Things They Saw in the Kingdom'.[14] Pantoja stressed the double nature of the eunuchs, for they could be very submissive and servile, but real despots if they were granted the emperor's favour (Zhang 1997: 51–64). In the imperial court, both Ricci and Pantoja would have a close-up of Chinese polygamy, according to Ricci one of the main obstacles to gaining converts among the great personages (OS II: 275). Although generally overshadowed by Ricci, Ruggieri still earned his fame as Ricci's companion in the first years of the mission. But that fame has been seldom accorded to the Spanish Jesuit Pantoja as one of Ricci's companions in his last years in Peking.

Ricci's TZSY, published in Peking, started to circulate widely and be discussed in literati circles. Another doctrinal text, the anonymous doctrine or *Tianzhu Jiaoyao* (TZJY), reprints of which were also entitled *Shenjing yuelu*, was a collective work in which Ricci took part, published in 1605 (Dudink 2002: 38–50). It is a compendium of the most important prayers – the Lord's Prayer, the Hail Mary and the sign of the cross, the ten commandments, the creed, a list of the seven sacraments, designed for literati catechumens preparing themselves for baptism.

By 1605 there were two hundred neophytes in Peking and Ricci claimed a total of more than one thousand converts. The Jesuits had four residences at the time: Zhaoqing, Shouzhou, Nanjing and Peking. But – Ricci suggested – one should not judge the situation by the number of Christians as there were only four priests in charge of the mission: Diego de Pantoja, Lazzaro Cattaneo, João da Rocha and Niccolò Longobardo (OS II: 262). However, Ricci did not miss the opportunity to mention that, with more labourers in the vineyard, they could start to spread the sacred teachings in the villages, as shown below. In his *storia* and letters, Ricci always tried to offset the meagre number of converts with the quality of the conversions. He stressed the high quality of the few converts in Peking, easily observed in the frequency with which they received the sacraments of communion and confession (OS II: 263).

And Ricci never ceased to fight against the 'idolaters', proudly claiming that the way they were attacked in the TZSY had no precedent:

> Many idol worshippers were upset, because the catechism disavowed their sects, which had never been attacked like this before. But they soon discovered how they had been deceived by the founders of those sects ... and came to our house to listen to matters concerning their salvation,
>
> (OS II: 263)

What Ricci did not mention was that he was harshly criticized for his vehement attacks. Indeed, the disapproval of 'idolatrous sects' – especially Buddhism – generated hostile feelings, which Ricci tried to dispel by writing another of his works, the Twenty-five Sentences or *Ershiwu Yan* (1605), based on Epictetus' *Enchiridion* about stoic virtue (Spalatin 1975). As Ricci himself explains, this work does not confute the other sects; it approaches virtue stoically, but always accommodated to the Christian faith. The *Ershiwu Yan* was highly welcomed by his Chinese counterparts, who – according to Ricci – saw in it a proper way of imparting catechesis, that is, without confuting or attacking their idols (OS II: 264). However, the Jesuit's attacks against Buddhism and Daoism generated annoyance among certain officials, who threatened to give the emperor a memo against the missionaries, or confiscate their funds. But everything was resolved 'because the Emperor was in favour of the Jesuits and finally the Fathers were given – says Ricci – what was owed to them' (OS II: 264). Being realistic, Ricci had no high hopes about the emperor's conversion, as he explains in a letter to his friend Giovanni Battista in his hometown, Macerata:

> I am now in the court of Peking, very close to the Tartar country [Manchuria], and seemingly I will end my days here because the King wishes that I stay here and he supports and defends us. We don't have many hopes of his becoming a Christian, but this should not matter because with this favour many are converted and our other fellow missionaries are safe in the seventeen or eighteen places where the Society is based: many others are with us in several places, around fifty.
>
> (OS II: 264)

During that period, in both his letters and *storia*, Ricci repeatedly refers to the circulation of his works in successive editions, like On Friendship or the *Mappamondo*, which had been reprinted several times by 1605. In August that same year the Jesuits managed to buy a fourth residence in Peking, after having lived in different houses provided by the imperial court. Ricci was also able to negotiate a tax exemption for a public licence. With this, 'in this Court, capital of the kingdom, the Church began to enjoy ecclesiastic immunity' (FR II: 356). In those years Ricci undertook the translation of the first books of Euclid's *Elements*, with the Chinese convert and friend Xu Guangqi, and at the end of 1607 they wrote a brief treatise on geometry, *Celiang Fayi* or Meaning of Measurements Methods (Handbook 739). According to Ricci, the translation of the Elements aroused great admiration:

> It was just the right thing to moderate Chinese arrogance. The important literati were forced to admit that they failed to understand this book written in their own language, even if they studied it with care. Nobody thought that this could ever happen to them.
>
> (OS II: 335–36)

Among his last 'moral works', as Ricci would call them, the *Jiren Shipian* – usually translated as 'Ten Paradoxes of an Exceptional Man' (hereafter cited as JRSP) – were a great success, as he himself said in a letter to his fellow Jesuit Girolamo Costa in March 1608. Some of the paradoxes are included in the TZSY, especially the sixth, which analyses fasting. Unlike Buddhism, animal killing is not forbidden in the teachings of the Lord of Heaven. This work had a great impact among the literati, who extended numerous invitations to debate the paradoxes. In the debates – especially with the Buddhists – Ricci claims that 'the dispute was grounded on reasons and not on authority' – *non in autorità* (FR II: 78–79). Ricci also stressed the enormous power of written works as a way of obtaining benefits in China. Some of the Chinese literati, avid consumers of the Jesuit's works, converted to the Christian faith. Indeed, during Ricci's stay in Peking some of the highest officials converted to Christianity. Maybe the paradigmatic example is Xu Guangqi (1562–1633), who held the position of *Gelao* – secretary of state, baptized with the name Paul in 1603. Li Zhizao (1565–1630) was baptized in 1610 with the name of Leon. Yang Tingyun (1557–1627), baptized as Michael, embraced Christianity after Ricci's death but met the Jesuit in the capital city probably in 1602, when called to court to accept the position of censor (Standaert 1988: 53). Other literati close to Ricci, like Feng Yinjjing (1555–1606), died without being baptized. Chapter Three analyses key aspects of the reception of the teachings of the Lord of Heaven by the Chinese literati. A few of them, those closest to Ricci, actively collaborated with the Jesuit in composing European scientific works. Ricci always stressed the importance of these close ties since

> All of them kept their positions at Court, which worked in favour of the Fathers and matters regarding Christianity, without our people ever needing to request or suggest, and giving a rare example and spirit of Christianity to all those who observed them.
>
> (FR II: 309)

There are also many references to dialogues between the Jesuits in Peking and the mandarins of the other cities like Nanking and Nanchang, which showed:

They had proof of the great authority and good reputation enjoyed by our fathers, who are favourites and are well treated by the important personages. This also acted as a barrier to those who wished evil to the Fathers in other residences, aware that the Fathers of Peking could easily do them wrong if they so wished, only needing to speak ill of them with the great Mandarins, our friends.

(FR II: 312)

Ricci was often summoned to Court, to adjust the clocks given as gifts. There were enough proofs that the emperor held the missionaries in high esteem and favoured them. While Ricci remained in Peking, the growing presence of Jesuits in China allowed them to spread to other cities and Christianity reached the people who lived in the outskirts and neighbouring towns, as mentioned above. Jesuit Niccolò Longobardo, who would succeed Ricci as superior of the China mission, sought to extend the scope of the Christian faith in Shaozhou, when he saw that others of his peers, like Diego Pantoja and Gaspar Ferreira, managed to make converts in villages at two or three days' distance from the imperial city. Ricci himself narrates how Longobardo worked in the residence of Shaozhou, approaching the surrounding villages – Ricci here refers to a specific village, *Majia*. Longobardo transmitted the doctrine of the Lord of Heaven as in the TZJY, and recited the Ten Commandments. And the principals – *i principali* – were requested to learn the doctrine for Longobardo's next visit (FR II: 193). In sum, Ricci was able to witness – or at least to be informed about – the conversion of ordinary men and women in China before his death. But it could be assumed that Ricci felt comfortable with the responsibility of protecting the mission by forging and maintaining smooth relationships with the higher levels of the scholar-officials of the empire. As shown above, Ricci was the first to understand the conditions that foreign religions had to meet in order to be able to exist and remain in the empire. It was he who outlined *ad hoc* arguments to take the edge off these concerns: Christianity offered virtues that would contribute to the 'good governance of the Republic' and have a positive influence on moral behaviour, thus making it fully compatible with Confucianism, which – in his eyes – had no idols. Ricci thus concluded:

This is not a structured law but a school [*academia*] established for good governance of the republic. Therefore, they can belong to this school and become Christians, as its essence contains nothing against the Catholic faith neither does the Catholic faith forbid it; on the contrary, it greatly contributes to the quiet and peace of the republic, as their books expect.

(FR I: 120)

Nevertheless, the Christian religion was on some occasions branded 'heterodox'. Between 1616 and 1617 there was a 'persecution', as the Jesuits would call it, of considerable significance in Nanking. The Nanking 'persecution' was conceived as an attempt to control Christianity in China at state level rather than to ban Christianity. The Minister of Rites, Shen Que, accused the missionaries of, first, spreading a heterodox teaching and – given the strategic location of their residence – of espionage, in addition to a private use of the calendar (Dudink 1995: 2–16).[15] Actually, Ricci had seen and heard signs of persecution already in 1607, when Christianity started to spread in the provinces. In summary, from Ricci onwards, missionaries had to constantly remind the ruling class that they were not a threat to public order.

Ricci's unceasing restless activity eventually drove him to death; and this he expressed with a certain sense of foreboding to the Superior of the Residence in Peking, Sabatino de Ursis, on 3 May 1610. Lying ill in his bed Ricci stated: 'this disease, caused by excessive activity, will be my death' (FR II: 537). And so it was: Ricci died a few days later, on May 11 1610. In an account of Ricci's death dated May 20 1610, Sabatino de Ursis explains the cause of Ricci's fatigue and death. Due to his fame and reputation, Ricci would receive candidates for the civil examinations in Peking, coming from different parts of China, who wanted to visit the famous Jesuit, and this, in turn, contributed to make him tired to death (AUG, N. 292, f. 181).

The missions in Peru and China became a space in which Acosta and Ricci proved how their education in Jesuit colleges provided them with various resources for their missions. Acosta was needed in Peru mainly as a theologian, while Ricci excelled at conveying his humanist and scientific knowledge to the Chinese with great versatility. His merit was his versatility, which indeed fed on his cultural background. Apart from their education, they both had a taste and vocation for power. As regards Acosta, it was always clear to him that, in Peru, he would collaborate with the Spanish crown and its representatives in his capacity as theologian, even if this caused frictions inside the Society in the Peru province. Right from the beginning, Acosta sharply detected where the power was and never fought against it, nor resisted it; he was actually a collaborator. In Spain he was one of the Jesuits active in the context of the 'Spanish crisis' that affected Acquaviva's government, part of a global crisis scenario in the structure of the Society of Jesus (Certeau 2006b: 172). Since Acosta was the theologian of the mission, the *Doctrina Christiana y Cate-cismo para Instrucción de Indios* (DCC), the title of the TLC corpus, fed from his *De Procuranda*, conceived as the project of the Society of Jesus in Peru. But, at the same time, it is totally in line with the needs of the Spanish *Patronato Regio* to unify and impose a single authoritative orthodoxy, harbouring Tridentine Catholicism in Peru for the first time, in an unprecedentedly harsh Counter-Reformation tone. In sum, Acosta's writing skills as a Jesuit, theologian and politician are present throughout the DCC.

While Acosta whittled his political skills in Spain in a double game with Rome, Ricci devoted his efforts to strengthening his ties with the scholar-officials of the Ming empire and with the emperor himself, totally absorbed by the Chinese world from which he would never depart. Though often not

Figure 1.3 Matteo Ricci's tombstone in Beijing
Source: Courtesy of USF Ricci Institute for Chinese-Western Cultural History

recognized as a 'politician', Ricci's greatest merit in this regard consisted in understanding the late Ming's political codes in order to guarantee the permanence of the mission in the empire. Ricci succeeded in capturing the interest of all those he consciously sought to charm: the Chinese scholars and the emperor, who did not convert but provided the Jesuits with the official protection that was a necessary requirement to guarantee the permanence and future of the mission in China. And, because of that protection the mission could expand and reach less sophisticated layers of society. In this regard, the TZSY is always trying to set the minds of the political authorities' at rest. The teachings of the Lord of Heaven contribute to harmony in the empire, not chaos.

These two 'selective' biographies show the extent to which the Society of Jesus offered its members countless opportunities in which to display their talents. Indeed, the expansion and extension of the Order relied on the combination of discipline and individual freedom (Fulop Miller 1929: 34). In this regard, the Society of Jesus created its own fields of tensions, marked by multiple identities as a result of local mediations by its members and their own strategies acting in different contexts, but within the requirements of the Ignatian legacy (Romano 2011).

As for their personalities, one element in these two 'selective' biographies is the melancholy mood shared by the two Jesuits. Acosta was described by his peers in these terms – which makes us think that he really was a melancholic – and Ricci describes himself as such; almost all mentions of a 'black humour' in his *history* are self-referential. Undoubtedly, all missionaries may feel nostalgia as a result of their condition of wandering pilgrims and travellers in unknown lands (Corsi 2008c: 172). Some – like Ricci – never returned to their homeland, although this might not have been a problem for him.

Notes

1 Founded close to the University, by 1546 the Jesuit College at Alcalá de Henares had already become one of the most important Jesuit colleges.

2 ARSI, Provincia Toletana, 12a, I, f. 36v. The triennial catalogue aimed to inform about both individual careers and capacities and the material conditions of the houses. It is three-fold; the first or *Primus* provides a) general information on each member, i.e. name, age, nationality, health condition, studies before entering the Society; b) studies in the Society and c) *ministeria*. The second or *Secundus* was reserved to the provincial and general; it comprises an appraisal of each individual: judgment, prudence, experience, temperament, behaviour. The *Tertius*, generally called '*catalogus brevis*', describes the expenses and income of each house. See ARSI *Glossario Gesuitico, Guida all'Inteligenza dei documenti*, Roma 1992.

3 ARSI, Fondo Gesuitico, mss 77 III, f. 111.

4 ARSI, Assistentia Hispaniae, 110, ff 251–252v.

5 Two expeditions sent to Lima preceded Acosta's: the first, with eight members of the Society of Jesus in 1568 and a second one, with a larger group, in 1569 together with Viceroy Toledo.

6 The accusations against De la Cruz were triggered by a sermon in the Santo Domingo Convent in Lima in honour of Saint Thomas the Apostle, considered to be the one who originally spread the Christian word in Peru. De la Cruz had taken

part in spreading the worship of Thomas the Apostle in the Titicaca region, where the Andean hero Tunupa was identified with the apostle (Estenssoro 2003: 185–88).

7 *Parecer sobre la Guerra de la China*, Méjico (EM: 331–33) and *Respuesta a los Fundamentos que Justifican la Guerra contra China* (EM: 334–45).

8 Those decrees condemning clergymen's commercial practices in the Indies were the most controversial (Astrain 1913: 516).

9 Ricci died before finishing his account, which reached Europe in 1614 thanks to Nicolas Trigault, a Belgian Jesuit who completed the manuscript in Latin. Between 1942 and 1949, Pasquale D'Elia SI entitled this account *Storia dell' Introduzione del Cristianesimo in Cina*, and edited it under the general title of *Fonti Ricciane*. See *Storia dell'Introduzione del Cristianesimo in Cina*, nuovamente edita ed ampiamente commentata col sussidio di molti fonti inedite e delle fonti cinesi da Pasquale M. D'Elia SI, Roma, La Libreria dello Stato, 1942–49, Vol. 3.

10 The Four Books are usually regarded as 'Confucian' because they were essential to Confucian learning, especially from the late Song period onward.

11 ARSI, Jap-Sin 13, 1: 46–46v.

12 This compendium experienced changes over time, since it was once also integrated by the Book of Music (*Yue Jing*), lost in the Qin dynasty (221–206 BC).

13 ARSI, Jap-Sin 14: 230; FR I: 336, note 1.

14 The original Spanish title is *Relación de la Entrada de Algunos Padres de la Compañía de Jesús en la China y Particulares Sucesos que Tuvieron, y de Cosas Muy Notables que Vieron en el Mismo Reino*.

15 Among the novelties brought to China by Western missionaries were liturgical calendars, which were pivotal in ordering ritual life. Such calendars introduced to the new converts the organization of 'Christian time' (Menegon 2005: 196–97).

2   The missions

The nature of political constraints in the Jesuit missions

This chapter focuses on the particular period when the Society of Jesus projected itself beyond European borders in new spatial layouts, into the new territories split between Spain and Portugal, under the jurisdiction of the Spanish *Patronato* and the Portuguese *Padroado* respectively. Both were the result of an agreement that stemmed from the promulgation of a number of Papal bulls in 1493 in which sovereigns were commanded to spread the word of Christ among the 'gentiles' in their overseas possessions, for which they were empowered to appoint ecclesiastical authorities and handle ecclesiastical matters. This chapter explores the relationship between the Society of Jesus and the Spanish *Patronato* on the one hand and the Portuguese *Padroado* on the other, with the Society branching off in separate directions as it accommodated to the instructions of the two crowns regarding evangelization in their respective colonies. But, before addressing these themes, it is necessary to outline a general overview of the origin of the royal patronage system in Spain and Portugal and its projection and effects in the sixteenth century.

Overseas expansion and inception of the Jesuit missions

This story starts – briefly – with the voyages of exploration carried out by Portugal, Columbus's expeditions and the announcement of his discoveries to the Catholic sovereigns Ferdinand and Isabella.

The travels of Vasco da Gama (1469–1524) and his discovery of a sea route from Europe to India round the coast of Africa transformed Lisbon into Europe's business hub, with a commercial route that linked it directly with Asia. In 1511, Portuguese merchants travelled to Goa and Malacca; in 1517 they entered the south of China via the estuary of the Pearl River, leading to Canton. There, they carried out a highly profitable trade, which consisted mainly in transporting spices from the Moluccas to China. Tomé Pires, the first Portuguese 'ambassador' in China, reached Peking in 1520, but the Emperor *Zhengde* (1505–21) of the Ming Dynasty died before receiving him (Boxer 1967: xxi). With the 'discovery' of Japan in 1542, the Portuguese greatly benefitted from their role as trade intermediaries between Japan and China. During the Ming dynasty (1368–1644), China had purposely erected a wall to isolate it from the onslaught of the *wokou* – Japanese pirates – on the Chinese coastline and the Portuguese presence in the south. Trading with Japan was officially banned in the 1480s. This had damaging effects on Chinese merchants, whose only alternative way of trading with Japan – other than the ever present option of smuggling – was by exploiting the Portuguese's role as middlemen. Besides their status as unique suppliers of European and Indian goods to the Japanese, the Portuguese also virtually monopolized the export of Chinese silk, which was no doubt the most profitable part of Chinese–Portuguese trade (Boxer 1948: chapters 1&2). Thanks to this commercial relationship with Japan, they obtained permission to establish themselves in Macao in 1557. Once trading became a regular activity, Goa was used as the departure point of the voyages and Macao was set up as a warehouse where the raw and finished silks acquired in Canton were loaded. Portugal thus played a leading role, combining maritime expansion with business interests. At the time, its motto was 'spices and souls', the latter being in the hands of the Dominicans in the early sixteenth century. In this context, according to David Brading, the fact that Columbus found support for his voyages in Spain rather than in Portugal or England changed the course of history, as, had it not been for his personal participation, Spanish America would never have existed (Brading 1991: 10). When Columbus informed the Catholic monarchs of his discoveries, Ferdinand and Isabella announced them to Pope Alexander VI, who promulgated four bulls during 1493 – the two *Inter Caetera*, *Eximiæ Devotionis* and *Dudum Siquide-muna*. *Inter Caetera* excessively tipped the scales in favour of the Catholic monarchs, because it excluded Portugal from American enterprises even though it had already set foot in what is now Brazil. The bull was therefore threatening and unacceptable to the Portuguese. The Catholic Monarchs negotiated with John II of Portugal (1502–57) and, on the basis of the Treaty of Tordesillas of June 1494, agreed to stretch the line delimiting Spanish territory further to the West, thus covering enough of the American continent to be able to grant Portugal title over Brazil. Notably, Spain extended its colonies beyond this legal framework when it conquered the Philippines in 1565. This expansion of Spanish rule to the Philippines was a severe blow to Portugal's monopoly in East Asia, with Manila trying to compete with Macao as Spain's future gateway into China. However, although according to the *Unión de Tomar* of 1581 the crowns of both Spain and Portugal reverted to Phillip II, the same did not apply to administrative matters with regard to the overseas possessions in East Asia under the Portuguese *Padroado*'s jurisdiction. This caused much annoyance among the Spanish Franciscans, Dominicans and Augustinians, who resented being excluded from China and Japan. Despite it being a well known fact, it should be noted that, from the very beginning, Portugal developed the strategy of connecting commercial points and skirting territories rather than penetrating them. The exception was Brazil in South America, where the Portuguese empire implemented extensive colonial control.

The royal patronage system changed the worldly and spiritual relationship between the papacy and the burgeoning modern states, especially in terms of the exercise of power in the period from the middle of the fifteenth century extending into the sixteenth century. These changes took place at two different levels. On the one hand, there was the exercise of papal authority over the Latin Church during the decline of the medieval *respublica Christiana*, and on the other hand there was the vigorous rise of modern states. So two parallel processes took place: the 'clericalization' of modern states on the one hand, and the 'laicization' of the papacy on the other. The process of 'clericalization' is reflected in the strong leadership by the Spanish and Portuguese crowns in the task of evangelizing their colonies and, in the case of Spain, in Phillip II's firm determination to implement the Tridentine decrees in both the Iberian peninsula and his overseas possessions in the mid-1560s (Prodi 1987: 157–81). In fact, during the time when the Tridentine reforms were implemented in Spanish America, the ecclesiastical authorities – particularly the bishops and their dioceses – had practically no contact with the pope and the Roman Curia. Any communications between the prelates and the pope were channelled mainly through the king and the *Consejo de Indias* – the Council of the Indies (Villegas 1975: 67 onward). Likewise, prelates in America showed great interest in attending the council, but the *Consejo de Indias* – with the king's approval – refused them permission to attend. The 'official' claim was that this would avoid prolonged absence from their dioceses to the detriment of the evangelization of the natives. However, the real reason was to avoid any kind of situation in which bishops could discuss the abuses that occurred as a result of the conquest (Aparicio 1972: 217 onward).

Undoubtedly, the responsibility and duty to evangelize the gentiles was simply one among the many ways of further strengthening the king's power and his active role in ecclesiastical matters in his colonies (Elliott 1984: 104). However, in the case of the Spanish crown, this process was justified by the fact that not everybody agreed on the legitimacy of its domain in America. This originated in the debates between Juan Ginés de Sepúlveda and Bartolomé de Las Casas in Valladolid in the period 1550–51. The reasons justifying the crown's power were grounded in the inner core of Thomist theology and the philosophy of the University of Salamanca and its major exponents, among them Francisco de Vitoria. Rejecting the canonical doctrine of universal papal monarchy, Vitoria, and later Las Casas, was of the opinion that the papal donation of 1493 was the ultimate justification for the Spanish empire in the 'New World'. And this did not imply recognizing that the pope – as Vicar of Christ – had worldly dominion over all the kingdoms of the earth, Christian and infidel.

The rulers of overseas empires summoned the Society of Jesus to evangelize their new subjects in this expanding world. Indeed, the first generation of Jesuits was committed to the promotion of *Christianitas* in their three countries of origin: Portugal, Spain and Italy. Six provinces were already active in 1553: India, Portugal, Castilla, Aragon, Brazil and Italy (see Introduction, note 5).

This meant that, from the outset, Jesuits were dependent upon the whims of secular authorities, compelled to rely upon the support and protection of the governments of the nations in which their Order served and to yield to the constraints they imposed (Alden 1996: 656). The Iberian Peninsula was the starting point for all Jesuit enterprises beyond Europe. The Portugal province was the first to engage in the missions overseas, ahead of the Spanish provinces, with Francis Xavier in the East in 1542 and with Manoel da Nóbrega in Brazil in 1549. Indeed, the first impulse to venture beyond the old world came from King John III of Portugal in 1540, the same year that the Society of Jesus was recognized by Pope Paul III.

From Xavier to Valignano: the Jesuits in Japan

In 1540, Francis Xavier and Simão Rodrigues went to Lisbon at the request of King John III. The king was anxious to host in his kingdom Jesuits appointed for the Christianization of the gentiles in his overseas possessions. Rodrigues set up the Order in Portugal on a permanent basis, whereas Francis Xavier sailed to India in April 1541. The king's appeal also responded to a need to improve the quality of religious life in the kingdom, where simony, absenteeism, cohabitation, slackness in spiritual duties, ostentation and worldly concerns were becoming too obvious to overlook. One of the main duties of the Jesuit colleges in Portugal – Santo Antão, the Order's first college in Lisbon since 1542, and subsequently the University of Evora in the 1550s – was to train missionaries for overseas missions. In 1542 Francis Xavier arrived in Goa, the city that would become the Society's most important teaching centre in East Asia and main recruitment centre for those who had received previous training in Europe. For two years, Xavier taught catechesis to the pearl fishermen on the east coast of Cape Comorín, using simple prayers he had translated into Tamil. In 1549 he arrived in Kyushu, Japan, where he stayed for two-and-a-half years. That same year the Province of the East Indies – *Indiarum Orientalem* – was separated from the Province of Portugal – *Lusitaniae*.

Xavier praised the virtues and intelligence of the Japanese, but word had it that the Chinese were even superior in culture and learning. As he wrote from Cochin in 1552, the year of his death, 'People from China ... they are wise, wiser than the Japanese, and extremely learned' (MS: 125). He therefore decided to enter the Middle Kingdom, a feat that he nevertheless failed to accomplish. Xavier died on Shangchuan Island in the South China Sea, on December 3 1552, a few miles away from his destination.

When Xavier departed from Japan in 1551, the mission was left in the hands of a small group of Jesuits. The Society in Japan was divided into three jurisdictions: Shimo, Bungo and Miyako, each with their houses and residences. From 1551 until 1570, the missions' Superior was a Valencian, Cosme de Torres (1510–70). Torres was responsible for some notable conversions, including the lord of Bungo, who permitted the Jesuits to establish the archipelago's first hospital at Funai – now Oita – in 1556. When Torres died, he left a Christian population that approached 30,000 (Alden 1996: 61). His successor, Francisco Cabral, took charge of the mission until the arrival of Alessandro Valignano, who undertook the first of three extended visitations to the archipelago between 1579 and 1582. Born in Naples, admitted to the Society of Jesus in 1566 and appointed Visitor of the Province of the Portuguese Indies by General Mercurian in 1573, Valignano was an imposing figure, whose influence was intensely felt in the missions to the East. He travelled regularly between India and Japan, making a total of three trips. As mentioned above, his first visit to Japan was in 1579 and he stayed until 1582. The second was from 1590 to 1592 and the last from 1598 to 1603. His *Sumario de las Cosas de Japón* [1583] (1954) – the Japan Summary, hereafter cited as Sumario – is the result of the first trip to Japan; the *Adiciones del Sumario* [1592] (1954) of the second one; and the *Apología de la Compañía de Jesús de Japón y de la China* (1598), the *Principio de la Compañía de Jesús de Japón y de la China* (1598) and the *Principio y Progreso de la Religión Cristiana en Japón* (1601–03) were written during the third visit. As a visitor in an order as centralized as the Society of Jesus, Valignano enjoyed full powers to oversee and rule the mission. He had the authority to accept, transfer or discharge members in his jurisdiction and to implement new missionary policies as long as the general approved them. In turn, the visitor was obliged to submit detailed reports of his activities and the policies implemented to the authorities in Rome and Portugal, and the General of the Society could overrule any of his decisions.

When appointed visitor in the Portuguese Indies by General Mercurian in 1573, Valignano stayed in Spain, recruiting suitable candidates for his great enterprise. He spent a brief sojourn in Portugal before sailing to Goa. Valignano was at odds with the Jesuits in the Portugal province, mainly facing problems on account of the numerous Spanish Jesuits that formed part of his entourage. Frictions with the Spanish missionaries in the Society were a sensitive issue at that moment, because of the conquest of the Philippines by Philip II. This enterprise by the Spaniards indeed caused alarm among the Portuguese magnates and in their business in the *Indias* (Lopetegui 1947: 24–25). Valignano disapproved of the harshness of the Spanish, which he found in overt contradiction with the *spirito soave* – mild spirit – of the Society, as an expression of the Ignatian spirit, that he would advocate in the East. The visitor was to later experience the bitter taste of similar disagreements in Japan.

Valignano conceived accommodation as the only possible way of bringing the Christian faith to Japan, and his ideas in this regard actually grew out of his disagreements with Cabral. The first aspect they disagreed upon was a local clergy. Additional manpower was needed for the growth of the Japan mission and, as Valignano concluded, the success of Christianity in Japan depended on the development of an indigenous clergy; Ricci would later support the same idea in China. Francisco Cabral strongly disagreed and remained sceptical regarding such a prospect. Indeed, the visitor was convinced that the time was fast approaching when Japanese should be admitted to the Order. However, ruler Toyotomi Hideyoshi's edict peremptorily ordering the banishing of the Jesuits in 1587 set a natural limit to that kind of optimistic prospect, as will be shown below (Alden 1996: 62–63).

When Valignano arrived in Japan in 1579 he noticed that the Japanese held a grudge against the Jesuits. This he attributed, amongst other things, to the severe discipline enforced by Cabral, his belief that the Japanese had to adjust to the Jesuits' methods, his ongoing critical attitude towards their customs and his refusal to learn Japanese except for the basics of communication (Ücerler 2003: 360–61). Right from his arrival, Valignano strove to reverse this trend by setting new guidelines: learning the local language, respecting Japanese etiquette and adopting their customs – from food to attire – and rituals. These rules would eventually be communicated to Michele Ruggieri and Matteo Ricci when they were preparing to enter China. The learning of the vernacular, i.e. Japanese and Chinese, was at the core of Valignano's directives on accommodation or adaptation, although he was always aware of the enormous effort that this implied. Valignano's appraisal of his disagreements with Cabral helped to shape the method of accommodation as he conceived it:

> since they [the Japanese] will not change their things, we are the ones to accommodate to them as seems necessary in Japan, and this means a lot of effort for us ... having to change our nature, the difficulty is on our side to try whatever it takes to reach them, and it is not on their side (Sumario: 211).

For all these reasons, the missions in Japan and China always summoned the Society's 'most virtuous men', as the visitor would call them. At that moment, the Society was alone in Japan and, as Valignano himself points out, it carried 'the burden of governing this entire new Church, which can definitely not be based on European laws' (Sumario: 136). This disagreement was sealed with Cabral's reassignment in 1579 and the appointment of a supporter of Valignano, Gaspar Coelho. By 1586 there were one hundred and thirteen Jesuits, twenty residences, two hundred churches and an estimated two hundred thousand Christians in Japan (Alden 1996: 63). However, some members of the Society did have certain qualms regarding Valignano's accommodation method imbued with the *spirito soave*. Indeed, some of the Jesuits in Japan resisted the visitor's vision, and even the general, Claudio Acquaviva, Valignano's friend, harboured serious doubts about its viability. Pedro Gómez, theologian of the mission and vice-provincial since 1590, had the task of introducing and adjusting the Society's Institute. Gómez could not hide his disappointment at Valignano's attitude, not putting his heart into reducing all the missionaries 'to the clean and pure behaviour of the Society'; accommodation interfered negatively in the procedures. The introduction of the *Regulae Instituti* of the Society in Japan became even more difficult with the arrival of a letter from Acquaviva in 1585, in which he was specific regarding certain methods, giving both his approvals and objections. By and large, the issue was about maintaining the 'purity of the Institute' and its adjustment in Japan, when sometimes it was hard for the two to be compatible with each other (López Gay 1972: 86). In sum, the factors that conditioned the accommodation of the Society in Japan originated in the heart of the Society itself rather than from the authorities empowered by the *Padroado*, an important contrast with the Spanish authorities and the Society of Jesus in Peru, as will be seen below.

The 'loneliness' of the Society in Japan did, however, have its bright side. In fact,

> Our Lord has reserved this big enterprise for the Society only … . And, as the Society is in charge of all the Christian community in this area, without the presence of others contradicting it and following other methods, everything is done in a way regarded as suitable.
>
> (Sumario: 134)

In his *Sumario de las Cosas de Japón* of 1583, Valignano made no secret of his preference for the exclusive presence of the Society in Japan and its implications in terms of sending ecclesiastical authorities, especially bishops. There were various reasons why there would have been no point in a bishop being sent to Japan, as Valignano stated in a letter of August 1580 to the Archbishop of Evora, Theotonio de Bragança (1530–1602):

> The first reason is that Christianity is scattered in different kingdoms, and their lords will not allow a bishop to have jurisdiction over their subjects. The second is that Japanese customs are so different to European, that Christians cannot be guided in the same way as in Europe. Japanese do not suffer the effect of heavy words or punishments, therefore no prelates could guide them without punishments or jurisdiction. The third one is that Japan is a very rebellious land, so there is no place a bishop could be safe if mistreated, just like us now. The fourth reason is that it would be extremely expensive to support the Church and its activities. Visits and gifts would always be necessary to obtain favours from the Lords, for nothing can be gained without them. The fifth and last, because this bishop would belong to the Society, and would not have other members of the secular clergy, so he could do no more than what the Society is already doing (LL, Cartas que os Padres e Irmãos da Companhia de Iesus Escreverão dos Reynos de Iapão & China, 1598: Part I, 478v–479, hereafter cited as *Cartas de Japão & China*; *Sumario*: 138–39).

What Valignano did not want was a bishop consecrated in Portugal, for the king could send a bishop with jurisdiction. During Everard Mercurian's years as general (1573–80), none of the members of the Society of Jesus was appointed bishop. But, unlike General Mercurian, Claudio Acquaviva considered appointing bishops for Japan and India. In 1588 the Funai diocese was created in Bungo. Phillip II, who was now King of Portugal, set new guidelines for Japan, as this diocese existed at his request. Philip II asked the pope to appoint a bishop in Japan, preferably a Jesuit bishop. In January 1587, Valignano suggested to Acquaviva that it would be better not to refuse, not only because any kind of criticism would be badly looked upon, but also because the pope would send someone anyway, so it was advisable to accept him (Santos Hernández 1999: 102). As Gaspar Coelho wrote to Acquaviva in a letter of January 17, 1588, Valignano had been consulting the Jesuits in Japan on this matter and, even though some time before nobody had been in favour of appointing a bishop in Japan, experience showed that it would be better to have one, as otherwise the Society could not ordain any priests there.[1] The bishop assigned a few years later was the Jesuit Pedro Martínez – also called Martins – confirmed by the Holy See in 1592, but he died shortly afterwards on a voyage to India. His successor, in 1598, was the Jesuit Luis Cerqueira, who resided in Nagasaki until his death in 1614.

Regarding missionaries from other religious orders, the Jesuits were not destined to remain alone in Japan. Their first competitors were a Spanish Dominican friar and several Franciscans. They arrived from the Philippines in 1592–93, when Hideyoshi was actively exploring possible trade relations between Japan and the Spanish islands. Although formal relations were not established, the Franciscans remained on Honshu – the largest Island of Japan – much to the annoyance of the Jesuits (Alden 1996: 65).

Visitor Valignano's restless versatility and ubiquity is remarkable. In 1582 he assembled an expedition consisting of four Japanese Christian boys from noble Kyushu families, several Jesuit escorts and personal servants. They departed from Nagasaki in 1582 and arrived in Lisbon two-and-a-half years later, in August 1584. Valignano himself accompanied the envoys as far as Goa, after which they sailed to Lisbon, travelling by land across the Iberian Peninsula and then sailing to Rome and journeying throughout northern Italy. Leading dignitaries everywhere, including the regent of Portugal in Lisbon, Philip II in Madrid, and Popes Gregory XIII and Sixtus V in Rome, received them warmly (Alden 1996: 64). In 1584, the Jesuit interpreter Diego Mesquita disembarked in Europe with the Christian Japanese Embassy organized by Alessandro Valignano. Besides showing Europe the achievements of the Society in Japan, one of the objectives of the embassy was to awaken the European vocation for the mission. This objective was indeed accomplished, for between 1584 and 1585 Japan became the destination most in demand among Spanish Jesuits, as reflected in the *Indipetae* (Maldavsky 2007: 51).

Valignano was also very concerned about doctrinal issues, especially when he learned about the diversity of 'sects' in Japan.[2] Therefore, in his *Sumario* of 1583 he advocated a 'uniformity' of doctrine, denouncing 'the faults and lies of their sects' and proclaiming the existence of one sole God who rewards and punishes souls (Sumario: 165). The visitor himself wrote a catechism, the *Catechismus Christianae Fidei*, with this aim in mind; it was first published in Lisbon in 1586 without the author's knowledge. It would later inspire Ricci's TZSY in China, as will be analysed in detail in Chapter Four. But Valignano's writing endeavours went even further. Together with Duarte de Sande, Valignano composed a treatise entitled *De Missione Legatorum Iaponensium ad Romanam Curiam* – On the Japanese Mission to the Roman Curia, printed in Macao in 1590, which narrates the journey of two ambassadors travelling around Asia and Europe. It was intended to be – as Duarte put it – an educational text for Japanese pupils in the Jesuit schools, as well as a compendium of useful information based on travelogues and on the experience of the four young Japanese men who formed part of the embassy to Europe. The information about China in this treatise was based on that provided by Ruggieri and Ricci. Apparently, Valignano composed the text in Spanish and Duarte de Sande, rector of the St Paul College in Macao, translated it into Latin (Loureiro 1992: 18). This is probably the second book printed in Macao with a European printing press (Braga 1963: 35–36). In 1599 it was translated into English in London by Richard Hakluyt with the title *An Excellent Treatise of the Kingdom of China*. By and large, there was a growth in perceptions of and information about China due to the circulation of letters, some of them with descriptions of the Middle Kingdom. One example is a letter that Ricci sent via Michele Ruggieri from Zhaoqing to Juan Bautista Román, Royal Representative in the Philippines, dated September 13 1584, containing a very detailed and articulate description of China. This letter was part of a selection of Jesuit letters edited in a book entitled *Cartas Anuas Titulado Avisos de la China y Japón del Fin del Año 1587, Recebidos en Octubre de 88, Sacados de las Cartas de los Padres de la Compañía de Jesús que Anda en Aqellas Partes* – Notices of China and Japan in Late 1587, Received in October '88, Taken from the Annual Letters from the Fathers of the Society of Jesus in Those Parts – published in 1589 in Madrid. It contains letters from Alessandro Valignano and Antonio de Almeida, and a long description of China by Ricci to Juan Bautista Román, among others (Ollé 2008: 50–51). In addition, we must not forget Juan González de Mendoza's account in the second half of the 1580s, *Historia de las Cosas Mas Notables, Ritos y Costumbres del Gran Reyno de la China*, which was also in circulation at the time but offered a different view and representation of China. Juan González de Mendoza never set foot in China; his chronicle fed on his fellow Augustines, Martin de Rada and Jerónimo Marín, 'who entered China and from whose account I took the things I state here' (González de Mendoza [1585] 1944: 48). Both Augustinians, Martín de Rada and Jerónimo Marín had been sent on an embassy to China, but they did not obtain permission to stay. Martín de Rada tried once more, but failed again. They were followed in the attempt by seventeen Franciscans who embarked from Seville to the Philippines (Colín [1663] 1904:159–66).

Jesuit 'geopolitics' in the East: the Philippines as a strategic hub

One of the attributes that Valignano observed in Japan was its capacity for self-government, whereby the visitor stated that 'the King of Spain does not have and will not have any form of dominion or jurisdiction there' (Sumario: 146). Even though Valignano was not originally against the presence of Spanish Jesuits, he later changed his mind and prevented the entry of Jesuits of that origin coming from New Spain or the Philippines. One telling example was the controversial Alonso Sánchez – already mentioned in the previous chapter – the missionary in the Philippines who was eager to declare war against China. In 1582 Sánchez travelled from the Philippines to China, appointed by the governor of those islands to carry out two assignments: one was to have Phillip II recognized as King of Portugal – an objective that he managed to fulfil – and the other was to establish commercial relations between the Philippines and China, in which he failed. In Canton, Sánchez met Ruggieri when the latter was negotiating the establishment of the mission in China. Alonso Sánchez showed him the papers he had brought with him, all of them addressed to the Chinese authorities of the Canton province, with whom he was able to communicate thanks to Ruggieri's interpreting skills. Ruggieri was aware of the difficulty of this enterprise, not only on account of the Chinese, who distrusted the Spaniards, but also because of the Portuguese in Macao, who were against the Spaniards entering China via Manila. In the end, Sánchez failed to achieve his purpose (Astrain 1913: 452). Unable to settle the deal between Canton and Manila, the two Jesuits were allowed to return to Macao. There, Sánchez met Visitor Valignano and informed him that Phillip II had been crowned King of Portugal. In 1584 Sánchez made another trip to Macao, in the company of the Royal Representative of the Philippines, Juan Bautista Román. In his *storia*, Ricci narrates that Sánchez and Román had gone from the Philippines to China to propose an embassy on behalf of Philip II to China. Previous to their arrival, Sánchez claimed that Ruggieri and Ricci had written to the governor in the Philippines, to the bishop in Manila, and to Sánchez himself informing them about the progress of the mission and also asking for financial help. The governor of the Philippines, Don Gonzalvo Ronquillo de Peñalosa, and the bishop in Manila decided to help the two Jesuits. In exchange, the latter wanted Ruggieri and Ricci's help in finding a place in the Canton province where they could send their ships to trade and thus make higher profits for the government. Therefore, 'to that effect they sent one of our Fathers, Alfonso Sanci [Sánchez] and the Spanish Royal Representative in those parts, named Giovanni Battista Romano' – here Ricci translates Roman's name into Italian (FR I: 214, note 4). But only Ruggieri met Sánchez in person at that time. As already mentioned, they soon realized that the possibility of any communication between Manila and China was out of the question.

General Acquaviva had already warned the Jesuits in the Philippines against going from there to China or Macao, to avoid mixing the trips from

New Spain with those from Portugal, something that Phillip II himself had also forbidden (Astrain 1913: 454). It was during this second voyage that Sánchez made those very controversial statements which prompted José de Acosta to confute them. When refuting chapters ten, eleven and twelve of Sánchez's memo, one of Acosta's arguments was the need to avoid greater harm by trying to overrule 'the powerful' – *mayores* – referring to the Chinese. There was also the need to

> try with other as peaceful means as possible, like the Fathers in Xauquin [Zhaoqing], who are learning the language, so they are not dependent on unloyal interpreters; to persuade those who rule about the truth of our faith, as if they convert, so will the others, and even if these means take longer, the benefit is greater, for it is true that the people in China will support their government and judgment of their nature, not alien, and that even if we seem to be soft, at the same time we oppress them and humiliate more than their mandarins (EM: 339–40).

Time would tell that Acosta was wrong regarding this last statement. But, by and large, he was an optimist when it came to the progress of the China mission, where 'the Italian Fathers are held in great esteem' (EM: 344).

In a letter to Acquaviva of April 1585, Valignano warned about the presence of Spaniards in the Philippines and their eagerness to enter China; he purposely mentioned Alonso Sánchez when referring to 'the other Fathers of the Society'. Valignano describes Sánchez as having a 'pilgrim-like spirit, which led him to commit so many indiscretions in his first visit – says Valignano – that I was shocked'.[3] And he was not the only one to advise Acquaviva about Sánchez. In an annual letter of November 30 1585, the provincial in New Spain, Antonio de Mendoza, said to Acquaviva that Alonso Sánchez was again toying with the idea of

> the conquest of China, for nothing will ever be achieved if it is not with the sword in one hand and the gospel in the other. And so he says, after witnessing the great progress in that kingdom, that Your Paternity can see in the account he sent. The 1,500 characters [*cuerpos*] printed in the Catechism [Ruggieri's Tianzhu shilu], are circulated throughout the whole kingdom, among the most important people, and it is held in great esteem. And what is indeed regrettable, is that he [Sánchez] made copies of his reports of his first and second trips, in which he grounds his idea of a war against China, and published them in Manila, before sending them here. And it would be probable that, through the Chinese traders, many of whom know our language, it be known that, there in China, the Spanish try to make war … which would be enough to kill the fathers who are now in China, and the Portuguese and Castilians who are now in

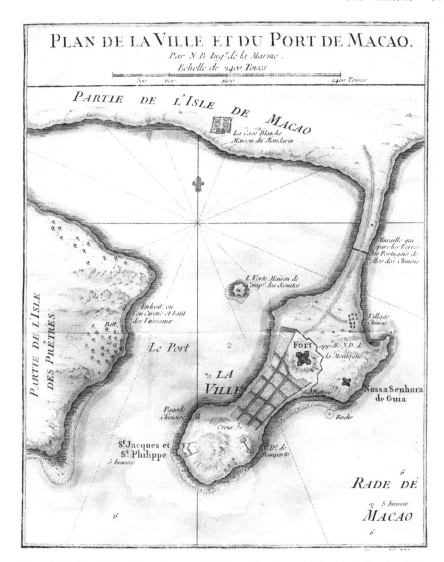

Figure 2.1 Plan de la ville et du port de Macao, by Jacques Nicolas Bellin (c. 1750)
Source: Courtesy of USF Ricci Institute for Chinese-Western Cultural History

Macao, or at least expel them and refuse to trade with them. And this
would be harmful not only for China, but also for Japan.

(Zubillaga 1959: 718–19, *Monumenta Mexicana (1570–1605)*,
8 vols, hereafter cited as MM II, etc.)

Valignano's change of attitude regarding the arrival of Spanish Jesuits in
Japan and China was mainly due to suspicions aroused in Japan about the

Jesuits' penchant for intrigue and conspiracy (Alden 1996: 63; Ucerler 2003: 336–37). In October 1587, the ruler Toyotomi Hideyoshi (1536–98), brusquely ordered the banishment of all Jesuits from the archipelago, which caught them completely off guard. They were required to leave the country within twenty days. No drastic measures were taken, but as long as the decree was in force the threat of expulsion was ever present, generating an atmosphere of instability that affected the permanence of the Society. This marked the beginning of 'persecutions' – from a Jesuit perspective – which climaxed in 1614 with the banning of the Christian faith under the Tokugawa Shogunate, in power since 1603. In a letter to Acquaviva, Gaspar Coello clearly states that the persecutions in Japan by the ruling tyrant – *tirano* – could harm the Jesuits in China, at that moment in the city of Zhaoqing. Indeed, even though the Jesuits in Japan considered sending some brothers to Macao so they could avoid death, in the end they decided not to do that, since

> The Chinese were so cautious about the government of their lands, and so suspicious of the Portuguese, that if they saw that ours [the Jesuits] were expelled from Japan, and hearing that one of the reasons for this is that we want to own and possess their land, they might think this holds true and will expel the Jesuits in Xauquin [Zhaoqing], and so we thought it was more convenient to die all of us here, than escape just some of us.[4]

However, in more general terms, the reaction against Sánchez's plan and the Spaniards in the Philippines was also a response to other kinds of rivalries and conflicts, mainly against the Spanish crown's expansionist ambition, which was implemented through Phillip II's control of the ecclesiastical jurisdictions. In fact, the project of conquering China, to which the Spanish authorities in the Philippines warmly adhered, demonstrated the Spaniards' expansionist strategy, which overtly threatened Portuguese commercial interests in the area. On the other hand, had it been successful it would have fulfilled the ideal of universal dominance on the part of the Hispanic monarchy, which in turn would have implied an even stronger pressure on Rome (Millán 2007). In his correspondence, we can see that Valignano became almost obsessed with the Castilians – *castellanos* – and all the damage they could do to the missions in Japan and in China. In sum, they could ruin everything that the Jesuits had built so far.

Valignano concentrated his distrust of the *castellanos* on the figure of Francisco Cabral, who succeeded as Provincial of India in 1592. In Valignano's letters to General Acquaviva of 1593, 1594 and 1595 there is a great deal about Francisco Cabral, almost all of it uncomplimentary. Valignano blamed himself for having Cabral sent to India as a provincial. As the visitor put it in a letter to Acquaviva in November 1595, Cabral 'lacks many necessary things to be a provincial in India, and he has many things that are intolerable for … this government.[5] In those letters sent to Acquaviva, with references to Cabral's personality, Valignano always reaches a point at which he ends up mentioning what seems to be a leitmotif in many of his letters: the disunion between the Portuguese and the Spanish, or more precisely the *castellanos*. And the union of the two crowns would not change anything in Valignano's opinion:

> between the Portuguese and the Castillians there are *repartimentos*, and differences with regard to the conquests, even though now all are subjects of the same King, each of these nations, they are still governed according to their own laws and want to have separate jurisdictions and limits of the conquest under their own reign, and crown, so they are not mistaken, but always apart according to the capitulations.[6]

Valignano is the key to understanding the entry of the Jesuits Michele Ruggieri and Matteo Ricci into the Ming empire in 1583. His insight and experience of the mission in Japan made him aware of the importance of mastering the Chinese language as a *sine qua non* for gaining access to the Middle Kingdom. In a letter to the superior of the Province of India in Goa, the visitor requested him to send a qualified man to Macao with the purpose of learning Chinese; he particularly mentioned Michele Ruggieri.

Valignano's imprint on the China mission

Like other missionaries who had tried to enter China, Ruggieri made more than one trip from Macao to Canton, trying to establish himself in China. Unlike his predecessors, he addressed the local mandarins in their own language when he requested permission to stay in that province, which triggered the officials' curiosity. After his arrival in Macao in July 1579, Ruggieri studied Chinese with great enthusiasm, but he managed only short sojourns in Canton when the annual Portuguese trade fairs took place. In June 1582, Ruggieri travelled to Zhaoqing with the auditor in Macao to help in the negotiations with the governor of Guandong and Guanxi Provinces, Chen Rui, who had threatened to expel the Portuguese from Chinese soil. Ruggieri's knowledge of Chinese contributed to making a favourable impression on Chen Rui, who approved the Jesuit request to establish a residence in Zhaoqing. Indeed, thanks to this protection, Ruggieri obtained a residence in Zhaoqing, in the Guandong province, along with permission for the entry of two of his brethren. As a result, Valignano summoned two other missionaries to Macao: Matteo Ricci and Francesco Pasio. Ruggieri made a first trip with Franceso Pasio but, after Chen Rui's dismissal, he had to return to Macao. In August 1583, Michele Ruggieri departed Macao for Zhaoqing with Matteo Ricci, after receiving permission from the new governor to travel there. Besides mastering the language, accommodation as conceived by Valignano in Japan largely consisted of adjusting to the local customs and habits – culinary and dress-wise – as well as the rules of etiquette. That directive would soon be echoed in Zhaoqing, where Ruggieri accepted the suggestion of a local Chinese official that they shave off their beards and hair and don the robes of Buddhist monks.

A couple of years later, in a letter to Acquaviva of April 1 1585, Alessandro Valignano proudly says:

> As for China, we know that Our Lord was rewarded for the directive adopted six years ago stating that Father Rogerio [Ruggieri] and another companion [Ricci] should study the Chinese language. It was not for nothing, since they were finally admitted in China ... in the main city called Xauquin [Zhaoqing] in the Canton province.[7]

Valignano then writes of how carefully the fathers – Ruggieri and Ricci – proceeded with conversions, in such a way that they not only caused no trouble when baptizing and catechizing but also gained recognition from the mandarins, who had a welcoming attitude (Ibid.).

Accommodation as conceived by Valignano was a response to the Jesuits' asymmetrical position in Japan, later replicated in China. In this regard, the frailty of the missions in Japan and China was in direct relation to their subjection to the decisions of the local political powers. Many situations that were out of the Jesuits' hands generated instability and jeopardized the progress of the mission in Japan. In fact, subjection to 'persecutions' and attacks stemming from the political decisions made during the Toyotomi Hideyoshi period (1537–98) and the final banning of the Christian faith under the Tokugawa Shogunate in 1614 helped turn the Society's eyes towards China. Ruggieri was the first missionary to China, following Valignano's command. In an account of the China mission in the years 1577–91, composed for the Superior General, Ruggieri states that Valignano was in India when, hearing things from China, and considering the great benefits that would result from the conversion of so many thousands of souls, he started to think of possible ways for the Jesuits to set foot there. Therefore, the visitor appointed some fathers to Macao to learn Chinese.[8] Ruggieri arrived in Macao less than fifteen days after Valignano's departure for Japan, in July 1579, perhaps around July 20.[9] In a letter to General Mercurian dated November 12 1581, Ruggieri narrates that Valignano had already left for Japan when he arrived in Macao, but the visitor had left written orders for Ruggieri 'to learn to read, write and speak Chinese as diligently as possible' (OS II: 401). During his very first visit to Canton from Macao with a group of Portuguese merchants in 1580, Ruggieri secured the unusual permission to stay on land throughout the trading season, rather than having to return to a boat every night like the Portuguese merchants, who were not permitted to lodge on land. Ruggieri narrates how the Mandarin who governed the city was so affectionately disposed toward him that he granted Ruggieri's supplication that he be allowed to live on land since – Ruggieri explained – it was not permissible 'to perform my sacrifices on the water' (Rienstra 1986: 16).

Valignano stressed the difference between Japan and China, especially with regard to the – Buddhist – garments the Jesuits wore. In a letter to Acquaviva from Macao, in October 1588, Valignano says that all the measures to be taken were out of sheer necessity, but

> What is said about the Fathers changing their attires here in Japan is false, except when it was the time of persecutions. It is true that in China our Fathers changed their habit to be able to enter and I think they deserved glory for that, since according to our Constitutions our habit is not determined but accommodated ... to that responding to the diversity of lands and proper to reformed priests, also because in China they do not change their attire to wear fancier clothes, but to wear long and modest garments accommodated to Chinese religious [people] so that, despite experiencing hardships, they can enter to save souls ... . And with regard to the adoption of strange and gentile names, this is so false that I do not know how anyone could think of it.[10]

Here, Valignano made reference to the fact that Jesuits did not have to wear a distinctive garb, but rather adopted the form of clothing that their leaders believed to be most appropriate in particular circumstances. Indeed, Ignatius of Loyola had decided against the adoption of a distinctive habit for members of the Society – a measure that at his time aroused disapproval – and Valignano raised that particular issue in his defence.

By now, we know that the Chinese could be suspicious of Western foreigners, especially when they arrived hostile and aggressive – *animosi e guerrieri*, as Ricci put it – which was exactly what they observed about the Portuguese: armed people with the largest ships they had ever seen. Beyond the particularities of the Chinese, if Valignano became obsessed with keeping the *castellanos* away from the East Indies, it was because, with their aggressiveness, they could ruin everything the Jesuits had built there. Eventually, Ricci became one of the visitor's best disciples, and he explicitly recognized Valignano as the first author of the Society's mission in the East – *il primo autore di questa missione* (FR I: 221). To Valignano's guidelines regarding accommodation Ricci added his own skills in observing and understanding the local scenario, as shown in Chapter One. In short, it was not only about avoiding any hostile attitudes. Ricci's perception of the local political rules on different scales and in different cities proved to be as or more important. For example, in 1609, a year before his death, Ricci wrote a letter to the vice-provincial Francesco Pasio expressing his concern about the future and per-manence of the mission. The way Ricci communicates the local peculiarities and the impossibility of solving issues through typically Western methods is most interesting. Making reference to Pasio's suggestion of sending a memo 'to the King' to secure and protect the mission in the Middle Kingdom, Ricci explained that the form of government in China is very different to the rest of the world. This he attributes to the presence of the eunuchs and their role as the king's intermediaries and to the impossibility of delivering memorandums without passing through the control of the magistrates – *gelao* – in strict keeping with the kingdom's laws and styles.

Ricci's prestige at court – due to which he enjoyed the favour of Emperor Wanli – contributed more than once to preventing other Jesuits scattered in the provinces from being 'persecuted' by the local authorities. In short, as Ricci put it, even if the first fathers or the emperor should die, the credit earned by the Jesuits was a positive fact when sending more missionaries to other parts of China (OS II: 377–81). As regards the other religious orders, the only missionaries in China were Jesuits until 1632, when – owing to a reversal of papal policy – other Catholic orders started to evangelize China, like Dominicans and Franciscan friars, who reached the province of Fujian.

The Society of Jesus during Viceroy Toledo's rule (1569–80)

The Jesuits in Spanish America were dedicated exclusively to ministry with the Indians. The General of the Society of Jesus, Francisco de Borja wrote an *Instrucción* laying down the principles for the missions in Spanish America, after a failed experience in Florida. In 1567 Phillip II requested General Borja to appoint twenty priests to establish the Society in Peru. The Vice-royalty of Peru spanned practically all of South America, except Brazil. The Jesuit Province of Peru was founded in 1568 and had the same boundaries as the Viceroyalty of Peru.[11] Francisco de Borja's premature death left his successor, Everard Mercurian – appointed general on April 23 1573 – in charge of appointing a visitor for the missions in Peru and Mexico. Mercurian named Juan de la Plaza as visitor in Peru and Mexico, and Alessandro Valignano as visitor in the Portuguese Indies.

The Society of Jesus in Peru never witnessed the events that the four preceding orders – Dominicans, Franciscans, Mercedarians and Augustinians – had had to live through: the atmosphere of unrest caused first by the Inca forces trying to push the Spaniards out of Cuzco in the late 1530s and soon afterwards by the clash of clans among the Spaniards. Indeed, open hostilities between the conquistadors Francisco Pizarro and Diego de Almagro for the division of spoils put the whole Spanish colonial enterprise at risk and so the Spanish crown dispatched the first Viceroy of Peru, Blasco Núñez Vela, who arrived in 1544. Among his royal instructions were the controversial New Laws – *Leyes Nuevas* – promulgated in 1542, concerning the *encomiendas*. The *encomiendas* were grants of indigenous towns to the first conquistadors, allowing them to demand taxes and labour from the Indians in return for military protection and religious instruction (Andrien 2001: 44). The New Laws demanded an end to Amerindian slavery and, equally importantly, that all the *encomienda* grants held by public officials and the clergy revert to the crown upon the death of the current holder. In addition to the laws promulgated by the embryonic colonial state seeking to weaken the conquistadors' might, the *encomienda* system was also weakened by the epidemic European diseases spreading in the Andean lands, i.e. influenza, smallpox, measles, etc., against which the Indians had no natural immunities. In sum, the early colonial order based on the extraction of surplus wealth and labour from the indigenous communities by the *encomenderos* was in danger of collapsing. The real issue at stake – to which the New Laws acted as a reflex – was the establishment of the Spanish empire in America; these laws were proof of the crown's decision to reaffirm its authority in those lands (Brading 1991: 72). In *De Procuranda Indorum Salute*, José de Acosta makes a distinction between Spain and Portugal and refers to the private enterprise dimension, so evident in the *encomiendas*. As regards the reasons for the origin of the *encomiendas*, it was not only that private individuals discovered and conquered a large portion of the 'New World' at their own expense but, 'since the conquered New World was so far away from the King, he could not have kept it under his might, had not the same people who discovered and conquered it kept it' (De Proc: 475). So, in Acosta's view, the first cause – paying for the work and expenses of the conquistadors – was a result of need rather than will or religion,

> Given that the Prince was unable, or hardly able, to reward their efforts with other means than dividing among them the power and financial gain of the New World ... [i]n the Portuguese Indies, as they were all conquered under the sponsorship and with the gold of their monarchs, the crown kept full control and power so the private individuals had no rightful cause of complaint. But the case of the Castilian Indies is very different because it was for the most part a private enterprise.
>
> (De Proc: 476)

Once the Spanish crown was able to set limits to the increasing power of the *encomenderos*, it became necessary to organize the Church in Peru. The First Lima Council in 1551–52 enacted the monarchy's main purpose: the submission of the Church in Spanish America. In turn, the ecclesiastical colonial system was enforced, recognizing Philip II as 'patron of the Churches and missions in the Indies'. The obligation to evangelize the New World as stipulated by papal bulls involved various concessions, which had gradually increased royal power over time. But the second half of the 1560s marked a turning point in the ecclesiastical sphere, especially after the official communication of the Tridentine decrees. The council's decrees had been ratified by the pope in January 1564, and on the July 12 of the same year Phillip II implemented them as law for the entire kingdom, the decrees reaching Lima on October 28 1565. The arrival of the decrees encouraged the organization of the Second Lima Council (1567–68) to carry out the consequent reforms. This second council had been repeatedly postponed, largely due to the absence of the suffragan bishops, who decided to ignore Archbishop Loayza's invitation as a way of showing their disagreement with the hard-line policy imposed through the *Patronato real*. Archbishop Jerónimo de Loayza (1498–1575) and his successor Toribio de Mogrovejo (1538–1606) were faithful advocates of the Spanish Monarchy and unpopular among the suffragan bishops.

Phillip II summoned a *Junta Magna* – Great Summit – in 1568, with the purpose of addressing a number of administrative and ecclesiastical matters. Among other things, the *Junta Magna* also helped reinforce the *Patronato real* in its basic requirements: the rights to receive tithes, to appoint priests in the different dioceses, to establish new dioceses covering the majority of the indigenous population and set their limits or modify those that already existed.[12] Francisco de Toledo was appointed Viceroy of Peru; he was determined to suppress the selfish *encomenderos* and to build a strong and powerful colonial state. He ruled Peru for twelve years, and came to know the land extremely well in the course of his numerous visits in Peru between 1570 and 1575. Thanks to his in-depth knowledge of the territory, Toledo implemented a series of changes known in colonial history as the *reformas toledanas* – Toledan reforms. After an extensive tour – *visita general* – of Peru, the viceroy carried out these administrative reforms by ordering all the Andean communities to be relocated into *reducciones*, i.e. large Spanish-style towns where the Indians were resettled. The process of congregating the indigenous population had already begun before Toledo's arrival, but he expanded it dramatically, to the extent of leaving an indelible mark on colonial Peru.[13] Toledo also organized the *reducciones* into six hundred and fourteen *repartimientos* – administrative districts – each headed by a *curaca* – i.e. regional Andean lord, frequently the intermediary between Spanish officialdom and the Andean community – and a town council of appointed Andean elders. With this forced relocation into the *reducciones*, Toledo could more easily impose effective labour, tax, and religious controls on the already overexploited Andean population. The *corregidores de indios*, or provincial magistrates, controlled the Andean communities and were put in charge of tithe collection and the administration of justice. Profound changes in the population under Toledo's rule were also brought about by the mining boom in Potosi, especially for Potosi silver, which was produced from a mercury-based alloy. The method was very work-intensive, the labour being supplied by the *mita* – a Quechua term for labour divisions – which resulted in major migrations to the Cerro Rico of Potosí and the Huancavelica mines. Besides responding to the multiple needs of the colonial government, the concentration of population that resulted from the *reducciones* facilitated the pastoral reforms implemented by Toledo where the crown had not yet interfered.

The colonial authorities were actively involved in organizing the dioceses and reforming the clergy. Although, as already mentioned, Phillip II had ordained compliance with the Tridentine decrees in all his possessions, he reserved the right to intervene in ecclesiastical appointments, which was alien to the spirit of the Tridentine dispositions. Moreover, Viceroy Toledo had personally undertaken the organization of the viceroyalty and was strongly determined to recover this patronage, taking different responsibilities from the hands of the bishops and clergymen. From that moment on, the bishops had to appoint and distribute their clergy under strict surveillance, with their organizational powers limited right from the start (Villegas 1975:107–11). Another big innovation was the development of parishes – *parroquias* – i.e. a Tridentine imposition consisting of a clearly delimited territory and a group of Indians assigned to a priest, which was essential for the conversion and pastoral care of the Indians. Together with the *reducciones*, the parish system was fundamental to the implementation of the Tridentine decrees in Peru; Toledo created hundreds of new parishes, making it easier to control the religious instruction of the Indians.

The *parroquias* were not as controversial for the newly arrived religious order, the Society of Jesus, as the *doctrinas*. As mentioned in the first chapter, Toledo's imposition of the *doctrinas de indios* as the preferred evangelization method in the province of Peru represented a serious attack on the Society of Jesus' mobility. Indeed, the *doctrinas de indios* required a commitment to spiritual control in the long term, so the Jesuits had to settle there. Moreover, in the *doctrinas* the parish priests received a stipend – tithes paid by the Indians – and the Society was against the collection of stipends.[14] While from Toledo's perspective the *doctrinas* were the main method for evangelizing the Indians in Peru, in the eyes of the Society they were a threat directly aimed at their Institute. There were other ways of Christianizing the Indians more to the liking of the Jesuits: *Colegios* for the sons of the *caciques* – or *curacas* in Quechua – the Andean lords; *misiones* – for Indian converts; and *entradas* – for the infidels (Albó 1966: 262–79). According to Acosta, the *doctrinas* implied two major drawbacks in relation to the figure of the *cura doctrinero* – the parish priest: the danger of incontinence resulting from loneliness and the greed that 'tarnished' his work. These were Acosta's words, referring to Viceroy Toledo's criticism:

> As in this New World the only evangelizing method used so far is the one parish priests use with their brethren, many are of the idea that if the priests of the Society do not adopt the *doctrinas* they will be unable to do anything for the salvation of their souls and their coming from Europe will have been in vain. Thus, they believe we should embrace this burden and cure Indians' souls and when they perceive our doubts they accuse us of being hesitant and prone to idleness, and of shunning the work and life of rural people to enjoy the delights of city life.
>
> (De Proc: 572)

Acosta's observations are also apropos one of the problems that emerged when trying to implement the Tridentine reforms: the uneven distribution of the regular clergy, who preferred to concentrate in the cities and avoid the *doctrinas* in outlying places (Villegas 1975: 110). However that may be, Viceroy Toledo wanted the Society of Jesus to be in charge of the *doctrinas*, and he made this explicit in a letter to Phillip II dated March 1, 1572:

it is necessary that Your Majesty urge his generals [of the Society of Jesus] to do this work, as they do all the other orders in compliance with Your Majesty's command, otherwise Your Majesty will understand that they are not useful in important matters but [only] in matters of secondary importance.

(*Gobernantes*, Levillier 1924: IV, 1–34)

The first *doctrina* that the Jesuits accepted was that of Santiago de Cercado, near Lima, in 1570. This *doctrina* was divided into thirty-five blocks and each of them was in turn sub-divided into one hundred and twenty-two sites according to the number of Indians who were distributed in *encomiendas*. There was an area allotted for public buildings and a main square at the centre. Viceroy Toledo had prohibited both the Spanish and black people from living in Santiago del Cercado. This *doctrina* was not subjected to the bishops' jurisdiction, but to the Spanish crown (Coello 2008: 56–57).

In 1570, during his inspection in Peru, Toledo arrived in the Huarochirí district and asked Provincial Portillo to accept this *doctrina*, which had previously been in the hands of the Dominicans. At the beginning of 1570 two Jesuits, Alonso Barzana and Blas Valera were sent to the *doctrina* of Huarochirí, but the project did not succeed so the Jesuits left in 1572. Indeed, Provincial Portillo had too many doubts regarding the *doctrinas* and summoned the Jesuits in Huarochirí to Lima. Viceroy Toledo resented Portillo for this decision, and – as one of the measures he took – dismissed the provincial as his confessor (Astrain 1909: 152–53). Moreover, displeased at the Jesuits' reluctance to accept the *doctrinas*, Toledo eventually took measures against the Society such as closing down colleges in Potosí and Arequipa and refusing permission to open one in La Paz. Toledo also punished the Society through the Inquisition, as shown in the case of Luis López.[15] In 1578, in Juli in the Chucuito province, Luis López sent Plaza a piece of writing entitled *About the Doctrinas*, in which he set out his negative views regarding both Toledo's favourite evangelization method and his policies in general. López was put on trial by the Inquisition, to which Acosta was consultant. Eventually, as already mentioned, this episode created divided opinions within the Society in Peru. Very soon afterwards a 'faction' was formed, headed by Visitor Plaza and Luis López, opposing Toledo's policies, as well as Acosta's compliance with them (Lisi 1990: 70). In this regard, as the theologian who had envisioned the evangelization process of the Society of Jesus in Peru, maybe it was more difficult for Acosta to tackle the royal authorities' impositions without compromising than for the other members of the Society in Peru. Right from the beginning, the influential Juan de Polanco (1517–76) – appointed Vicar-General on Borja's death while waiting for the new general to be elected – advised Portillo to show the Constitutions to

the Viceroy and the Archbishop, so they can see how much better we will serve and how much more suitable it will be to his Divine Majesty and to the King and the good of souls if we are allowed to carry out the missions according to our Institute instead of making them disappear in those residences and the way they were implemented.

(MP I: 501)

But Acosta was fully aware of the fact that Viceroy Toledo would not welcome Juan de Polanco's request to Portillo, which did not mean that the Jesuit was in favour of the *doctrinas*. Acosta's presence in Peru would cool down the frictions with Toledo; with Acosta as provincial, in 1576 the Jesuits accepted the *doctrina* in Juli in the Chucuito province, previously in the hands of the Dominicans. Thus, even though Acosta mentions the drawbacks of the *doctrinas* – e.g. parish priests' incontinence and greed – he does find a half-way solution: 'With all these issues, I claim so far, and until we see anything better, that the Society must neither accept parishes recklessly nor reject them altogether' (De Proc: 574). Acosta compromised, indeed, but he still found a way of stating clearly the methods favoured by the Society. He did nothing to hide the Society's preference – and his own – for the itinerant missions – *misiones* – which he defined in *De Procuranda*:

from the missions [*misiones*] one can expect great usefulness. I call missions the excursions and pilgrimages that go from town to town spreading the word of God, the benefits and authority of which are much greater and more far-reaching than men think.

(De Proc: 575)

The *misiones* – itinerant missions – were the method most used by the Jesuits in Europe, and Acosta depicted them as the method most cherished by the Society, the most adequate and in conformity with the spirit of the founding members of the Order (Broggio 2004: 108–09).

Through Acosta, the Society adjusted to – and finally accepted – the conditions imposed by the colonial authorities, specifically regarding the *doctrinas*, which, in fact, the Society eventually incorporated as an evangelization method. To go no further, the missions in Paraguay stemmed from the *doctrina* in Juli. In short, Acosta's intervention as the main theologian of the mission was both conciliatory and instrumental, as there was no possible way that Toledo would let the Society impose its preferences when it came to the principal Christianization methods in Peru. Toledo's beliefs therefore conditioned the Society's 'way of proceeding'. In 1580, Phillip II issued a document from Badajoz with orders to hold a third provincial council when the new Archbishop of Lima, Toribio de Mogrovejo, and the new viceroy, Martín Enríquez, were due to arrive. Eventually, the bishops who were assembled in the *Audiencia real* – royal audience – in 1583 would no longer refer to the Third Lima Council as summoned 'in conformity with the holy council of Trent and with what Your Majesty has ordered', but as being carried out 'by command of Your Majesty'. This reveals how Phillip II made the most of the attributes granted by the *Patronato regio*, leaving Rome aside (Villegas 1975: 192 onward). Indeed, the *Consejo de Indias* – Council of Indies – controlled all the missionary work in Spanish America, together with all the bulls and commands issued from the Vatican to America and from America to Rome. In this regard, it can be said that right from his arrival in Peru, Jesuit José de Acosta accommodated the mission to the guidelines of the *Patronato regio*, especially during the tenure of Viceroy Toledo, always uncompromising and inflexible. And, as shown in the previous chapter, Acosta turned the TLC into a new opportunity to express his loyalty to the Spanish crown.

The starting points in this chapter were the Spanish *Patronato* and the Portuguese *Padroado*, both conceived as spatial frameworks that harboured the Jesuit missions from the second half of the sixteenth century.

The arrival of the Jesuits in the Portuguese *Indias*, mainly in Japan, was analyzed by focusing on the figure of Valignano and his performance as visitor of the Order in the East. Valignano's guidelines were mainly based on his experience of accommodation as he conceived it in Japan. His method was the result of his awareness of the Jesuits' impotence in Japan, a fact he never intended to hide, as we can clearly see both in the *Sumario de las Cosas de Japón* – the Japan Summary – and his correspondence. However, his sincerity does not belie his uncontested preference for this method. In this particular context, accommodation is the product of two main factors: on the one hand, the absence of conditioning factors from the authorities empowered through the *Padroado*, especially in those missions where the Portuguese colonial and ecclesiastical administration was weak or inexistent. And, on the other hand, accommodation was a possible and sensible solution to the restrictions and perils imposed locally in *ultra gangem* missions, i.e. Japan and China. In sum, the conditioning factors that restricted the Society's mission at the local level in Japan and China contrasted with a considerable freedom within the *Padroado* framework. However, this overadaptation triggered disagreements on how to introduce the Society's Institute in Japan, which reached General Claudio Acquaviva. In time, the Castilians, as Valignano called them, the *castellanos*, became a threat, be they Jesuits or not. And so Valignano, with Acquaviva's support, halted their entry. There is no doubt of the strategic value the Philippines played in the 'geopolitical currents' throughout the Jesuit missions in the East, for the Spanish always conceived of the islands as a springboard to China, not counting on Macao for that purpose. Finally, the Japan mission as shaped by Valignano can only explain the inception of the China mission, when Ruggieri and Ricci implemented the visitor's directives. But then each of them conceived his own ideas of how to carry out his guidelines; time and personal experiences would do the rest, as the next chapter will show.

In Peru, as seen in the previous pages, the *Patronato real* and the extent to which it empowered Phillip II and his representatives in the colonies conditioned the Society's mission in different ways. The first years after its arrival, coinciding with the years of Viceroy Toledo's rule (1569–80), were very rough. As the Order was in charge of carrying out evangelization in Peru while having to deal with an uncompromising Toledo at the same time, the Society experienced internal frictions because of the viceroy's commands. Acosta's *De Procuranda Indorum Salute* subtly reflects these disagreements about the most suitable missionary methods to apply in the province. However, as shown in these pages, Acosta chose to placate and compromise.

In a speculative vein, we could claim that Visitor Valignano's role in Japan can be compared to Toledo's in Peru, in terms of both the effects and impacts of their guidelines in their respective missions and the controversies they aroused in the Society regarding the adjustment of the Society's Institute. However that may be, it is clear that no comparison is possible between the equivalent offices of Visitor Valignano in the East and Visitor Plaza in Peru. Viceroy Toledo embodied the attributes of the *Patronato Real* in Peru, to which the Society responded, when even Rome had remained silent in the Council of Trent with respect to ecclesiastical matters, clearly under the exclusive control of Phillip II and his representatives in his overseas possessions. To conclude, beyond geography and distance-related factors, the Society of Jesus in Peru and in China attempted to establish the missions in line with the requirements of the sovereigns who had appointed them, making use of their flexible *forma mentis*, and also according to their 'way of proceeding'. Accommodation in East Asia was a paradigm of Jesuit flexibility, but even in the far more restrictive context of the mission in Peru, the Society also proved to be flexible, and accommodated to the royal representatives in general, and to the inflexible Viceroy Toledo in particular.

Notes

1 Archivio Romano Societatis Iesu (Roman Archives of the Society of Jesus) Jap-Sin, 1585–87, 10–12, f. 315 –hereafter referred to as ARSI.

2 These 'sects' were, by and large, Shintoism, which was born in Japan, and then Buddhism, which arrived from China. The latter spread very fast, especially when it became part of the religious life in the court in the sixth and seventh centuries. In the ninth century new Buddhist schools started to appear and continued to bloom. Some of them eventually merged with Pure Land Buddhism. Confucianism did not spread in Japan; it had some influence in the period corresponding to the Tang Dynasty in China (AD 626–910), but it remained confined to a small academic and aristocratic circle.

3 ARSI, Jap-Sin, 1585, 10–11, 25v.

4 ARSI, Jap-Sin, 1588, 10–12, f. 315.

5 ARSI, Jap-Sin, 1595, 12–2, 298v.

6 ARSI, Jap-Sin, 1595, 12–2, f. 311.

7 ARSI, Jap-Sin, 1585–88, 10–11, f. 025.

8 M. Roggiero SJ, *Relatione del Successo della Missione della Cina dal Mese di Novembre 1577 sin all'Año 1591 del P.ᵉ Michel Ruggiero al Nostro Rᵈᵒ P.ᵉ Claudio Acquauiua Generale della Comp.ᵃ di Gesù, 1577–1591* (Account of the China Mission from November 1577 to 1591 by Father Michel Ruggiero to Our Reverend Father Claudio Acquaviva, General of the Society of Jesus, 1577–91), ARSI Jap-Sin, 101.

9 ARSI, Jap-Sin, 8, I, f. 248r; *FR*, I, 148–49, n. 1.
10 ARSI, Jap-Sin, 1588, 10–12, f. 337.
11 Between 1605 and 1607 two new Jesuit provinces were created: Nueva Granada – which included Quito until 1609 – and Paraguay, including Chile and Argentina.
12 Tithe donation was imposed by Pope Alexander VI (1431–1503) in 1501 to support divine worship, thus subjecting the ecclesiastics' economy to the crown. Later on, Paul III (1468–1549) entrusted the royal power with establishing the jurisdictions of dioceses and parishes.
13 A well-known precursor of Toledo's reforms is Juan de Matienzo (1520–79), appointed President of the Royal Audience in Charcas in 1561. Matienzo organized the resettlement of the Andean inhabitants himself. His work, *Gobierno del Perú* (1567) is considered a synthesis of both the colonial measures and institutions later implemented by Toledo (Presta 2008: 396–400).
14 It is important to distinguish between the concepts of *doctrina de indios* and *parroquias de indios*, which are quite often used interchangeably, even though there are some differences. Fernando de Armas Medina focuses on this distinction, stating that the terms *doctrina* and *parroquia* are not equivalent. The *doctrina* stems from the *encomienda*, from the duty of an *encomendero* in charge of more than one thousand Indians to pay a priest for their religious instruction. He points out that the *doctrinas* are not actual parishes since they are not included in the beneficiary ecclesiastical regime. Therefore, even though the *doctrineros* could be priests, there was not a direct bond between the ecclesiastical authorities and the office holder (Armas Medina 1952: 101–29).
15 Moreover, frictions arose between Viceroy Toledo and the Society regarding the University of San Marcos when Toledo centralized all the studies in this institution in 1575, also asking the Society to adapt the syllabus to that of San Marcos (Vargas Ugarte 1941: 88 onward).

3 The tricky concepts of Hispanicization in Peru and 'accommodation' in China

The missions that the Society of Jesus established around the globe inevitably exposed it to alterity. Broadly speaking, the equality between Europe and China in terms of their cultural, economic, institutional, intellectual and material complexity was a key element that marked the encounter between them. Another characteristic of the European–Chinese contacts that came about through Christianity is the fact that external power was extremely reduced. Although the missionaries remained dependent on material support from ecclesiastical institutions and the colonial administration, it was the Ming administration – and later the Qing – that ultimately decided whether or not they could enter and stay (Standaert 2001b: 83–85; Standaert 2002: 2).

As the missions expanded, encounters with different cultures gained in complexity. The Columbus voyage – or rather the date 1492 – sparked the Catholic monarchs' claim to sovereignty, riches and mission in America. The claim set off a rush towards European imperial rivalry and indigenous disaster, and towards the building of power and prosperity on foundations of racial dominance and violence (Stern 1992: 4). That moment marked the beginning of – paraphrasing de Certeau – a 'hermeneutics of the Other' (de Certeau 2006a: 217–18). One of the natural outcomes of the conquest was 'Occidentalization', meaning the setting up of European institutions, beliefs and practices in the 'New World', which went alongside both the exploitation of its resources and energy and the transformation of its natives (Gruzinski 1999: 502 onward). The process of Occidentalization that started in 1492 enabled an expansion of the space for enunciation; that is, it extended the 'legitimate' space for the relocation of other imaginary constructs, such as Orientalism and the Far East (Mignolo 1995: 39). Of course, the process of Occidentalization was far from linear and unidirectional, and ran parallel with other processes. As Indian communities were continuously exposed to Western practices, these elements were in turn adapted to or integrated into a local logic. At the same time, the Spaniards were subject to local contingences, such as biological and cultural interbreeding. Nevertheless, overall, the conquest was imposed on a decimated Indian population that became a minority while being the majority (Gruzinski and Wachtel 1997). This chapter focuses on one – of the many – specific ways in which

Occidentalization unfolded, with the indelible imprint of the conquest: the *Hispanicization* of the Indians, which was intimately connected to their Christianization. Right from the beginning, in the first instructions by General Borja for Spanish America, the General advised working first with the Indians who were 'officially Christian' (MP I: 122). In the first years in Peru, Acosta envisioned Hispanicization in his own way, laying the foundations for a gradual Hispanicization of the Indians, thus preserving certain customs and traditions, as will be shown in this chapter.

Meanwhile, as shown in Chapter Two, in his *Sumario de las Cosas de Japón* (1583) – Japan Summary – Alessandro Valignano clearly expresses the improbability of the Japanese accommodating to the Jesuits, so accommodation had to work the other way around. Apart from it being constitutive of the Ignatian spirit, another of the founding members of the Society, Francis Xavier, was the first to realize that some sort of accommodation was necessary in Japan. And it was Valignano, a true disciple, who envisioned this adaptation in the missions where both Portuguese military presence and ecclesiastical administration were weak or inexistent, and where Christianization was not identical to 'Portugalization' (Zupanov 2003: 20). Last but not least, accommodation was the alternative – probably the only one – that the Jesuits had in those missions where they had neither political nor coercive power on their side. As already mentioned, in the Japan Summary, Valignano conveyed a realistic notion of accommodation, distant from attitudes like those shown by Cabral in Japan.[1] Time and experience would give concrete meaning to Valignano's general directive of accommodation when carried out in China. Ruggieri and Ricci were the first to implement it, each in his own way. This chapter examines their different ways of interpreting and implementing Valignano's directives, when time, experience and personal appraisals would deal with the rest. Finally, this chapter proposes to analyse an intersection point in which Hispanicization and accommodation, as envisioned by Acosta and Ricci respectively, meet. As two religious men in the sixteenth century, they were both concerned – or obsessed – about idolatry, 'finding' its specific manifestations in their respective missions.

José de Acosta and the Hispanicization of the Indians in Peru

Civilizing and educating the Indians in Spanish America

The conquest in Spanish America converted the Indians into subjects of the Catholic monarchs. From that moment on, their *Hispanicization*, together with Christianization, was mandated, starting with the obligation to learn Spanish as one of the first directives.[2] A series of royal *cédulas* from the mid-sixteenth century onwards imposed the use of the Spanish language on all the Indians.[3] At the same time, the conquest of a whole 'New World' opened the floor to a series of debates in Spain relating to its legitimacy. Aristotle's theory of natural slavery provided a model to explain Indian backwardness, which was in turn used to prove the legitimacy of the conquest. Simply put, in European eyes, these people could be classified as 'barbarians' and their culture and society as clearly inferior to those of white men (Pagden 1988: 35 onward; 76). Hand in hand with their Christianization, the Indians were soon required to achieve a civil and political status. They had to be civilized, a requirement that the Spaniards expressed with the word *policía*. The term *policía* was incompatible with, or opposed to, the vices of the Indians, which were those of beasts, contrary to natural reason and thus condemned. That is why Christianization was not exclusively a religious problem; faith and a civilized state – *policía* – eventually became the same thing, both necessary requirements for a 'Spanish civil society' (Estenssoro 2003: 45–46). Many years later, the imposition of the TLC corpus, published between 1584–85, would continue to instruct the Indians in proper and civilized customs – *de policía*. Resorting to a great deal of everyday vocabulary and expressions, the Third catechism by sermons – *Tercero catecismo por sermones* – was involved in this battle (Taylor 2003: 69). In one of the sermons, addressing 'the Spanish and all men, civilized and of good judgement', it was suggested that they 'pay great attention that the elderly be honoured by the young … . And those with children … preach the Doctrine every day, before taking them to bed … bathing and cleaning and dressing them' (DCC: 615–17).

One of the key factors working against *policía* and civilized standards was the Indian custom of living in scattered communities. In colonial Peru, the *reducciones*, i.e. the resettlements of the population into villages, carried out by Viceroy Toledo, disrupted the political and socio-economic organization of the indigenous world, facilitating both forced Indian labour and Christianization. In the urban areas, Western domination turned the defeated Indians into a republic, la *república de indios*, as opposed to the *república de los españoles*, to finally reduce it to a minority. Both the *república de indios* and the *Juzgado de Indios* – a judiciary body – led to its juridical differentiation from the rest of the population. It was a distinction that purposely overlooked the pre-Hispanic differences within the indigenous world of a multitude of ethnicities and states with distinct languages and origins (Gruzinski-Wachtel 1997: 232).

Since the conquest, the strategy of educating the sons of the *caciques* – the native lords, as the Spanish called them – was strongly encouraged. These lords, who in Peru were referred to by the Quechua term *curaca*, became key figures connecting the two worlds, that of Spanish officialdom and the Andean people, in order to encourage the incorporation of Indians into the labour market and the mining drafts, as well as their Christianization. Hispanicization was soon channelled through the education of the *curacas'* offspring. The constitutions of the First Lima Council (1552) advised gathering in the parishes

all the caciques and principals' sons, as well as three or four skilled boys from the other towns for indoctrination, with care and diligence, in the truths of our holy Catholic faith and to teach them how to pray in the morning and when they go to bed, and bless what they eat and drink, as well as other proper and civilized customs [*policía*], and to read and write, and sing ... and to learn our Spanish.

(Mateos 1950: 52)

The *encomenderos* were often in charge of controlling these children's compulsory attendance at the schools, which had first been in the hands of Dominicans and Franciscans since the 1530s. The purpose was to make sure that these boys were not deprived of Christian education, especially because their parents – the *curacas* – were sometimes reluctant to send their offspring to the schools (Borges 1960: 399–412). Over time, towards the end of the sixteenth century, the educational institutions stopped being exclusively conceived for the Indian elite, and mass education for Indian children gained prominence. However, by and large, there were different attitudes towards the education of Indian noble children. In New Spain – modern Mexico – in the late sixteenth century, Viceroy Mendoza founded a school for noble Indian children in Michoacán. But it was a mixed school, i.e. the Indian noble children and the Spanish received the same education. This would avoid, for instance, the problem addressed by the Franciscans in New Spain of mixing noble and 'plebeian' Indian boys. In Peru, Viceroy Toledo opened two colleges, one in Cuzco and another in Lima, exclusively for the Indian elite (Borges 1960: 414–15).

The *mestizos* – mixed blood – were also students in these *colegios*, many of them sons of leading conquistadors who married their native concubines. The *mestizo* Inca Garcilaso de la Vega, son of a leading conqueror who served as *corregidor* – provincial administrative chief – of Cuzco and of an Indian princess, Isabel Chimpu Occllo, the grand-daughter of the Inca ruler Tupac Yupanqui, received a Spanish education in company with other mestizos and sons of Inca nobles. Later on, men like Garcilaso de la Vega inquired about the Inca past, haunted by its memory. Garcilaso's work fed on Jesuit Blas Valera's lost works and it is to date the only reliable access to Valera's view of a pre-Hispanic past. The son of Luis Valera, a Spanish conqueror and *encomendero*, and a native woman, Francisca Pérez, from whom he learned Quechua, Blas Valera was born in the province of Chachapoyas in 1544. He was admitted to the Society of Jesus in Lima soon after the Jesuits established themselves there. It was in the Jesuit residence in the same city that he would be imprisoned in 1583 for three years, for reasons still unclear, later leaving the underground jail cells for house arrest. Finally – thanks to a request by Acosta to Acquaviva – Valera was transferred to Spain, although he had originally asked Acquaviva to transfer him to Rome (Hyland 2003). The question of whether or not Blas Valera was the *Jesuita anónimo* – the Anonymous Jesuit – author of the anonymous chronicle *De las Costumbres Antiguas de los Naturales del Piru* of the late sixteenth century, has been a matter of debate, but there is not enough proof of Valera's authorship of the treatise, probably written between 1580 and 1594 (see Anónima 1968).[4] In his historical narrative *Comentarios Reales de los Incas* – Royal Commentaries of the Incas – Garcilaso did not deny that the Indians lived in a state of savagery, scattered across the land and practising unnatural vices, etc.[5] Garcilaso – through Valera – compared the Incas, the authors of civilization in Peru, with the ancient Romans for all their achievements, focusing on those aspects of Inca culture that defined it as an advanced civilization. Nevertheless, Garcilaso did not call the conquest into question. He was a *mestizo*, the acknowledged son of a leading *encomendero*, raised and educated in his father's house and influenced by his father's class (Brading 1986: 14). At almost the same time as Garcilaso's work, the Indian chronicler Felipe Guaman Poma de Ayala wrote his *Nueva Coronica y Buen Gobierno* – New Chronicle and Good Government. Guaman Poma has the vision of a man from the provincial indigenous nobility, a powerful connoisseur and observer of Andean culture who was also a zealous Catholic and an avid reader of European sources (Ramos 2010: 45).

The different views of Hispanicization in Peru

The Society of Jesus was the favourite religious order of Viceroy Toledo, one of the staunchest allies of Philip II in the Viceroyalty of Peru and also friend of General Francisco de Borja. As soon as they arrived in Peru, the Jesuits had an enormous responsibility regarding the education of the Indians.

Ignoring what the future would bring, one of the first directives that the General of the Society, Francisco de Borja, gave to Provincial Portillo before his departure in 1567 was to

> Be alert and notice what kind of people they are, which errors and gentile sects they follow, their dispositions and vices, if they have learned men or men of authority among them, so they can be positioned ahead of the rest, and which remedies for all these things could and must be used.
>
> (Zubillaga 1943: 61; MP I: 123)

When Acosta arrived in Peru a few years later – in 1571 – he expressed his agreement on these policies and suggested gaining 'the will of lords and *curacas*, showing them how those whom they rule would serve them more properly, according to our law'. That is why Acosta regretted Atahualpa's death. Had his will been conquered, the faith would have been warmly welcomed throughout the whole empire, since 'the barbarians are incredibly subjected to their princes or lords' (De Proc: 458).

Acosta's *De Procuranda* offers a possibility to observe the order of priorities the Jesuit established with regard to evangelization in the *Indias Occidentales*, more precisely in Peru. The evangelization of the Indians comes after civilized customs, proper to men, as subjects of the 'Christian princes'. Acosta follows Aristotle's *Ethics* when stating that in the barbaric nations cruelty abounds; it is a vice that makes beasts out of men, and these habits are closely related to mores. In sum, in Acosta's view, first and foremost, the 'barbarians' – the Indians – first learn to be men and then Christians; this was so essential a principle that it became of utmost importance for the question of salvation or ruin of souls. Acosta concludes that the first fundamental responsibility of the rulers is to attract these wild – *silvestres* – and fierce men to human life, make them more accommodated to civilized manners and behaviour for, otherwise, teaching the celestial and divine to those who do not understand 'human' is a futile business (De Proc: 491–92). But this did not mean banning all the Indians' customs, if they were not against natural reason or the Gospel. In the last chapter of *De Procuranda*, Acosta claims that:

> It is our responsibility to introduce the Indians to Christian customs and discipline and end without question their superstitious rites and sacrileges and their habits of barbaric fierceness; but in those particular aspects in which they do not oppose religion or justice, I do not think it is convenient to change them; on the contrary, it is about keeping all the paternal and gentile in them, inasmuch as they do not oppose reason, and then rule according to the law, as established by the Council of the Indies [*Consejo de Indias*] regulations.
>
> (De Proc: 502)[6]

Acosta applied this same criterion with regard to education in the Jesuit colleges two years later. In the Rules for the Colleges for Caciques – *Reglas para el Colegio de Caciques* – dated October 1578, by Visitor Plaza and Provincial José de Acosta, which included 'Notices for those with positions within the colleges' – *Avisos para el que ha de tener cargo del collegio de caciques* – the fifth notice warns that:

> It is not advisable to disregard the laws and customs and modes of government that they have in their land which are not contrary to Christian and natural law; nor is it convenient to make them Spanish in every aspect because, apart from being very difficult and thus leading to failure, it will do great harm to their government and republic.
>
> (MP II: 460)

However, Acosta was not the only one to promote a gradual Hispanicization of the Indians. The Dominicans before him, and Francisco de la Cruz in particular, pointed out that not all Indians customs and rites should be uprooted, and that some funerary rites, or their dances – *taquies* – had to be allowed. Indeed, the Dominicans in Peru welcomed the *taquies* – and indigenous songs, e.g. the *haylli*, triumphant songs for the celebration of military feats or events in the agricultural calendar – during the procession of the holy sacrament that they had established in Peru. The pre-Hispanic rituals thus turned into indigenous expressions of legitimate Catholic devotion with no ruptures with a pagan past, which welcomed and became the Christian present (Estenssoro 2003: 145). This responded, to a great extent, to Barto-lomé de Las Casas's view of pre-Hispanic religions. Las Casas was among the first to establish that the Inca rule, according to an evolutionary sequence, drew a demarcation line regarding Andean political and cultural modes, since the Incas represented the most complex political and religious organization known in those lands. They had introduced organized cults to the Andes, taking as a starting point their own cult of the sun. In this sense, religion was not exclusively defined by a set of doctrines, but by political and cultural changes. And the knowledge of God was not produced only by revelation, but in a series of steps that constituted a *praeparatio evangelica*. Some said that the Apostle St Thomas had been in Peru, as proof of a Christian presence in pre-Columbian America. The identification of local characters from Andean tradition with the apostles of Christ, like St Thomas, led to a game of similarities that re-evaluated Andean religions (MacCormack 1993: 212–13; Marzal 1993: 316 onward).

From a different angle, Acosta's above mentioned statement reflects the influence of the Corregidor of Cuzco, Polo de Ondegardo (1520–75), whom Acosta met during his first trip around Peru between 1573 and 1574. Polo de Ondegardo had provided the Jesuit with a great deal of the information which was included in his *Historia Natural y Moral de las Indias* – especially in the fourth book. Ondegardo was in favour of preserving all those elements of local culture that would not contradict natural law and Christian religion. In fact, part of the contents of Polo's treatise *Tratado y Averiguación sobre los Errores y Supersticiones de los Indios* (1559) were later included in the confession manual for priests contained in the Third Lima Council catechetical corpus – *Confesionario para Curas de Indios* – under the title Errors and Superstitions of the Indians, taken from Polo's treatise – *Los Errores y Supersticiones de los Indios Sacados del Tratado y Averiguación que Hizo el Licenciado Polo*. This is one of the main characteristics of Polo's influence upon the Society of Jesus and, more precisely, on Acosta, i.e. his insistence on the importance of gaining insight into the Indians' rites and beliefs, which did not necessarily exclude violence and punishment when it came to Christianization and building a civilized state – *poleçía* (Duviols 1977: 293–310). There was also an economic aspect to Polo's statements, when he proposed turning to the Indian tributary system based on labour and thus eliminating a fixed rate on products. This measure would help maximize Indian tributes and not be subject to the consequences of years of bad crops (Assadourian 1988: 138 onward).

Always setting an aggressive tone, Viceroy Toledo would not be an exception to the main concern of Hispanicization of the Indians in Peru. Toledo had the firm conviction that the extirpation of Indian idolatry was absolutely necessary for a full Hispanicization of the Andean people and, most importantly, it was an issue in the hands of the state (Duviols 1977: 145 onward). During his government (1569–80), the harshest measures were taken against Indian idolatry. When Toledo arrived in Peru, he encountered the

Andean movement known as the *Taki Oncoy*, or 'dance sickness'. This movement expanded throughout the central-southern Andes in 1562, thanks to itinerant Indian preachers – *dogmatizadores*, according to the Spaniards – and inspired the first attempt at the extirpation of idolatry in the region of Lima. Toledo took reprisals against the 'idolaters' usually portrayed as *hechiceros* – sorcerers (Griffiths 1998: 93–105). In 1572 Toledo dispatched an expedition to the stronghold of Vilcabamba to capture the last claimant to the Inca throne, Tupac Amaru. His aim was to eradicate the Inca dynasty. He did so with the help of Sarmiento de Gamboa and his *Historia Indica*, a work whose purpose was to prove that the Inca empire had been a merciless tyranny. Thanks to a letter that Jesuit Luis López sent to General Borja, it is known that the Jesuit Barzana had served as Tupac Amaru's confessor in the Inca's final days, having also pled before Toledo for Tupac Amaru's life to be spared. Luis López also wanted the Inca to be reprieved. But all these requests were hopeless, for Toledo had decided to execute Tupac Amaru, who was brought to Cuzco on September 21 1572, catechized and beheaded in the main square of Cuzco three days later (Mateos 1949: 150 onward).

Let us now go back to Acosta's statements advising the preservation of all those customs and traditions not contrary to Christian and natural law.

The blurry boundaries of Hispanicization

As the theologian who shaped Tridentine Catholicism in an Andean setting, Acosta grew suspicious that certain pre-Hispanic rituals and dances were idolatrous, thus widening the gap with the pre-Hispanic past. However, when the first expeditions of the Society arrived in Peru, before Acosta's arrival, some Jesuits might have been closer to the Dominicans in their view regarding religious celebrations, welcoming Andean religious customs. This can be observed in a letter of 1571 that Father Juan Gómez sent to General Borja, narrating a Corpus Christi celebration that incorporated Andean dances, in particular Inca dances, and costumes – a lively ceremony well described in this letter (MP I: 410–24). However, even though in *De Procuranda* Acosta is never precise regarding the specific pre-Hispanic customs to be preserved, *De Procuranda* is – once more – a starting point to trace them. In the *Proemio*, the preface, Acosta establishes distinctions between different categories of 'barbarians' which, in turn, would lead to different modes of evangelization for their salvation, the ultimate goal. Acosta places the Indians from Mexico and Peru in the middle between the Chinese and Japanese, who belonged in the first category, and the nomads – i.e. the Indians in the Caribbean – similar to beasts, in the third. The second group, according to Acosta, may have had empires and republics, laws and institutions, but they lacked a writing system – a key difference regarding the first group of Chinese and Japanese. Nevertheless, they found in the *quipus* – knotted string devices – a means of recording their memories and history, their laws and genealogies, as well as figures and numbers. Indeed, Acosta stated that the *peruanos* had artfully replaced writing with the *quipus*, a pre-Columbian memory technique used for all those purposes. This system of knotted strings has been extensively analyzed by scholars, who have both focused on *quipus* as a non-alphabetical writing system and also laid stress on the relationship between writing and orality (Boone and Mignolo 1996; Salomon 2001; Urton 1998).

Acosta furthers the information regarding *quipus* in Peru in his *Historia Natural y Moral de las Indias*:

> The Indians in Peru did not have any kind of writing system before the Spanish arrived, nor letters, characters or figures, like in China or Mexico; but not because of that did they not keep the memory of their past [*sus antiguallas*], because they were very diligent in keeping their memory. Apart from this diligence, they [the Indians] replaced the lack of writing and letters, in part with paintings, like Mexico, although in Peru they were very coarse and common, but mostly with *quipos*. *Quipos* consist of records made with strap, in which different knots and colours mean different things. And it is incredible what they achieved with *quipos*, for what the books can tell regarding history, and law, and ceremonies and accounting, they replace all of that with *quipos*. Offical deputies, called *Quipocamayo*, were in charge of *quipos*, like the notaries here [in Spain].
>
> (HNyM: 189)

Acosta's positive appreciation of the *quipu* can also be observed in a letter to General Mercurian of February 15 1577, when referring to their use in the *doctrina* in Juli:

> I forgot to say how in these boys who learn the doctrine I find many more skills than I thought. After just one week some of them know how to cross themselves and also the Our Father, Hail Mary and the Creed and the Salve in the language [Spanish] so they all sang it during the procession on Sunday; and many men and women and boys and girls are all day with their *quipos*, like students repeating a lesson.
>
> (MP II: 276)

The Society of Jesus encouraged a religious use of *quipu*; and it was not the first order to do so. Before the Jesuits, the Mercedarian Diego de Porres recommended their use for each village to have both the resolutions by the FLC in 1551 and the list of the commandments (Estenssoro 2003: 217). So distant from European modes of expression, the Toledan reforms of the 1570s had aimed at replacing *quipus* with alphabetic records, but they were not very successful in this respect (Durston 2008: 69). The problem resided in the interaction between Andean and Spanish records and record-keepers – by no

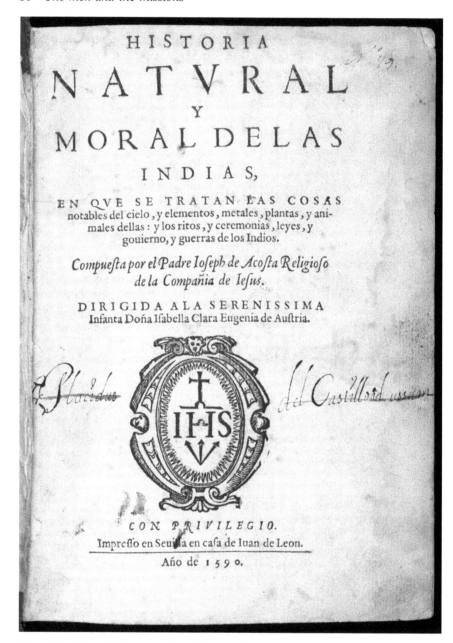

Figure 3.1 Historia Natural y Moral de las Indias (front cover), Seville (1590)

means always amicable, especially when the central issue became who – natives or Spaniards – was to be in control of public records in the colony. In that regard, in the TLC's constitutions the *quipu* were classified as idolatrous objects that had to be burned (Vargas Ugarte 1951: 358; Castillo Arroyo

1966: 91; Urton 2002: 6–10). But the TLC catechetical corpus made of the manufacturing of *quipu* a *sine qua non* for a thorough confession. In short, what was allowed exclusively was a Christian usage of *quipu* and none other that could serve 'the Indians' superstitions'. In sermon twelve of the Third catechism, part of the TLC corpus, on how Indians should confess their sins to be forgiven, it is recommended that they record their sins with *quipu*. So the sermon addresses the Indians by saying:

> For your confession to be good, and please God, the first thing you have to do, my son, is to make a *quipo*, just like you make them ... of what you give and what people owe you. So you make a *quipo* of what you have done against God and against others, and how many times, if many or a few. And not only is it about deeds, but also about your thoughts ... if you desired to commit sin with a woman and you looked at her with that purpose, if you want to steal a blanket or someone's ram.
>
> (DCC: 482)

In short, the *quipu* proved to be effective for the Indians to both record their sins before confession and remember doctrine. And Acosta, through *De Procuranda*, his correspondence and the TLC corpus left sufficient proofs of both their efficiency and approval. However, Acosta did not stop short of providing information regarding other alternative writing systems in Peru. Jan Szeminski has studied these pre-Hispanic writing systems – *qillca* in Quechua – by analyzing catechetical texts in Quechua and Aymara, currently used to date in Bolivia. In most of the cases, the authors were people who did not speak Spanish nor were knowledgeable of the Latin alphabet. One of these alternative writing systems is a catechetical pictography, presented on a round surface – 'clay pizzas' – with a sequence of clay figurines, pebbles and other elements representing prayers and some variants of the catechism (Szeminski 2010: 129–86). In the *Historia Natural*, Acosta describes:

> Beside these *quipos* made of strings, they [the Indians in Peru] also have pebbles, through which they learn the words they want to remember by heart, and very old men can be seen with a wheel made of pebbles to learn the Our Father, and with another one the Hail Mary, and with another for the Creed, knowing which is the right stone.
>
> ... if this is not wit and if these men are beasts, it should be judged at everyone's own discretion; as for myself, what I gather is that these things they apply, they are of great benefit to us.
>
> (HNyM: 190)[7]

In sum, Acosta, and the Jesuits in Peru, might have been tolerant and in favour of keeping these systems because they were practical; if the missionaries wanted the Indians not to repeat doctrine parrot fashion and to be thorough when recording all their sins, time proved that *quipu* were effective.

We can gather from these statements by Acosta that the idea of keeping certain pre-Hispanic customs might have been encouraged by a pragmatism which, in turn, set some boundaries in the process of Hispanicization of the Indians.

Acosta never dismissed coercion as a means of achieving certain goals, like Hispanicization; it was justified by the Indians' condition as subjects of the Spanish crown. Indeed, Acosta finds a justification for force and coercion in the evangelization and salvation of the Indians in their condition as subjects of the 'Christian princes'. However, with all its ambiguities, *De Procuranda* conveys a search for a balance between persuasion and coercion. This was not a new conundrum, indeed. Sabine MacCormack established some parallels regarding religious coercion in Peru and in the Roman empire, as a by-product of the church's involvement with the state. In late ancient Rome, the debate about conversion and persecution/coercion could raise the question of the possibility of religious tolerance because the participants in the debate shared the same culture. However, the question of religious tolerance would not arise in Peru because it could only be discussed among people who viewed each other as equals in some respect. Those who pleaded the cause of the Indians therefore concentrated on proving that in various ways they were equal to the Spaniards; such is the case of Francisco de la Cruz (MacCormack 1985: 463–64). A manifestation of the cultural difference can be observed in Acosta's rejection of Indians being ordained priests, as he clearly states in *De Procuranda*. Acosta quotes St Paul, who claimed that a neophyte should not preside in the Church because, being vain like the devil, he could fall (De Proc: 601). In short, Indians should not be admitted to the priesthood or any other status in the Church, but only help with inferior services, e.g. sing in the choir.

Shaping accommodation in the China mission

Interpreting Valignano's directives

The tension between persuasion and coercion never reached China; no conquest would shape the encounter between the Jesuits and the Chinese. As mentioned above, one of the characteristics of the European–Chinese contacts that came about through Christianity is the fact that external power was extremely reduced, it being the Ming administration – and later the Qing – who ultimately decided whether or not they could enter and stay (Standaert 2001b: 83–85).

In his Japan Summary, Valignano commented how the mission in Japan was the most important and fruitful among the ones in those lands in the East. This was for many reasons. The first, is that it is a very vast Province that 'harbours sixty-six kingdoms, inhabited by white people, very civilized [*de mucha policía*], with prudence and understanding and subject to reason' (Sumario: 131). Valignano was convinced that the kind of missionary needed in the missions to the East were those who could be assimilated to learned men, who would accommodate to their civilized inhabitants. However, as he said to Acquaviva in a letter of 1595, Valignano did not consider it was necessary to send literati – *letrados* – to all the missions in the East, specifically India, while it was necessary for the other missions like Japan and later China.[8] Valignano was not aware of the existence of famous schools of thought in the interior of India at the time (Schütte 1980 I: 130–31). Some years later, inspired by the adaptation propagated by Valignano and Ricci in China, the Italian Jesuit Roberto Nobili implemented his own adaptionist practice in Madurai, India. He studied Sanskrit, approached the Brahmans and dressed like them (Zupanov 2003).

China was a world unto itself and saw itself as synonymous with civilization, inclined to think that outside its borders nothing existed but barbarism. And one of the countless challenges that Ruggieri and Ricci had to cope with was to prove to the Chinese that they were not 'barbarians'. The spread of Western scientific knowledge proved useful for that purpose as a response to these contingencies in certain mission contexts, at the same time representing actual knowledge produced by the Jesuits in those spaces (Romano 2008: 276).

Chapter Two ended with a focus on Ruggieri's first steps in the China mission. In August 1583 Michele Ruggieri left Macao en route to Zhaoqing with Matteo Ricci, after receiving permission from the governor to travel to that city. In Zhaoqing Ruggieri accepted the suggestion of a local Chinese official to shave off his beard and hair and don the robes of a Buddhist monk; and Ricci did likewise. More than ten years later Ricci switched the dress and personal appearance of a Buddhist monk to that of a Chinese scholar-official, a mandarin, who Ricci regarded as exclusively 'Confucian'. However, as early as 1585, the sense of a full adaptation to that 'other world of China' can be perceived in a letter to Father Giulio Fuligatti in 1585, in which Ricci said he had turned into a Chinese – *fatto un cina* – in the external aspects, from garments to etiquette (OS II: 72).

While making those trips from Macao to Canton, in the very first years, Ruggieri had begun to translate 'a very small book' – *un libro molto piccolo* – on the moral virtues 'transcribed hastily in bad Latin', which was enclosed with a letter to General Mercurian dated 12 November 1581 (Rule 1986: 6–7).[9] Ruggieri tells General Mercurian:

> It was through divine favour that I have already learned fifteen thousand figures, with which, little by little, I read their books and lately in this year of 1581, in Canton ... I have transcribed this Chinese book that I am sending you so you can see the kind of letters these people have, together with the wit and skills that our Lord gave to these gentile and barbaric people, who can profess moral virtues ... . They do not have philosophy, but sentences and conclusions produced as reason mandates. And despite not having knowledge of God, they live morally ... as you will gather from this book transcribed in bad Latin.
>
> (OS II: 401)

According to Ruggieri, the problem that may arise in converting the Chinese 'is the resistance found in their will, because they do not have any difficulty in understanding the things of God' (OS II: 403).

It is difficult to say how good Ruggieri became at speaking and reading Chinese in the course of the eight-and-a-half years he lived in a Chinese language milieu. It is true that both Valignano and Ricci's statements regarding Ruggieri's bad Chinese were made near the time of the plan of sending Ruggieri back to Rome, in 1588. However that may be, it holds true that Ruggieri had written Chinese poems and translated into Latin the basic Confucian set of works, the Four Books (Chan 1993; Lundbaek 1979). Antonio Possevino, appointed secretary of the Society of Jesus in 1573, printed a small part of Ruggieri's translation of one of the Four Books, the Great Learning, in his *Bibliotheca Selecta* (1593), his great encyclopaedic work. After returning to Italy, between 1591 and 1592, Ruggieri sat down to revise his translation of the Four Books. In those years he frequented the company of Possevino, whom he told about his experience in China. Ruggieri was the only man in Europe who had worked in China as a missionary and knew its language. Chapter nine in Possevino's *Bibliotheca Selecta* contains some of the information about China based on material that Ruggieri provided, including information on politics, agriculture and transportation, as well as on poetry, philosophy and physics, among other topics. As mentioned above, Possevino also reprinted a section from Ruggieri's translation of the Confucian classic, the Great Learning. The passages have the distinction of being the earliest Confucian classic to appear in print in Europe (Donnelly 1988: 195). As seen in the previous chapter, however, after having made Ruggieri the first Jesuit missionary in China, Valignano did everything in his power to keep him in the background, even when he was back in Italy.

On December 10 1593, Ricci wrote to Acquaviva from Shaozhou saying that Valignano had asked him to make a translation of the Four Books. In 1596, Valignano himself wrote to the General informing him that Ricci was going to translate these works – in 1594 Ricci had shown the visitor large parts of the translation already finished. Valignano added that he had heard of Ruggieri's translation of the Four Books and that the latter wished to have them printed in Europe. Valignano firmly advised against that, in the letter to Acquaviva of 1596 mentioned above (see Chapter Two). When the editions of *Bibliotheca Selecta* appeared – 1593, 1603 and 1607 – China had not yet become an object of intellectual curiosity in Europe. For the common reader, there was only González de Mendoza's *Historia del Gran Reyno de la China* (1585), which became a best-seller. But it portrayed China only from the impressions of a few Franciscans and Augustinian missionaries on very short visits to certain coastal areas and from hearsay among the overseas Chinese in the Philippines, as seen in Chapter Two (Lundbaek 1979: 3–7).

Following Valignano's guidelines, Ruggieri had pioneered the process of accommodation, as a bonze from the West, and diverted it into the natural channel of Chinese popular religion. By and large, in late Ming China Buddhism offered a less hierarchical, and less patriarchal, identity. No educated layman, however devoted to Buddhism, could forsake his Confucian persona, which was also a mark of social power (Brooks 1993a: 188 onward). Even though this role of a bonze from the West had also been suggested by Chinese officials in the first place, there is no evidence that Ruggieri questioned it (Rule 1986: 10). The aspect to be underscored here is that both Ruggieri and Ricci's accommodation has been conceived as generally trapped in an 'either-or' approach, i.e. Buddhism or Confucianism, although in the years that Ruggieri spent in China, he did not seem to adopt such an exclusivist view of 'the Chinese sects' as Ricci did. Ruggieri could dress like a Buddhist monk and try to translate the 'Confucian' books, and confute Buddhism in his TZSL. In that regard, Ruggieri seemed to be 'more Chinese' than Ricci, in the sense that he did not adopt such rigid divisions between the main schools of thought in China. What is true is that Ricci gained deeper insight into Confucianism, possibly because he stayed much longer in China than Ruggieri. And probably because – simply put – he was indeed attracted to what he interpreted as Confucianism, which he conceived as the cornerstone of Chinese lettered culture, with political power on its side: a perfect match.

Ricci's interpretation of Confucianism

According to Matteo Ricci, the uniqueness of China resided in the key role that letters played in the kingdom, to the extent that 'if philosophers are not kings, it is true that kings are governed by philosophers' (FR I: 36). Many of these 'philosophers' were those who participated in the civil service examination to obtain official posts within the empire, which proved to be successful in capturing the fancy of ambitious men and their families in such a way that one of the defining characteristics for gentry status became examination success. Indeed, the civil examination system was designed to test the merits of young men, most of whom came from literati or merchant backgrounds. Exclusion of those who lacked sufficient cultural and linguistic resources for training their sons was successfully defended by the imperial ideal of open competition to select the 'best and the brightest' to serve the emperor (Elman 2000: 240 onward). The term 'literati' can be applied to the large group of scholars who participated in the official examinations, although they were not always successful in passing the final grades. But a considerable group among them were also 'officials', i.e. they occupied an official position in the local, provincial or central government. Those who did not pass the official examinations could be employed in various other positions, such as clerks or private tutors (Handbook: 474). The better-learned citizens of pre-modern China, even those who had failed the examinations or had passed but never held office, enjoyed a familiarity with the 'Confucian' books that afforded them a common store of knowledge.[10] One of the differences between Ruggieri and

Ricci is that the latter had the opportunity to gain a deeper insight into these circles in different cities and this was, indeed, due to his longer sojourn in China. And he shaped an interpretation of Confucianism, which is not possible to assess in Ruggieri's works.

Ricci's view of Confucianism as a moral system useful to govern the empire wisely, also fed on an alleged non-idolatrous gentility that Ricci ascribed to it. And he interpreted the rituals performed by the scholar-officials in that same vein. Indeed, in Ricci's opinion, the performing of rituals was also part of the administrative duties of the officials; and thus part of their intellectual equipment. It is a well-known fact that this interpretation by Ricci would have consequences in the seventeenth century, in what became known as the Chinese rites controversy. In sum, according to Ricci, Christianity and Confucianism were compatible at a moral and ethical level, and Christianity would provide Confucianism with a supernatural base. Last but not least, Ricci was convinced that the Chinese Classics, imbued with a 'pure' Confucianism, contained evidence of an ancient monotheism, free from Buddhist influences. This is another difference between Ruggieri and Ricci; not only in knowledge about Confucianism, but in the fact that Ricci's interpretation was meant to provide a local anchorage for Christianity. Buddhism could also provide it, indeed, but – with Valignano's support – it was not what Ricci had in mind. Actually, as Gernet points out, it was the Buddhist element of the ethics of the time that was most in tune with Ricci's own teaching. Buddhism preached contempt for the world and the senses, which were the cause of attachments and rebirth. Buddhist, like Christian, morality is prohibitive and ascetically inclined (Gernet 1985: 143). But Ricci sought to differentiate from this 'sect', which he abhorred, as much as possible, as shown below.

It was essential for Ricci to legitimize his interpretation on the basis of textual evidence, thus he resorted to the Four Books, which he then translated into Latin (see Introduction, note 9). Ricci regarded Confucius as the Sage, 'another Seneca' – *un altro Seneca* – and the Four Books as 'good moral works', *buoni documenti morali*. And this perception also served as an impulse for Ricci to compose humanistic writings proclaiming wisdom from the West, on the basis of sayings by 'ancient saints and sages'. The first writing of this kind produced by Ricci was inspired by a theme that he saw was common to – and would bring closer – both cultures: friendship, and more specifically virtuous friendship. Indeed, a proof of this insight is his first treatise in Chinese, On Friendship, or *Jiaoyou lun* [1595] (2009). Friendship was a topic of great interest to late Ming intellectuals, which suggests that Ricci was attempting to participate in, and to benefit from, a discussion that was already taking place in China (Ricci 2009 (1595): 5). Male bonding as intellectual and elitist was fundamental to Ming men, who pursued their masculinity as scholar-officials and would participate in the intellectual debates of the time in literati associations e.g. literary clubs and assemblies for philosophical debate (Huang 2007; Lam 2007: 84). In sum, the friendship among literati was the type that Ricci was interested in, not only to write about but also to experience. In the concluding maxim of his 'On Friendship', Ricci portrayed himself as a 'philosopher', a *'filosofo'* in the Italian version, from the Western mountains.[11]

On the side of Orthodoxy

It was in Nanchang that Ricci was introduced to the less official aspects of Confucianism, the world of academies and discussion circles. He was beginning to appreciate that Confucianism was not a monolithic orthodoxy but a living doctrine with a variety of sometimes conflicting tendencies. And he started to interweave them with Christianity, which in its Chinese version became the doctrine of the Lord of Heaven. We know from his letters that he was working on his definitive book, *Tianzhu Shiyi* – hereafter cited as TZSY – in those years. Although not printed until 1603, it was the fruit of the Nanchang years. Over time, Ricci became acquainted with some literati who were not satisfied with a dominant Neo-Confucian orthodoxy at that moment, since it was too impregnated with Buddhism.[12] These dissenting literati became part of Ricci's closest circle until his death in 1610. We can find among these prominent officials those who came to be called 'the three pillars of the Church': Xu Guanqi (1562–1633), Li Zhizao (1557–1630) and Yang Tingyun (1557–1627). They offered Matteo Ricci patronage, protection and friendship. Yang Tingyun was an active member of the Donglin Academy – *Donglin Shuyuan* –, which proclaimed a return to an orthodox Confucianism, at that moment too impregnated with Buddhism. And the Donglin movement – *Donglin Xuepai* – itself was a manifestation of a considerable crisis that Neo-Confucianism went through in late Ming China (Standaert 1988: 36–37). Yang Tingyun observed both differences and similarities between Confucianism and Christianity. Despite the differences, the basic assumption is that the relationship between the two doctrines is one of congruity and complementarity, provided that Confucianism is 'cleansed' of Neo-Confucian speculations. Christianity was presented to serve as a 'complement to Confucianism' – *bu ru* – an expression that appears to have been coined by Xu Guangqi. According to Yang, the Heavenly Teachings – *Tianxue* – can be practised in a way through which Confucianism and Christianity find mutual support, serving a three-fold aim of complementing and furthering the ruler's civilizing influence, supporting the methods of Confucianism and correcting the errors of Buddhism (Zürcher 1994: 45–47). By and large, these literati converts, Xu Guangqi, Li Zhizao and Yang Tingyun, shared a concern about the decadence of morals and public life, along with a search for alternatives, and the doctrine that Ricci expounded, the doctrine of the Lord of Heaven, became one of them. This confluence was defined by Jacques Gernet as a 'happy conjunction' between the teaching of the Jesuits and the tendencies of the period and it was as much a political as a philosophical and moral reaction (Gernet 1985: 23).

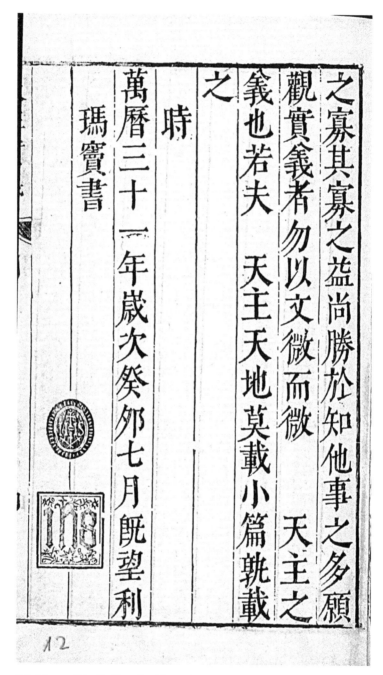

Figure 3.2 Matteo Ricci's *Tianzhu Shiyi* (True Meaning of the Lord of Heaven; front cover) (1603)
Source: Courtesy of USF Ricci Institute for Chinese-Western Cultural History

Ricci's TZSY explicitly expresses the congruity and complementation between Confucianism and Christianity. But it went further than that. As conceived by Ricci, the teachings of the Lord of Heaven claimed to offer its own interpretation of Confucianism itself. Let us remember that, in the Confucian tradition the nucleus of right thought and action is called *zheng*, i.e. correct, legitimate – usually translated as 'orthodoxy'; it is contrasted with the 'heterodox' principles – *xie* – of non-Confucian religious systems, notably Buddhism and Daoism, and with sectarian cults and rituals that are regarded as potentially subverting the moral order and therefore considered 'heterodox'. In Ricci's view the sphere of *zheng* was limited to the officially recognized interpretation of the Confucian canon. However, there were several strongly divergent trends and schools led by influential masters who expounded ideas that differed from the official exegesis on fundamental points, without being branded as heterodox or 'heretical' (Zürcher 1997: 615–21).

Summarizing, in his TZSY, Ricci inaugurates a strict and exclusive division between orthodoxy and heterodoxy, attempting to legitimise the new doctrine of the Lord of Heaven through the Confucian concept of orthodoxy. Ricci thus condemned Buddhism and Daoism as 'heterodox' sects, according to his own interpretation of these categories but in line with many of the Christian converts' statements. In doing this, Ricci was no exception in conveying an exclusivist view of religions, and an ecumenical orthodoxy, although neither of these things related to the Chinese context. However, he went further by shaping the congruity between the teachings of the Lord of Heaven and Confucianism, as an intellectual-oriented accommodation in China.[13] From Ruggieri onward, accommodation also implied that the Jesuits preached their ideas by using the Chinese language. In this process, they accepted or rejected certain Chinese concepts, ideas and trends very selectively, and would not always agree on the choices. Conversely, this process of interpretation also occurred on the Chinese side. When the Chinese came into contact with Christianity, Western-Christian thought had already been translated into Chinese. Building on these efforts, they interpreted Christianity by basing their reasoning upon their own concepts, and selecting, accepting or rejecting ideas (Standaert 1991: 9).[14]

Over time, Ricci forged a monolithic view of Confucianism, which is reflected in his TZSY, but which never did justice to the real experience of the literati circles he became acquainted with. Apart from Buddhism, Ricci grew vehement toward the syncretistic trends in late Ming China. The Three Teachings, the *San jiao*, attracted some of the late-sixteenth-century intellectuals associated with what became known as the *Taizhou* School. The goal of their philosophical effort was to search for an inner essence that would render insignificant the distinctions among Buddhism, Daoism, and Confucianism (Brooks 1993b: 19–20). But Ricci's rigid division into the three 'sects' dismissed and rejected these schools and intellectual traditions.

Hispanicization and accommodation in dialogue with idolatry

As religious men of the sixteenth century, Acosta and Ricci were concerned about idolatry and they both gave a specific cultural content to the more abstract idea of devilish idolatry (Rubiés 2005: 244–64). Their views were shaped by Scholasticism, based on Augustinianism and Aristotelianism, which gave the devil an important role in the world. Both Jesuits formulated their impressions in their respective catechisms, the DCC and the TZSY. For both of them, the devil was always behind the scenes, pulling the strings to deceive people, be they Indians or Chinese. But the problem lies in how the missionaries responded to the problem of identifying idolatry in non-Christian societies.[15] As shown in the first section of this chapter, Acosta set some boundaries to the mandate of Hispanicization. Undoubtedly, the Indians' idolatry would always pose a threat to its implementation, and no Spaniard on Andean soil had any doubt that it had to be 'extirpated'; when it came to idolatry, persuasion was not an option. However, in the time of Acosta the worst was yet to come. By the end of the first decade of the seventeenth century, the Catholic Church's confidence in the success of its efforts to convert the Andean population to Catholicism was severely shaken. The Indians' attachment to their own religious system had been – as the contemporary rhetoric put it – 'discovered' or 'unmasked'. The solution was found in 'extirpation visits', which amounted to a series of inquisitorial investigations held in the Indian parishes. The Jesuits supervised the instruction and detention of the principal religious offenders from the beginning of these campaigns in the second decade of the seventeenth century. Meanwhile, in China, despite the fact that coercion was not an option, nothing stopped Matteo Ricci from shaping the dark side of accommodation to Confucianism: a virulent rejection of 'Buddhist idolatry'. In short, Acosta and Ricci were not that different in certain aspects, or at least not to the extent that some scholars have chosen to believe. These pages will examine both the 'soft side' of Acosta's view of idolatry and Ricci's aggressive tone against 'Buddhist idolatry'.

In *De Procuranda Indorum Salute*, by making use of the deutoro-canonical Book of Wisdom, Acosta analyzes the rites and superstitions in Peru (Rubiés 2006: 590). He also follows and cites John Damascene's typology of the different kinds of idolatry: worship of celestial bodies by the Caldeans; worship of the dead by the Greeks; and that of animals, stones and wood by the Egyptians. According to Acosta, all these types were present in the Andes, embodied in the *huacas*, a native Andean deity often associated with nature in the form of hills, water, caves and stones, and ancestors in the form of mummies, etc. (De Proc: 559).[16] Acosta insists on the omnipresence and ubiquity of idolatry on Andean soil, based on the worship of *huacas*, to which he also refers in the fifth book of the *Historia Natural y Moral*. Indeed, *huacas* were the most general kind of idolatry in Peru, and one that Acosta regarded as typical of the land:

This pernicious pest of idolatry is in the mountains, valleys, villages, houses, paths, and there is not even a small portion of Andean soil free from this superstition ... whoever wants to read the chronicle [*historia*] so carefully written by this noble man Polo [de Ondegardo] will see that in Cuzco alone there were more than three hundred and sixty [*huacas*].

(De Proc: 561)

And this is reflected in the catechisms in the TLC corpus, in which monotheism is contrasted with the worship of natural phenomena. In the Greater catechism, the worship of *huacas* breaks the first commandment 'I am the Lord your God ... you shall have no other gods but me'. In a question and answer format, it says:

Who breaks the Commandment of loving God?
He who worships any creature, or has idols, or *guacas*, or believes in false sects, and heresies, or dreams ... they are all the Devil's schemes.

(DCC: 135 onward)

This reference to 'idols *or huacas*' allows us to infer that Acosta does not establish a clear-cut assimilation between the two. In the *Historia Natural y Moral de las Indias*, the fifth book in particular addresses the religion and superstitions of the Indians, to later focus on their similarities with the works of the devil, especially from chapter twenty-three onward. Here Acosta focuses on the emulations of the sacraments by the devil, as well as on celebrations like Corpus Christi and their similarities with the *Intyraimi*, the Andean 'celebration of the Sun'. But Acosta's standpoint is somewhat ambiguous, since all these imitations by the devil in turn helped the Indians to receive Christianity:

The Indians' subjection to their kings and lords was indeed of no small help for the Indians to receive the law of Christ. And the same servitude and subjection to the Devil and his tyranny ... [were] all rendered in a great disposition to supreme Wisdom, as of the same evil the good can be extracted.

And what in our law is so difficult, which is to believe in high mysteries, it became easier among them, with the Devil telling them much more difficult things; and the same things that he stole from our evangelical law like their way of communion and confession ... they all help them to receive the truth of what they have received before as a lie; God is wise and wonderful, and He defeats his enemy with his same weapon.

(HNyM: 174)

Like many of Acosta's statements, this one is ambiguous and contradictory regarding pre-Hispanic religions; and it has inspired different opinions from scholars. Pierre Duviols holds that Acosta and, in more general terms the Society of Jesus, both embody the struggle between two opposite standpoints: on the one hand the idea of using all the pre-existing favourable aspects of pre-Hispanic culture to their advantage and on the other hand the fear that such appealing foundations are corrupted by the devil (Duviols 1977: 304). In a similar vein, Anthony Pagden states that the only satisfactory explanation that Acosta found for pagan religious expressions was that of the devil's intervention. However, even though the highest category of 'barbaric nations' in the *Historia Natural y Moral de las Indias*, i.e. the Incas and Aztecs, were those most devoted to the cults of the devil, they were closer to the civilized Christian world than other nations. Therefore, once satanic rites were separated from their source of origin, they could be shaped as Christian rites (Pagden 1988: 234–39). More sceptically, Carmen Bernand and Serge Gruzinski consider that these analogies and a taste for similarities in Acosta – e.g. the Corpus Christi and the similarity with the *Intiraymi* – were reduced to an evil parody of all these points in common (Bernand and Gruzinski 1992: 75).

In Ricci's case, it has been shown that the other side of the coin of his interpretation of 'orthodox' Confucianism was 'heterodox' Buddhism and Daoism. Let us move forward to Buddhism as 'idolatrous'. The omnipresence of Buddhist idols led to Ricci's rejection of this 'sect', which he saw as nothing other than the incarnation of idolatry in China. In his TZSY, in a dialogue between a Western scholar – Ricci himself – and a Chinese scholar, the latter asks Ricci about the benefit of worshipping images of the Buddha – *bai fo xiang* – and reciting Buddhist scriptures – *nian qi jing*. Ricci – apparently – had no choice other than to answer that, far from benefiting, it would undoubtedly harm orthodoxy – *zheng dao* (TZSY, VII: 592, IV–V). Ricci laments that, although Confucians – *ru zhe* – wanted to get rid of Buddhism and Daoism, the latter were still erecting temples and worshipping 'idols', literally images – *xiang* – which the Jesuit clearly interpreted as 'idols' (TZSY, VII: 592, V–IX). There was one specific Buddhist precept that Ricci attacked: that of reincarnation. Right from the beginning, Ricci identified Buddhists with the Pythagoreans, but found that they distorted Pythagoras' concept of the transmigration of souls. This is something Ricci denounces in both catechisms, the TZSY and the brief Latin version sent to Rome. He had to convince the Chinese of the immortality of the soul; and when trying to impose this Christian truth, Ricci attacked the Buddhists. Buddhist reincarnation, according to Ricci, was nothing but a distorted – and plagiarized – version by Sakyamuni of the Pythagorean theory of the transmigration of souls (TZSY: 492). Ricci also denounced the 'idolaters' in China, in the brief Latin version of the TZSY sent to Rome, for distorting Pythagoras' theory – *nostro Philosopho antiquo* – and including it in their books (Ricci 1985 [1603]: 467). In sum, when it came to idolatry and harsh condemnation of it, whatever language was used to express it, both Acosta and Ricci – as men of their times – shared identical concerns. However, Ricci's interpretation and adaptation to

Confucianism prevented him from seeing idolatry spread throughout the Middle Kingdom, while Acosta could afford to see idolatry everywhere. This was not only because the *huacas* were everywhere, but also because coercive power fed on and endorsed these views. However, it is reasonable to think that Acosta's ambiguities regarding pre-Hispanic religions and culture marked a distance from men like Viceroy Toledo, who were blinded by the obsession of idolatry. In China, Buddhist 'idols' were omnipresent, but Ricci made of Confucianism – metaphorically speaking – a 'sight for sore eyes' – and a peaceful backwater. What separated Acosta from Ricci was a matter of scope: the scope of the projection of idolatry onto the missions.

To conclude, in his *Historia Natural y Moral de las Indias*, Acosta opines that, should anyone despise the Indians' rites and customs as foolish – *necios* – or hate them as inhuman and devilish, they should consider that the Greeks and the Romans had similar rites and customs, and even worse. But it is true that these ancient gentiles' natural knowledge exceeded the Indians'. In sum, the Indians lacked the supernatural light as well as philosophy and natural doctrine (HNyM: 139). However, Acosta found a way to accommodate to them. In *De Procuranda*, in one of the last chapters of the Fourth book entitled 'On the catechism and how to alleviate the catechist's tediousness', Acosta claims it is difficult to find anyone who wants to be among the Indians and persevere in their instruction. He states that:

> Tedium and sadness usually originate from both the catechizing labour itself, and the capacity and condition of the Indians. It is unpleasant to instruct those who are rude, because the same things have to be repeated over and again ... without elevating to major things ... . The remedies against this illness, nobody will provide with better medicine than St. Augustine in that book he wrote to evangelize rude people, where he says: 'If we get tired of repeating things to children over and again until they know them in general, and that is convenient for them, we have to accommodate to them with love ... , and joining our hearts to them, we will start to conceive those things as new, for so powerful is the sympathetic spirit, when they become affectionate to those who teach them, and we to them who learn.
>
> (De Proc: 539)

Within the Jesuit tradition, Ricci's accommodation in the East has been 'naturally' conceived as accommodation to the well-learned Chinese men, while there were other modes of accommodating to gentiles, as Acosta claims, in an Augustinian vein. But accommodation to the Indians did not imply, as in China, a close contact with the Indian converts or potential converts. It was not for nothing that two Jesuits, Matteo Ricci in the late sixteenth century and Martino Martini (1614–61) in the seventeenth century, wrote on friendship.[17] In sum, Jesuit accommodation has been praised in a world of letters, as part of an Ignatian spirit, but it had a 'dark side', i.e.

condescending, by approaching the Indians, portrayed as affectionate children, using unsophisticated truths to transmit the Christian faith. In this sense, many of the complexities of Andean culture that the Spanish observed and described at that time, like the non-alphabetic writing systems, served evangelization and its purposes in a practical way, outside the 'world of letters'.

In a letter that Acquaviva sent to Baltasar Piñas on June 15 1584 regarding the missions in the Peru and Mexico provinces, the general makes reference to those vast provinces that still exist without God, even if those poor souls – *pobres animas* – had received baptism. The problem Acquaviva notices is that the fathers of the Society who are sent from Europe to those missions cannot resist the temptation, inherent in their nature,

> of getting carried away by things more fitted to their taste and inclination, which is relating to the people of the same nation, dealing with people more civilized, all matters that give more satisfaction and consolation than work, and in which the will is not harmed for finding in them less repugnance, and the senses find a better entertainment due to the comfort and taste of the body, and for being an enterprise more apparent and striking to the human eye.

So Acquaviva insists that 'our fathers' put all their effort into those parts, understanding that otherwise they are depriving themselves of the glorious goal that their missions expect from their painstaking endeavours among the Indians.

In Spanish America, the Jesuits belonged to – quoting Angel Rama – the 'lettered city', as opposed to the colonized society. This lettered city regarded cultural diversity as a threat to the cultural homogeneity that colonialism – domestic and overseas – tried to impose. From this perspective, the lettered city viewed the 'others' like stereotypes without any kind of specificity, sharing a series of negative characteristics: a lack of letters – or an existence of symbolic languages representing wicked beliefs; a lack of laws – or an existence of those of devilish origin; a lack of government – or an existence of illegitimate government; a lack of mechanical arts and crafts – or their purposive use for Satan. Regarding the first of these characteristics – the lack or presence of letters – the elite denied their existence among the colonized groups like the Amerindians (Adorno 1987: 21–22). Acosta showed interest and, we might say, respect for the Andean non-alphabetical writing systems, such as the *quipus*, and all his statements regarding these knotted-string devices prove he was in favour of keeping and using them for both a genuine indoctrination and confession of the Indians. Indeed, the Andeans recorded their lives through the tactile and visual world connected to orality, as they were not inclined to writing and images accompanying texts to express themselves (Cummins 1998: 95 onward). But only an exclusively Christian usage of the *quipu* was allowed, and none other that could serve the Indians' superstitions outside the 'lettered city'.

Notes

1 As mentioned in the introduction, the term 'accommodation' has most commonly been applied to the Jesuit missions to the East and to Ricci's approach in particular and became central to missionology in the 1950s and 1960s. See for instance Johannes Bettray SVD (1955) and George Dunne SJ (1962). In Dunne's view, Alessandro Valignano gave an entirely new direction to the enterprise of the mission to China, restoring the concept of cultural adaptation – based upon respect for native cultures – to a central position in the world mission of Christianity. This meant a definite break with the mindset of exaggerated Europeanism of the time, i.e. a narrow and arrogant assumption of the finality of 'national' cultural forms (Dunne 1962: 17–19).

2 Among some of the traits that help define the process of 'Christianization', as John Van Engen has analyzed for medieval Europe, Christianization implies the putting in place of the means to structure Christian profession and practice, that is, the rituals and institutions that religious authorities supervised and, second, the degree to which time, space, and ritual observances came to be defined and grasped essentially in terms of the Christian liturgical year. Slowly and fitfully such ritual and juridical structures were put in place. Third, came religious instruction to close the gap between 'implicit' and 'explicit' faith; for men and women to go beyond the status of merely baptized to securely won salvation required regular participation in the sacraments, especially confession and the eucharist, or entry into the formal religious life. Both instructions and the sacraments required an ordained priesthood (Van Engen 1986: 537–49).

3 Real Cédula to Virrey del Perú, Valladolid, July 7 1550, in *Colección de Documentos Inéditos Relativos al Descubrimiento, Conquista y Organización de las Antiguas Posesiones Españolas de América y Oceanía*, 42 vol., Madrid, 1864–84, XVIII, 472, cited in Borges (1960: 214).

4 Among some of the scholars who claim that Valera was the Anonymous Jesuit see M. González de la Rosa (1907: pp. 184–200), León Lopetequi (1942: 88–89) and Sabine Hyland (2006).

5 The Royal Commentaries by Garcilaso were printed in two parts: the first in 1609 and a second part in 1617.

6 There are other previous references to this issue in De Procuranda:

> As they present such monstrosity in their rites, customs and laws, and the licence among the subjects to deviate from commands, it is with great difficulty that they will receive the illuminated gospel and adopt customs proper to men ... provided that they are constrained by a superior power. That is why reason itself and the Church authorities have established that those who have embraced the Gospel be subjected to Christian rules and magistrates, but only if they are not deprived of full possession of their fortunes and goods, and they are allowed to keep the laws and possessions that are not against reason or the Gospel.
>
> (De Proc: 393)

7 Szeminski points out that in this passage Acosta might be referring to the *pizza* found in the Museo de la Universidad de Cochabamba, where it is kept nowadays (Szeminski 2010: 135).

8 ARSI, Jap-Sin, 1594–96, 12–2, 298v.

9 It is uncertain which work this was. Following Henri Bernard-Maitre, Paul Rule suggests it might be the Confucian *San zi jing* – Three-character Classic (Rule 1986: 7).

10 Beginning in Han (206 BC–AD 220), state-sponsored classical learning – often dubbed 'Confucian' when, according to Michael Nylan, 'orthodox' or 'official'

would be more appropriate – drew freely on the teachings of many non-Confucian thinkers to better cope with the complexities (many unforeseen by Confucius) of ruling an empire. The Classics can properly be called Confucian in only two senses: Confucius and his followers may have used some – but not all – of them as templates for moral instruction. And, second, early traditions ascribe to Confucius the tasks of compiling, editing and, in a few cases, composing the separate parts in this repository of wisdom, although modern scholarship generally disputes those pious legends. Until late in the Song period (960–1279), the Five Classics – the Odes, the Documents, the Rites, the Changes, and the Spring and Autumn Annals – were generally considered more essential to Confucian learning than the collection of Four Books (Nylan 2001: 1–10).

11 *Nell'anno 23 del Re Vanlie' s'anno che si chiama Devi, nella 3 luna un filosofo delli monti dell'Occidente Matteo Ricci da Macerata pose insieme queste cose*, MSS, AUG 292, f. 200 (maxim 78).

12 The term Neo-Confucianism does not exists in Chinese; in this language it is referred to as *Daoxue*, i.e. the Study of the Way. By and large, there are two 'Neo-Confucian branches': one is the Cheng-Zhu tradition, after its leading exponents Cheng Yi (1033–1107) and Zhu Xi (1130–1200), which is often described as 'rationalistic' since it stressed the notion of *li* (principle). This is why it is also called the School of Principle. The second tradition or school is 'Lu-Wang Neo-Confucianism', named after its two leading representatives: Lu Xianshan (1139–93) and Wang Yangming (1472–1529), also called X*in Xue* or School of Mind. The particular variety of Neo-Confucianism as systematized by Zhu Xi (1130–1200) enjoyed official status from the early fourteenth century.

13 David Mungello stresses the intellectual emphasis of Ricci's accommodation method, which could be described as 'intellectually flavoured Christianity', this being a flavouring of Confucianism (Mungello 1985: 62 onward).

14 N. Standaert points out the major differences between 'accommodation' or 'adaptation', and 'inculturation'. In accommodation it is the missionary, the foreigner, who is the main actor, adapting himself to the new culture, whereas in inculturation the main actor becomes the local culture, which gives a new form to the gospel (Standaert 1991).

15 David Brading was among the first to assess the differences between Acosta and Ricci with regard to the idolatry of the gentiles in their respective mission spaces. According to Brading, while Acosta – inspired by Augustine – saw all Indians as sons of the devil and idolatry everywhere, Ricci established the theological grounds of the mission in China in which the observance of natural law was not contaminated by idolatry (Brading 1991: 184–95).

16 The concept of *huaca* indeed challenges a brief and clear-cut description and definition. In extremely general terms, *huaca* refers to regional Andean deities. The *huacas* could be natural stone forms, mountains, shrines, ancestor's bodies – *malquis* – or burial sites, to mention some of their varied forms. The *huacas* were related to ancestors or/and protectors, and – being sacred – they were worshiped and deserved reverence.

17 Martino Martini's treatise on friendship *Qiuyou pian*, translated as The Search for Friends, was published in Hangzhou in 1661.

Part II
The missions and their texts

Introduction to Part II

A world of doctrinal texts

From Augustine to Erasmus

This second part of the book will focus on two Jesuit catechisms: the *Doctrina Christiana y Catecismo* (1584–85) (DCC), with José de Acosta as the main author of the Spanish text, and Matteo Ricci's *Tianzhu Shiyi* or True Meaning of the Lord of Heaven (TZSY) in Chinese. But before analysing these catechisms in the respective missions in Peru and China, this introduction will provide a brief overview of the catechism as a genre, as well as its versatility as such within the Society of Jesus, in and outside Europe.

It was during the sixteenth century that catechisms were finally shaped as a genre in Europe, but their origins can be traced back to ancient times, when Greek Christians gave the name 'catechesis' to the teaching of religion and to its contents. Augustine's *De Catechizandis Rudibus* is one of the early references. In the Middle Ages, the term 'catechism' took on the meaning of religious instruction in general. In the ninth century, the first texts for transmitting the faith employed a question-and-answer format, containing the Sacraments, the Creed and the Lord's Prayer. Eventually, works that dealt with the Christian doctrine in greater detail were called *Liber synodalis*, and covered the main elements of the doctrine: the Sign of the Cross, Lord's Prayer, Hail Mary, Salve Regina, Creed, articles of faith, Ten Commandments, Holy Sacraments, Works of Mercy, capital sins, theological and moral virtues, powers of the soul and the bodily senses (García 1986: 211).

In the fifteenth century a new concern about instructing the faithful in 'the art of Christian living and dying began to emerge in some parts of Europe. Erasmus (1469–1536) became a prominent figure in this context. In 1512 he edited the *Christiani Hominis Institutum* as a reworking of the *Catechyzon*, the work of his English friend John Colet (1466–1519). Erasmus exerted a strong influence in the period that preceded the Council of Trent, before orthodoxy was clearly outlined. The pastoral ideal in Erasmism had a powerful effect on the young Society of Jesus and its missionary impulse through the figure of Juan de Ávila, a reformer influenced by Erasmus (Bataillon 1977: 155). De Ávila published his catechism in Spain, perhaps as early as 1527. It was written in verse and meant to be set to music – *Doctrina Cristiana que Se Canta*. De Ávila developed a Christological mysticism; his spiritual experience was centred on the humanity of Jesus (Criveller 1997: 16). He articulated principles of catechetical pedagogy that stressed the necessity of accommodation of the teacher and lesson to the audience and insisted on the establishment of an affectionate and trusting relationship between teacher and pupil. There were other catechisms of Erasmian influence circulating at the time, like those by the Protestant Spanish theologian Constantino Ponce de la Fuente in the 1540s.[1] In 1554, two talented disciples of Juan de Ávila – Diego Guzmán and Gaspar de Loarte – were accepted into the Society. From 1554 until his death in 1585, Guzmán laboured as the most important and influential cate-chist in Italy. For the rest of the century in Spain, the Jesuit schools used Avila's catechism. Chapter One made reference to the fate of the Dominican Francisco de la Cruz in Peru, one of Avila's disciples, due to his Erasmian tone, and the charge of Lutheran heresy by José de Acosta. Let us also remember that Jesuit Alonso de Barzana, one of the most outstanding *lenguas* in Peru, had been a follower of Juan de Ávila, who, as he did with other disciples, encouraged Barzana to enter the Society of Jesus. In New Spain, now Mexico, the Franciscan Juan de Zumárraga, whose *Doctrina* was printed in 1544 or 1545, was under the Lutheran influence of Constantino Ponce de la Fuente. Robert Ricard establishes a difference between the Franciscans and Domini-cans in Mexico, as the former limited themselves to translations of Spanish catechisms. However, Zumárraga, the first archbishop of Mexico city, encour-aged the Dominicans to also translate the doctrinal texts into Náhuatl. The result was the *doctrina larga* – lengthy doctrine – which was printed in 1548 in a Spanish-Náhuatl bilingual edition and included the main prayers, the articles of faith, the Ten Commandments, the Sacraments, the Works of Mercy and the capital sins (Ricard 1995: 191–94). The first printing press in Spanish America was established in Mexico at the request of Viceroy Antonio de Mendoza and Juan de Zumárraga; and the first book in Spanish America was printed in 1539. One of the first printers, the Italian Antonio Ricardo, moved to Peru at the request of Juan de la Plaza, Visitor in Peru (1574–79) and then appointed provincial (1580–85) in Mexico. We shall return to Plaza's activities in New Spain below.

The 'first Jesuits', as portrayed by John O'Malley, had to a greater or lesser degree been influenced by aspects of the humanist traditions at Alcalá or Paris, or both places. The influential Juan de Polanco, appointed secretary to Loyola in 1547, for instance, while a student of theology at the University of Padua, studied Erasmus's *Ecclesiastes: On the Art of Preaching* and copied out excerpts from it for himself. In fact, by 1552 Xavier in India was using, among others, a catechism by Constantino Ponce de la Fuente, in which Xavier, unlike the Spanish Inquisition, did not perceive any heterodoxy; and he wanted to take it with him to China (O'Malley 1993: 118).

Doctrinal texts amidst a myriad of changes in the sixteenth century

In general terms, the second half of the sixteenth century marked a great change in catechesis. First, what had previously been a preoccupation of relatively few individuals and of elite circles exploded into widespread action that eventually touched every social stratum. The teaching of catechisms became a more highly organized enterprise than ever before and it moved from the hearth into the public arena. The printing press was a key element in this phase, allowing a wider circulation of texts. Another major change, again thanks to the printing press, was a movement away from the fundamentally oral character of catechesis, in which the lesson was conveyed by lectures or sermons and learned in verses often set to tunes, to studying from printed texts. The question-and-answer format practically drove out all other forms (O'Malley 1993: 117 onward). The Jesuits appeared just as these changes were taking place and consolidated a new literary genre themselves: the Spiritual Exercises of Ignatius of Loyola, published in 1548.

In the mid-1550s, Jesuit catechesis began to be affected by concerns and assumptions stemming from the Reformation. More than twenty years before, Martin Luther's *Kleiner Katechismus* and *Grosser Katechismus* in 1529 had powerfully stimulated a radical change in the history of catechesis. When Jesuits worked in those parts of Europe where the catechisms of the Protestant reformers were in use, the catechism devised to respond to Luther's by Peter Canisius (1521–97) in Catholic Germany gained wider currency in the Society, especially in its schools. In 1554, Canisius delivered to King Ferdinand, the emperor's brother, a first version of his catechism entitled *Summa Doctrinae Christianae*, a project requested by Ferdinand and commended to Canisius by Loyola. However, the catechetical tradition of Juan de Ávila remained strong in the order at the same time. Therefore, even though the Jesuits much appreciated Canisius's labours, they adopted no master text, just as they adopted no uniform format. In short, they 'accommodated to times, persons and places'. Soon afterwards, the Tridentine era started, imposing its own catechism, which would serve as a model for the coming Catholic catechisms.

The Roman Catechism, which appeared in 1566, managed to unify the contents and to consolidate a genre that had so far not been directly recognized as 'catechism'. Its original complete title was *Catechismus ex Decreto Concilii Tridentini ad Parochos Pii Quinti Pont. Max. Iussu Editus ad Editione Romae A.D. MDLXVI Publici Iuris Factam Accuratissime Expressus*. Immediately after the Council of Trent (1545–63), Pope Pius IV appointed a team of theologians and archbishops to draft a first edition under the supervision of the cardinal archbishop in Milan, Charles Borromeo (1538–84). The humanists Giulio Poggiano and Paolo Manuzio were in charge of the translation into classical Latin and Cardinal Sirlet of the final revision of the text. It was published for the first time in Rome in 1566, in Latin and Italian.[2] Rather than to the congregation, the catechism was addressed first and foremost to the pastors – *ad Parochos* – in other words, the preachers. This characteristic is also found in the DCC in Peru.

The consolidation and spread of this new 'catechism' genre expanded in the 'war' scenario between Protestants and Catholics. One of the first challenges missionaries had to deal with in the Tridentine era was the sensitive issue of translating religion. Indeed, the Council of Trent carried out the important task of supporting these initiatives from the moment it established that religious instruction should be imparted in the vernacular in distant places like East Asia. But translation also became visible in Europe, expressed in a rapid rise of published translations remarkably promoted by the Society of Jesus. More than a thousand translations from vernaculars into Latin were made between 1500 and 1800, of which some 40 per cent were religious works. In the early modern period, the Society produced more than six hundred printed translations into European languages. For instance, Roberto Bellarmino's catechism was translated into twenty European languages, along with seventeen non-European ones (Burke 2006: 30–31).[3]

The Society's linguistic offensive

Along with the Tridentine mandates, the Jesuit authorities in Rome encouraged the missionaries not only to learn local languages, but also to compose grammars and dictionaries, and to send copies of such works to Europe. With Everard Mercurian, who succeeded Borja as General of the Society in 1573, and the appointment of Alessandro Valignano as visitor in the East that same year, a linguistic offensive started in the missions in India, China and Japan. Before these new policies were implemented, in the Portuguese *Indias* the intention of a 'Portugalization' was present. One of the key works to carry it out was the *Gramatica da Lingua Portuguesa* by João de Barros, printed in Lisbon in 1540. The *gramaticas* – a genre that also spread in Spanish America – were texts not exclusively related to the learning of the language, but also conceived of as means to learn Christian doctrine. Once in Goa, in 1542, Xavier wrote a Small Catechism, a basic prayer book in Portuguese, a large part of which was taken verbatim from Barros' *Cartinha*, in the introduction to the *Gramatica*. Not a native speaker of Portuguese himself, Francis Xavier, the first Jesuit missionary in Asia, was ready to teach the world Portuguese if that was how the Christianization of the world was to proceed, but he was also 'indifferent' enough – in the Jesuit sense of the world – to adopt and adapt any other language if necessary (Zupanov 2003: 119–20). The Jesuit João Nunes Barreto (1517–62), missionary in Morocco and India and patriarch of Ethiopia, brought a printing press to the Saint Paul College in Goa in 1556, which also benefited from the printing of materials for its students. Meanwhile, in Brazil, the other mission under the jurisdiction of the Portuguese *padroado*, the native Brazilian language in most widespread use, Tupí, was quickly adopted by the Jesuits. Indeed, as soon as Manoel da Nóbrega arrived, in March 1549, he started working on translations of prayers into the Indian language. Subsequently, there was an increased production of catechisms in Tupí for the use of missionaries in the 1570s.[4]

Going back to Valignano's era, during his first stay in India, i.e. 1574–77, the visitor promoted the development of a native literature, especially catechisms, and booklets on confession and the lives of the saints. In fact, he personally wrote two short catechisms, which he sent to all the Jesuits in India and later ordered that they be translated into the native languages. Valignano encouraged the missionaries to write similar booklets and created a plan for composing books on apologetics (Schütte 1980: I, 30–39). From that moment onward, translations of doctrinal texts, e.g. catechisms, confession manuals and lives of the saints, would be printed in the vernaculars. And, along with these translations, a whole process of adaptations to the local language commenced, so the receptor language could produce its own signification, imagery, cognitive patterns, and religious identity (Zupanov 2003).

Composing and printing doctrinal texts in the China mission

As we already know, thanks to Valignano's instructions, the first task for the missionaries sent to the China mission was to engage in the study of Mandarin and, eventually, to search for referents to translate Christian terminology into the local language. The Jesuit literature in China can be divided into two different genres. First, there was the genre 'catechism' or *Catechismus*, based on natural theology, which tried to explain fundamental notions through argumentation and to convince people of their truth according to the principles of natural reason. The second genre, the 'doctrine' or *Doctrina Christiana*, was a full account of Christian truth for catechumens and believers; this complete catechetic instruction was only given to those who truly desired to embrace the Catholic religion. Regarding the catechisms, written in the form of a dialogue, they often had an apologetic nature; they were much more substantive than prescriptive and much more intellectual and philosophical in approach. The earliest example of such a catechism is Michele Ruggieri's TZSL (1584), as is shown in the next chapter. But, since the TZSL also contains a detailed presentation of Christian doctrine, for some authors the boundaries between 'catechism' and 'doctrine' blur in this work (Shih 1964: 52). In 1603, two years after establishing the Jesuit residence in Peking, Ricci published his TZSY, written in the form of a dialogue between a Western and a Chinese scholar. Ricci clearly stated that the only doctrine to be taught in the catechisms is the one that 'can be proved with natural reason and understood with the same light of natural reason' (FR II: 292–93). As for a translation of the *Catechismus Romanus*, promulgated by the Council of Trent, this was made far beyond Ruggieri's and Ricci's times, during the 1720s in China and printed as *Xinyi Yinmeng wenda*, often being used in the missions in Sichuan province (Handbook: 611). There are no doubts that, as the genres were shaped in China, Ricci's TZSY is a catechism. The *Dottrina Christiana*, instead, is rather a small booklet, in Chinese usually called *Tianzhu jiayao* (TZJY) or sometimes *Shenjing yuelu*. To a large extent it corresponds to what is understood by 'catechism' in modern times and includes the most important prayers.[5] Dealing with revealed truths and the mysteries of faith, the doctrine and similar texts were destined to catechumens, those who were preparing for baptism, as well as converts, and promoted a Christian life heavily based on the complete set of Christian doctrine (Criveller 1997: 39 onward). However, as Criveller points out, the distinction between 'catechism' and 'Christian doctrine' does not necessarily concern the entire literature and apostolate of the Jesuits in China (Criveller 1997: 109). Moreover, by and large, this demarcation line between 'catechism' and 'doctrine' was also hazy in Europe itself – even in the Tridentine debates, in which the *methodus doctrinae christianae* and the *catechismus* were both discussed.[6]

Regarding the printing of doctrine in late Ming China, Ruggieri and Ricci immediately noticed that the printing press was already available for their works and took advantage of an ancient written culture. The expansion of the mission owed much to the printing press, which enabled standardization and reproduction over time and space. Ricci realized this early on and seized on printing, which operated on quite a massive scale. He was amazed at how much more powerful the written word was in China, since 'books could get to places the Fathers could not reach' (FR I: 198). Ricci shared a love of books and printing with the Chinese literati. So the Western books – material exponents of Renaissance culture – that the Jesuits had taken with them to China for their personal use provided one of the most effective ways of gaining recognition from the Chinese literati (Standaert 2003: 371).

Framing and printing doctrine in the Peru mission

In the first decades of the mission in Peru, missionary texts were written in Quechua, especially those of the Dominicans. They often fell into the category of *cartillas* or *pláticas* and circulated in written form. The *cartillas* were generally used for the learning of reading and writing, not directly connected to religion. Catechisms in Spanish America included some sort of brief *cartilla*, for it was not just a question of learning to read, but to read *the* Christian doctrine, for which the *silabeo* – pronunciation by syllables – contained in the *cartillas* was essential (Resines Llorente 1992: 21). The earlier texts were written in the 1540s and are attributed to Juan de Betanzos (1510–76), a Spanish chronicler who learned the Quechua language and spent years translating a Christian doctrine – probably a *cartilla* – and composing two dictionaries, a number of *colloquiums* and a confessionary, apparently by royal commission. Unfortunately, none of these texts still exists. In 1540, the Dominican Domingo de Santo Tomás arrived in Peru; some years later, he was to represent his Order in the FLC. In the 1560s under royal patronage, Domingo de Santo Tomás composed the *Plática para Todos los Indios*, a brief history of creation, and a dictionary, for which he used terms borrowed from Quechua. But the attitude towards pre-Hispanic languages as reflected in Domingo de Santo Tomás was short-lived. The fact that all people may recognize the existence of God through reason and that they know general moral principles in their rational conscience implied that they 'could also be misled by the devil'. Moreover, loan terms from local languages were ruled out, as Andean languages were also 'perverted by the devil' and could not be used to express Christian dogma (Delumeau 2002: 394). The arrival of the Tridentine decrees played a key role in this shift regarding translation policies. Far from conceiving of translation as an act of accommodation, as in the first decades of the missionaries in Peru, the translations of the TLC corpus into Quechua and Aymara were intended to reach the Indians through a clergy which was not devoted to learning the vernaculars. They thus made good use of those translations. In this regard, according to Durston, even though translation is an act of accommodation in itself, it can imply – at the same time – a minimization or even the end of the interaction between local religious traditions and Christianity, and such was the case of Peru in the TLC era, as will be seen in the next chapter (Durston 2007: 13, 206 onward). Unlike in Peru, the Jesuits in China did not have to deal with a secular clergy that had to be permanently disciplined with regard to the learning of the vernaculars.

Along with the imposition of the DCC, the colonial authorities – from Toledo onward – removed and banned all the previous doctrinal texts that had circulated in manuscript form. Reformed Catholicism in Peru made full use of printing: the printing press was introduced specifically for the publication of the TLC corpus, or DCC. In fact, the TLC's preference for print was such that it banned manuscript copies of its own catechetical texts. José de Acosta was also involved in the printing of the TLC corpus, first obtaining permission from the royal authorities, then represented by the *Royal Audiencia*, to print these works before receiving the royal permit that had already been requested.[7] In effect, in 1583, the TLC authorities had written to Philip II asking for authorization to print the *cartilla* and catechism on the grounds that errors would occur if the texts were copied by hand and that even the smallest variations could have dire consequences (Durston 2007: 100). These delays and requests were a consequence of the printing ban in Spanish South America at that time. The Society of Jesus became the guardian of doctrinal contents, protecting them from being altered or copied, as printing was carried out in the Lima College, the place of residence of the writers and translators of the works in question. The printing of the DCC was supervised by two of the translators – presumably one for each language, Quechua and Aymara, by the Provincial of the Society in Peru at that moment, Juan de Atienza, and by José de Acosta; but the latter played the leading role (Lopetegui 1942: 540), not only because Acosta was the person who most pulled the strings to obtain the permit but also – and more importantly – because he was on excellent terms with the *Royal Audiencia*, as was any other Jesuit in Peru at the time.

The legacy of the TLC eventually reached the Mexico province thanks to Juan de la Plaza, who had previously been visitor in Peru. Once in Mexico, Plaza was appointed rector in Tepotzotlán, but his presence was immediately requested in the capital to attend the Third Mexican Council of 1585, in which he played a key role. One of the urgent tasks on the agenda was that of producing a catechism during the council. There are many similarities between the Third Mexican Council catechism of 1585 and the TLC corpus, which suggests that Plaza might have used the TLC catechisms as a reference (Resines Llorente 1992: 647–48).[8]

Notes

1 Constantino Ponce de la Fuente composed the following doctrinal texts: *Suma de Doctrina Christiana* (1543), *Exposición del Primer Psalmo* (1546), the *Catecismo Cristiano* (1547) and the *Doctrina Christiana* (1548).

2 The Roman Catechism is organized as follows: 1 the Symbols of faith; 2 the Sacraments; 3 the Ten Commandments; 4 the Lord's Prayer. However, the Roman Catechism did not decree that the doctrine had to necessarily follow that order (Varo 1990/92: 549–51).

3 A long way behind come three texts, each of which was translated into eleven languages: the Catechism by Peter Canisius, the *Exercicio de Perfeción* by Alfonso Rodrigues and the *Pensées* of Dominique Bouhours, translated not only into Tagalog – the language of the Philippines – but also into Greek by a German Jesuit. Regarding the fashion in which translations were made outside Europe, Burke distinguishes between a medieval culture of translation and a post-medieval one. The medieval regime was largely dominated by 'word-for-word' translation (*verbum pro verbo*). In contrast with medieval practice, translators from Leonardo Bruni onwards emphasized the need to translate sense for sense (*sensum de senso*).

4 Apart from language, music became a basic component of indoctrination in Brazil. From the time of their arrival in 1549 until their expulsion in 1759, the Jesuits made extensive use of music in their attempt to convert the Indians to the Catholic faith. One of the problems that Nóbrega and his companions experienced was the opposition of the Bishop, Pedro Fernandez Sardinha, who did not accept the use of traditional Indian music, showing a preference for Christian music as the only type allowed in the Jesuit establishments (Castagna 1999).

5 i.e. the Lord's Prayer, the Hail Mary and the sign of the cross, the Ten Commandments, the Creed, a list of the seven Sacraments, the fourteen Works of Mercy – material and spiritual – the eight beatitudes, the seven capital sins and the seven opposing virtues, and usually other short items, which vary from edition to edition, such as lists of the five senses of the body, the three faculties of the soul, the three theological virtues, and – since 1619 – the four precepts of the Church.

6 Even though there is not an explicit difference between 'catechism' and 'doctrine', with regard to the content, for Ignatius of Loyola the teaching of the Christian doctrine was not confined to a mere memorization of the basic contents of faith. Unlike the catechism, its explanations are not based on memory, but are rich in spirituality and not limited to the simplest elements of faith. Moreover, the theological implications of Christian doctrine are more biblical in their interpretations and meditations (Catto 2003: 24–26).

7 The *Royal Audiencia* governed at that time, due to the death of Viceroy Henriquez, who had succeeded Toledo when the latter returned to Spain.

8 Resines has studied the similarities between the two texts very thoroughly. Plaza was not in Peru when the TLC was held, so he could not have taken the TLC corpus with him to Mexico. A traveller, either a missionary or not, might have

taken it and given it to Plaza. Resines also suggests as a hypothesis that, when composing the TLC corpus, previous texts were used, specifically those composed by Alonso de Barzana. At that time Plaza was in Peru, so the latter might have taken those catechisms with him to Mexico and have added them to the catechism he proposed to the Third Mexican Council of 1585.

4 The craftsmanship of Jesuit catechisms in Peru and in China

Both José de Acosta and Matteo Ricci undertook the task of composing catechisms with the purpose of redirecting a previous doctrinal path by replacing catechetical texts they found no longer suitable in their missions. Of course, theirs were not one-sided decisions, and neither were Acosta and Ricci alone in these undertakings, as this chapter shows.

In Peru, the doctrinal guidelines and texts preceding Acosta's *Doctrina Christiana y Catecismo para Instrucción de Indios* (1584–85) (DCC) had been provided by the First Lima council (1551–52) (FLC) and the Second Lima council (1567–68) (SLC). Both councils aimed to impose a single and authoritative catechism but, as we shall see, they failed in the attempt. The Trent decrees came into force for all the overseas possessions in October 1565, after which a Tridentine atmosphere was expected to inspire the composition of an authoritative catechism. As theologian of both the Jesuit mission and – unofficially – the Viceroyalty of Peru, Acosta laid the foundations for a new doctrinal and theological ground, starting with his *De Procuranda Indorum Salute*, setting new principles and guidelines for the solution to a key and tricky problem: the salvation of the Indians. As we shall see below, to a great extent the DCC fed on Acosta's *De Procuranda*.

At that time in China, the Counter-Reformation and Rome were a long way away. Unlike the Peru mission with its overwhelming presence of representatives of the royal jurisdiction, the Portuguese *Padroado* gave the Jesuits in China much more freedom to decide on doctrinal contents. Chapter Three focused on Ricci's interpretation of Confucianism and how it was reflected in his TZSY. But the particular policies regarding which catechism should be in force or not also depended on internal decisions of the Society. Ruggieri's TZSL, published in 1584, had been a first attempt to present the Christian faith in a Chinese context. The first part of this book showed how the TZSL stopped being regarded as acceptable, not because it was rejected by the Chinese, but by Visitor Valignano. And, with all his support, Ricci's TZSY aimed to replace Ruggieri's TZSL. As shown below, Valignano's catechism, the *Catechismus Christianae Fidei* ([1586] (1972), hereafter cited as Catechismus), was one of the sources that inspired Ricci's TZSY.

The purpose of this chapter is to witness the craftsmanship applied to doctrinal texts along the respective paths leading to orthodoxy followed by Acosta and Ricci. Interestingly, both their catechisms present a more aggressive tone against idolatry. In the case of Peru, there was an early set of colonial doctrinal texts predating the Jesuits; but in the China mission we discover a doctrine that the first Jesuits did not find, but created. What they found, what they created, and what they considered needed to be redirected. That is what this chapter is about.

Leaving behind a pre-Hispanic past: the Jesuit José de Acosta in Peru

The first evangelization in Peru and its associated texts

In general terms, the 'first evangelization' or *primera evangelización* in Peru can be defined as one of accommodation, expressed in diverse and flexible pastoral practices, less focused on formal catechesis (Estenssoro 2003). This implied, for instance, a very limited administration of the sacraments. In this first stage, many different evangelizing projects and approaches converged in Peru, and they were in turn reflected in various doctrinal texts. The texts of the *primera evangelización* are limited in number, for many of these manuscripts did not survive. Indeed, when the printing press was officially approved to print the TLC corpus in Lima in 1584, it was decreed that no text should be printed without the permission of the Council of the Indies – and all the previous doctrinal texts, now regarded as 'harmful' – *dañinos* – had to be removed from circulation (Villegas 1975: 77). However, some texts from the period previous to the TLC survived.[1] The purpose here is to focus on the particular aspects of some of these texts that shed light on Acosta's doctrinal works, to discover what he took from this preceding doctrinal tradition and what he ruled out.

Among the very first texts we find the *Instrucción de la Orden que Se Ha De Tener en la Doctrina de los Naturales* – Instruction for Indoctrinating the natives – a set of missionary and pastoral guidelines issued by Archbishop Loayza in 1545, which were included in the constitutions of the FLC – made public in January 1552 – with some changes. As for the vernaculars, the *primera evangelización* welcomed the appropriation of native cultural terms to translate key Christian concepts. Two examples are provided by the Dominican Domingo de Santo Tomás; first, the *Plática para Todos los Indios* that Santo Tomás inserted at the end of his *Grammatica o Arte de la Lengua en General*, a Grammar, printed in Valladolid in 1560, but composed immediately after the FLC (Santo Tomás [1560] 1951: 188–207); and, second, the *Lexicon o Vocabulario de la Lengua General del Peru and the Grammatica o Arte de la Lengua General de los Indios de los Reynos del Peru* – also printed in Valladolid in 1560 – which contains a General Confession at the beginning (Santo Tomás [1560] 1951: 18). But there were earlier, non-surviving, texts in Quechua, like the *Cartillas* – a compendium of basic prayers – and *Diccionarios* composed by Juan de Betanzos (1510–76), who seems to have been commissioned by the crown to write them. Finally, we have two other documents from the corpus of the *primera evangelización*, both from 1567: the first of these is a *Suma de la Fe*, added by Juan de Matienzo to his *Gobierno del Perú*, and the second is the SLC's own version of a *Suma de la Fe Catolica* intoduced immediately afterwards. (Estenssoro 2003: 583–85). In those years, the *Gobierno del Perú* demanded a thorough and ambitious reform, a particularly influential immediate political decision. Chapter thirty-six of Matienzo's work comprises a small evangelizing manual (Matienzo [1567] 1967: 119–22).

As mentioned above, as early as 1545, Archbishop Loayza issued a set of preliminary missionary/pastoral guidelines entitled *Instrucción de la Orden que Se A De Tener en la Doctrina de los Naturales* [Instructions for Indoctrinating the Natives]. More detailed instructions were later produced by the FLC, the first Council celebrated in Latin America between 1551 and 1552, conceived and created, among other purposes, to unify doctrine and erase contradictions and divergences. Treating the constitutions for the Spanish and the Indians separately, the first constitution for Indians of the FLC 'On the Order of Indoctrinating the Indians', states that

> where the Holy Gospel and things of our holy faith are preached, it is necessary by all means to avoid anything that could lead to error … because the capacity of understanding of the natives in these lands is very limited. [The Indians] might think that our faith is not stable … and the same could happen if they are not taught just one thing with the same style and language (Vargas Ugarte 1951: 7).[2]

This first constitution also commanded 'under pain of excommunication or fifty *pesos*, to all of those in the *doctrina de indios* in the whole archbishopric and suffragate bishoprics, to teach one same doctrine, and the *pláticas* should be according to the *Instrucción*, following these constitutions'. The same guidelines are repeated in the thirty-seventh constitution for the Indians of the FLC. After considering this main purpose of one sole doctrine, two other key aspects unfold with the *Instrucción*: first, the language of catechesis and second, the contents of catechesis; they are intertwined but for practical reasons let us look at them separately.

Regarding the language of doctrinal texts in the *primera evangelización* in Peru, they were largely in Spanish and Latin. In Loayza's *Instrucción* of 1545 there is a mention of various *cartillas* in the Indian language, saying that there was no proof of their conformity with the true faith, so the Indians must be taught the doctrine in Latin or Castillian Romance, following the printed *cartillas* brought from Spain. For the time being, they should not use those *cartillas* in their language 'until we, together with their authors and other people knowledgeable of their language, examine these texts, and then those [*cartillas*] already composed can be edited and become one' (Vargas Ugarte 1952: 142). The FLC, however, refers to a *cartilla* and some *coloquios* composed in 'the language more commonly used by the natives' – i.e. Quechua – and authorized their use, but imposed a penalty for any other version used (Vargas Ugarte 1951: 7; Mateos 1950: 17).

The second aspect to be addressed is that of the contents of catechesis. Catechesis consisted of the memorization of the basic prayers, i.e. the Apostle's Creed, the Lord's Prayer, the Hail Mary and the Ten Commandments, expressed in *cartillas* and in *pláticas* – brief, simple sermons. Both the *Instrucción* of 1545 and the version included in the FLC proposed a basic doctrine which was to be standardized, but this failed to be done (Durston 2008: 55). The very first version of the *Instrucción* did not mention either the Trinity or Christ, although the FLC included them, e.g.by mentioning the Trinity and the Incarnation (Estenssoro 2003: 58–59).[3] As for the sacraments, according to the FLC, they were to be limited to baptism, marriage, confession and – eventually – confirmation (Vargas Ugarte 1951: 14–15).

Memorization played a key role in the Christianization of the Indians and this is why there was an urgent need for one unique text; but in the meantime the Indians could memorize the prayers. So the *Instrucción* ordered that after the offertory the priest had to recite the Creed, the Lord's Prayer and the Hail Mary out loud so the Indians who were present could recite them too, as well as preaching the commandments and articles of faith (Vargas Ugarte 1952: 147–48). It is true that in the *primera evangelización* the needs in terms of spreading doctrine were still very basic. For instance, churches had to be built for the Indians to have a place to learn Christian doctrine and pray, as the second constitution of the FLC establishes. In that respect, the ideal solution was to build churches where the *huacas* were, so the third FLC decree commanded that 'all the idols and worship places in villages be burnt and destroyed; and if it is a decent place, that a church be built or at least a cross shall be erected' (Mateos 1550: 19). The Tridentine parish would have to wait until the SLC to become an important setting for evangelization in Peru.

The minimal contents required for salvation of the Indians constitute an essential feature of the texts of the FLC period. This was partially reversed after the SLC and, finally, the TLC banned those texts forever. However, there was one basic need or concern that helped connect the first three Lima councils, i.e. a unified doctrine to be transmitted to the Indians. It was a double concern: first, the Spanish priests were not transmitting just one single consolidated doctrine; and second, as a consequence, the Indians – because of their limited capacity – could think that the Christian doctrine was not unified.

Regarding the texts in Quechua, both of Santo Tomás's works, the *Lexicon o Vocabulario de la Lengua General del Peru* and the *Grammatica o Arte de la Lengua General de los Indios de los Reynos del Peru* contain complete doctrinal texts, presented as samples of the language he is describing. The Lexicon contains a General Confession, at the beginning, and the Grammar contains the *Plática para Todos los Indios* at the end. Additionally, the grammar quotes fragments of the Creed and the Ave Maria to exemplify how theological terms and expressions with no equivalent in Quechua could be translated using paraphrases. The Quechua versions of the General Confession, the Creed and the Hail Mary used by Santo Tomás were probably similar to the *cartilla* approved by the FLC that was mentioned above. Santo Tomás – who arrived in Peru in 1540 – participated in the FLC as the official representative of his order, and was elected its provincial in 1553. Therefore, according to Alan Durston, it seems unlikely that as a prominent Dominican he would have flouted the council's ban on other *cartillas* in a printed work intended for circulation. It also seems nearly certain that he was one of the translators of the official Quechua *cartilla*. Moreover, the *Plática para Todos los Indios* can be matched point for point with the outlines of catechetical contents contained in Loayza's 1545 *Instrucción* and in the decrees of the FLC, which suggests that it was one of the *pláticas* or *coloquios* approved by the council (Durston 2008: 69).[4]

Quoting Plato and the idea that men must serve the Republic – as otherwise their lives are wasted – Domingo de Santo Tomás presents his *Grammatica* as the result of fifteen years of learning 'the language of the kingdoms of Peru'. His intention is to turn it into an art, something not just for his own benefit so that he could teach the doctrine to the Indians in the new church, but for others too so that they could learn the language and preach the Gospel as well (Santo Tomás [1560] 1951: 3–4). As already mentioned, the *Plática para Todos los Indios* in Spanish and Quechua is attached at the end. According to Gerald Taylor, the most outstanding features of Santo Tomás's *Plática* are its intellectual quality and lexical creativeness. The summary of the *Doctrina Cristiana* is almost poetic as a myth of origin, and is free of the aggressiveness of similar future texts, i.e. the TLC corpus. This can be observed, for instance, in the inclusive 'us' he uses uniting Spaniards and Indians. Even though Santo Tomás emphasizes the Indian's worship of the *huacas* as a reflection of the devil's schemes, he does it without insistence. With the exception of the words for 'God', 'horse' and 'Christian', all the key words of the new religion and the philosophical concepts on which they are based are expressed in Quechua (Taylor 2003a: 19–25). The mention of Indian idolatry is absent in Santo Tomás's General Confession, in both Spanish and Quechua, which was added to his Lexicon of 1560. The sins of the Indians are reduced instead to childish vices, i.e. wasting their time with games and eating and drinking excessively (Taylor 2003b: 17–20).

The official reception in Lima of the decrees of the Council of Trent took place in October 1565. In 1567–68 the SLC was held in order to apply the Tridentine decrees in Spanish America. Meanwhile, Juan de Matienzo had finished his *Gobierno del Perú* [1567] (1967), which in those years represented an ambitious plan for reforms at every level. Chapter thirty-six of this work comprises a small evangelization manual. In this manual, Matienzo supports the idea of minimum doctrinal contents for the Indians to learn, without mentioning either Christ or the Trinity, since 'to introduce them [the Indians]

to higher things will stop them from believing, because they cannot understand nor grasp them, until they understand and make the most of them over
time' (Matienzo [1567] 1967: 121; Estenssoro 2003: 169).[5] This is the great
difference to what Acosta would impose later, as we shall see below. For
Acosta, the limited capacity of the Indians to understand the mysteries of
faith could not be a reason to deprive them of the sacraments, since 'nobody
becomes a Christian through baptism if he ignores the mysteries through
which he became a Christian' (De Proc: 554). Matienzo did not ignore the
problematic issue of the language to be used. Clergymen cannot be useful nor
take part in the *doctrinas* if they have not learned the general language of the
Indians, for the latter would not listen to them willingly; but Matienzo did
not specify which language should be learned (Matienzo [1567] 1967: 119).

The SLC constitutions – in Latin – dedicated to the administration of the
sacraments contrast remarkably with the FLC in terms of their number. A
major change, in accordance with the Council of Trent, was that priests were
required to administer Easter Communion and the last sacrament to those
who had acquired some understanding of the Eucharist (Vargas Ugarte 1951:
I, 186–87). As for the contents for salvation, the council introduced two
absolute novelties: the mystery of the Trinity and the Incarnation, which all
the Indians now needed to know to be baptized and when they were about to
die (Vargas Ugarte 1951: I, 176). In addition, while they waited for the
unique catechism imposed by the Council of Trent for all the churches,
bishops were allowed to compose a catechism   or approve one – to be used
exclusively by priests in their parishes (Vargas Ugarte 1951: I, 160–61).

A harsher attitude toward Indian customs and rites can be seen in the SLC.
Indeed, several constitutions command the destruction of *huacas* and idols,
both public and private, and the abolishment of Indian customs regarding
their heads, hair and ears in their funeral rites. Moreover, their habits of
drunkenness – *borracheras* – *taquíes* – dances – and devilish ceremonies had
to be abolished and punished, although a milder tone was used for the
curacas, their banquets and *borracheras* (Vargas Ugarte 1951: I, 205–14)[6]
Another major difference to the FLC is that the SLC instituted the Tridentine
requirement of knowledge of the vernacular for priests. This is a recurrent
theme throughout its constitutions. Priests are obliged to teach the main
prayers for the Indians to memorize both in Spanish and 'in their language',
i.e. Quechua (Vargas Ugarte 1951: I, 175–76). And they must know the
Indian language very well in order to confess them; otherwise they can
be helped by the diocesan at the price of part of their stipend (Vargas Ugarte
1951: 184). Last but not least, the third constitution for the Indians establishes that priests who are negligent in learning Quechua should lose a third
of their stipends in the first year, with the penalty increasing in the second and
third years (Vargas Ugarte 1951: I, 161).

Some years later, in a letter to Philip II, dated February 8 1570, Viceroy
Toledo complained about the priests not knowing the local language and he
also complained about the lack of priests in the *doctrinas*. He claimed to have

found seventeen *doctrinas* without a priest, and in those where he found priests in charge they did not know the local language. Interestingly, in this same letter Toledo says that in the *doctrinas* he visited he had found just one Dominican able to speak the language, while all the other priests relied on the *yanaconas*, 'who do not interpret the prayers in our language – *en nuestro bulgar* – properly' (Levillier 1921: 380–97).[7] In sum, the parish system was not only essential for the implementation of Tridentine standards of instruction and administering the sacraments, requiring that priests be able to monitor and keep records on individual parishioners, but also for them to learn the vernaculars. It was the SLC that made the major attempt to impose the Tridentine concept of the parish, i.e. a clearly defined territory demographically limited to four hundred heads of household assigned to a specific priest as the basic institution for the conversion and pastoral care of Indians. The parish system was part of a hierarchical order of the duties of the Indian church, dependent for pastoral work on the organization and demarcation of the dioceses in the hands of bishops.[8] But, as we shall see later, all these resolutions regarding the learning of the vernaculars were insufficient to bring about change, as Acosta clearly states in De Procuranda.

Even though the SLC introduced major innovations, all inherited from the Council of Trent, its impact on Andean soil was limited. Many of these reforms would finally coalesce in the TLC, with the cumulative reforms of Viceroy Toledo in between. One of the least known legacies of Toledo's government was a concrete programme for the creation of standard vernacular catechetical materials, something that would not be achieved until the Third Lima Council (1582–83) (TLC). Toledo argued that, in spite of the problem of linguistic diversity, a single catechism had to be imposed. And a translation of it was to be made into a variety of Quechua that, Toledo claimed, had been widely imposed by the Incas.[9] This translation would then be printed in Mexico or Spain and a large number of copies brought back to Peru, thus reducing the risk of modifications that could produce doctrinal errors (Durston 2007: 80–81). At that time Toledo could not imagine that the printing press would be brought to Lima with the same purpose: to control the printing and circulation of doctrinal texts to keep dogma unblemished. Indeed, the printing press arrived in Lima in 1581, at Visitor Plaza's request. It was brought by the Italian Antonio Ricardo to the Jesuit college of San Pablo, but it was officially approved in 1584 for the exclusive purpose of printing the TLC catechetical corpus, the *Doctrina Christiana y Catecismo para Instruccion de Indios*. Without it, the campaign for both textual and linguistic standardization would hardly have been possible. In fact, the TLC preference for print was such that it banned manuscript copies of its own catechetical texts.

The Society of Jesus' first catechisms in Peru

Right from the beginning, the Society of Jesus had some *lenguas* in Lima who were skilled enough to prepare doctrinal texts in Quechua and Aymara, as stated by Jesuit Sebastián Amador in a letter to General Borja of January 1570. The Indians were taken to the church, where they were asked questions both in Spanish and in their language, and an exhortation or *plática* was 'made by one of our Brothers who understand them and speak well' (MP I: 345). Although the Jesuits who already knew the languages were Barzana, Valera, Contreras, Pérez de Aguilar and Joseph González Ruiz, Amador might well be referring to Barzana, who had composed catechisms and sermons in Quechua.

When laying the theological foundations for evangelization in Peru, Acosta insisted on the learning of the vernaculars – quite a problematic issue as 'faith cannot be preached and spread by those who do not know the language; nor can they administer the sacraments or understand the Indians' confessions'. In short, according to Acosta, the problem lay more with the labourers in the vineyard than with the Indians.[10] His exhortations were not only inspired by the Tridentine precepts regarding the vernacular; Acosta was also inspired by the example of Francis Xavier in the *Indias Orientales*, spreading doctrine in the local language, guided by the *Constitutions* of the Society, which prescribed this.

In the first two Jesuit congregations, both held in Cuzco in 1576, the Society of Jesus developed an enterprising programme to compose catechetical texts in the vernacular that comprised both a brief catechism for memorization and a more thorough one for the religious instruction of the Indians: a *cartilla* and a *confesionario* – confession manual – to be translated into Quechua and Aymara (MP II: 67). At the same time, in *De Procuranda Indorum Salute*, which he composed the same year, Acosta pointed out the need for a brief catechism – *catecismo breve* – summing up all the things that were necessary for the Indians to know and a longer one where the same things were stated more thoroughly. The latter would also be very convenient for the parish priests to communicate doctrine in the Indian parishes, especially when their knowledge of Quechua and Aymara was scarce. In sum, a trilingual catechism was part of Acosta's proposal in *De Procuranda* and he also suggested a *confesionario* to enable poorly prepared priests to purge the Indians' consciences (De Proc: 568). In his annual letter of 1577 from Lima to General Mercurian, Acosta made reference to the two catechisms at the Colegio de Cuzco, whose students were 'so wise and skilled that they know both the long and brief catechism in their language' (MP I: 223).

The early stress on Quechua instead of Aymara for the composition of catechetical texts was justified by the fact that the Quechua-speaking areas were larger. The problem, according to Durston, was which Quechua to translate. In the beginning all the efforts focused on coastal Quechua, which was used by Domingo de Santo Tomás, but, in the 1570s and 80s, the language of pastoral texts changed to the variety of southern Quechua, near Cuzco, which Durston defines as 'colonial standard Quechua' (Durston 2007: 37–49). This change was due to demographic and economic developments in those decades, especially due to the mining boom around Potosí and the *mita* system of mandatory public service, which connected the Quechua to Cuzco. The Jesuits became part of this scene when they headed to Cuzco soon after their arrival and targeted the elite with their various evangelizing strategies.

From *Acosta's* De Procuranda Indorum Salute *to the* Third Lima Council

For José de Acosta, as the main theologian of the mission, Tridentine Catholicism precepts were essential for the achievement of the Society's major goal in the *Indias Occidentales*: the salvation of the Indians, as the title of Acosta's first work emphasizes – *De Procuranda Indorum Salute*. Apart from the continuing eradication of the cultural expressions of the pre-Hispanic past, to render salvation of the faithful possible it was also necessary to redefine doctrinal contents and leave the minimal natural law contents of the *primera evangelización* irreversibly behind. A first aspect to stress is the Christocentric nature of *De Procuranda*, which is essential to the understanding of both *De Procuranda Indorum Salute* and the DCC, the former being a precedent for the latter. The strong Christological leaning in Jesuit theology starts with the very name of the Society, the Society of Jesus (Corsi 2008b: 29). Let us also remember that the *Imitatio Christi* was one of the works which inspired Ignacio de Loyola's devotion. Moreover, apart from *De Procuranda* and the TLC corpus, the Christologial nature in Acosta's works was still present when he was back in Spain, in two theological works, *De Christo Revelato* and *De Temporibus Novissimis*. Their contents probably informed the curricula of the Theology courses Acosta taught at the University of San Marcos in Lima (Saranyana 2007: 38–39).

In the first chapter of the fifth book of *De Procuranda*, Acosta claims that salvation is only possible through the knowledge of Christ, reached through faith, and throughout this fifth book Acosta almost obsessively underlines how atrocious it was that among the Indians who called themselves Christians, the knowledge of Christ was so rare. In this regard, Acosta states that St Thomas, and then the Council of Trent, decreed that nobody can be justified without faith in the mystery of Christ (De Proc: 545–50). Independently of theological implications that are beyond the scope of this book, what needs to be stressed is that Acosta redefines what a Christian is: 'all Christians are Christians as they profess [the doctrine of] Christ, so teaching that all men have to be Christian to be saved but without regarding knowledge of Christ as necessary is nothing other than daydreaming and nonsense' (De Proc: 551).

Just like faith in Christ, the sacraments also lead to salvation. Again, we see how Acosta, profoundly inspired by the Society of Jesus and of course the Tridentine spirit, shaped doctrine and orthodoxy on Andean soil. The administration of the sacraments was one of the most important ministries of the Society of Jesus for the spiritual consolation of the faithful, although the Eucharist and confession were the only ones that they would administer in normal circumstances (O'Malley 1993: 134). Let us remember how the

Catholic Church insisted on the power of the sacraments in the context of the debate on justification during the Council of Trent. Most of the canons relating to justification by faith expressed condemnation of the Protestant position that men are without free will but subject to divine action. For the Catholic Church, men are saved through faith and good works, not through faith alone – *sola fide* – as Luther taught. While for Luther the sacramental rite was a confirmation of salvation for those who receive it, the Catholic Church, and Trent in particular, strongly disagreed. Since salvation was not granted automatically and men could be saved or not depending on what they did with the grace they received, the channels through which the latter flows – the sacraments – became essential (Delumeau 1973: 12–18). Peru was not an exception to this, so the Society of Jesus imposed the administration of the sacraments, enhancing the role of confession and incorporating the communion to consolidate an evangelization grounded on positive theology. This is one of the main contrasts that we find with the previous religious orders in Peru, specifically the Dominicans. They favoured the minimum of doctrinal contents for the Indians, because they had to embrace Christianity gradually, saving such complex dogma as the mysteries of the Trinity or the Incarnation for later. Acosta, however, insisted that, although the Indians were not required to understand the mysteries of faith, they needed to know them and receive the sacraments in order to be saved.

Acosta focuses on the importance of the administration of the sacraments to the Indians in the sixth – and last – book of *De Procuranda*, setting a scholastic tone of disputation. As his interest is the Andean context, his intention is 'not to dispute with the heretics' (De Proc: 580). The sacrament of the Eucharist was imposed by the Jesuits; the two sacraments of communion and confession lay at the heart of the Jesuit's charisma in Peru – something that stands out in the DCC.

The further Acosta went in shaping the new doctrinal contents for the salvation of the Indians, the more he tried to undo what the FLC and its doctrinal texts had proposed. In many of the statements in *De Procuranda* we can see how much Acosta abhorred the direction the FLC had taken. Amongst the FLC constitutions that Acosta found outrageous, was the fifth on baptism for Indians on the point of death, and for the elderly or those with difficulty in understanding – the *rudos*. There was no requirement of explicit faith in the mysteries of the Trinity or the Incarnation to baptize the *rudos*; just an implicit and global faith was needed. Acosta's rejection of the FLC at the same time reinforces the role played by the SLC – which he quotes in *De Procuranda* – as, for these same cases, constitutions thirty-three and thirty-four clearly state all the doctrinal contents to be taught after baptism, including the mysteries of the Trinity and the Incarnation (De Proc: 557). Instead, the SLC – for which Acosta shows a preference – prescribed that priests should not deny the Eucharist to Indians who had knowledge of this sacrament and wished to receive it (Vargas Ugarte 1951: 186). In short, the

SLC also served as a guide for *De Procuranda* (Mateos 1947: 521–22; Saranyana 2007: 34).

José de Acosta and the TLC catechetical corpus (1584–85)

The TLC of 1582–83 made an old dream come true: that of imposing an authoritative catechism embodying a unified doctrine in Peru, as well as in the suffragan dioceses. Indeed, this general catechism, in a Spanish version translated into Quechua and Aymara, was for use in all the provinces.[11]

The TLC corpus or DCC begins with some introductory documents, which remind us of those in Pius V's catechism, in addition to the royal provision stating that it was due to Philip II's zeal that the TLC council was celebrated. A council epistle introduces the authoritative catechism as having a twofold purpose: being for the benefit of both the priests and the Indians. As priests were not sufficiently prepared to indoctrinate the Indians, a single doctrine made it easier for them to know what they had to teach more easily, allowing them to avoid shallow digressions. Once again, the little or no knowledge the parish priests had of the vernaculars is denounced right from the beginning. As for the Indians, a single unique catechism would prevent them from thinking that the holy law was variable (DCC:12–14).

As for the substance and order of the catechetical corpus, it was to follow as much as possible that of Pius V's, also called the Roman catechism. Regarding the style, the TLC council was to accommodate it to the Indians, clearly following one of the Roman catechism's first premises, that instruction should be accommodated to the capacity of the hearer. The Indians could memorize it and could thus recite it in church or when they were working. However, since not all of them had the same capacity, there is also a brief catechism for the hard of understanding – the *rudos*. Following a decree of the Provincial Council in Latin, an epistle on translation opens with St Paul and his teachings on the need to preach doctrine in the language that the listeners understand, once again raising the issue of the incapacity of the clergy to preach in the vernaculars, something that easily led to errors of faith (DCC: 16–17). The last document is a decree in Latin about the translation of the Christian doctrine and catechism into Quechua and Aymara – *linguam Cuzquensem, sive Aymaraicam.*

Let us now focus on the structure and sections of the TLC corpus, which can be divided into two parts: doctrinal and disciplinary (Estenssoro 2003: 249–50). The first doctrinal part contains two catechisms, Brief and Greater – *breve* and *mayor* – the *Doctrina Christiana*, the *Suma de la Fe Catholica* and the *Plática Breve.* The *Doctrina Christiana*, in three languages, comprises the main prayers that the faithful have to memorize.[12] As for the two catechisms, the Brief and the Greater, both of them are presented in a question-and-answer format, the difference being in the number of questions: seventeen questions in the Brief catechism and one hundred and seventeen in

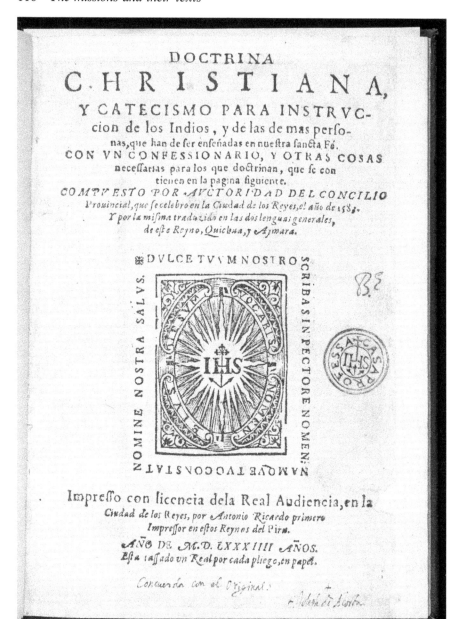

Figure 4.1 Doctrina Christiana y Catecismo para Instrucción de Indios (front cover), Lima (1584)
Source: Courtesy of Lilly Library, Bloomington, Indiana University

the Greater catechism. The catechumen always answers, proving his knowledge to the catechist. The Greater catechism takes the Roman catechism for its general structure and thematic order, but is adapted to Andean space.[13] Interestingly, the treatment of each sacrament is different, being more or less thorough according to the sacrament. The questions and answers on baptism and the Eucharist are more detailed and numerous than those on confirmation and extreme unction, but the more disciplinary ones, like penance and matrimony – marriage to siblings and polygamy were major concerns – receive more detailed and explanatory treatment. The shortest dialogue is, of course, about the sacrament of Holy Orders, as the Indians were not candidates for Orders, something that had already been stated in the seventy-fourth constitution of the SCL (Vargas Ugarte 1951: 192). The *Summa de la Fe Catholica* again reflects the influence of Acosta's *De Procuranda* on the DCC. This brief *Summa* contains what had to be taught 'to those who are baptized in sickness, and also the old and ignorant, not capable of learning a longer catechism', according to what was established in the SLC and the third and last council' (DCC: 43). *De Procuranda*'s imprint can be observed in the inclusion of the mystery of the Church – together with an only God, the mystery of the Trinity and Jesus Christ – something that, as Acosta says, most of the catechists do not take into account (De Proc: 556–57).[14]

This doctrinal part culminates with a separate section on criteria for Quechua and Aymara translations, entitled *Annotaciones o Escolios sobre la Traducción en las Lenguas Quechua y Aymara*.[15] The sub-section on Quechua makes reference to two extremes of the spoken language: first, the unrefined and corrupted language used in some of the provinces and second, the Quechua spoken in Cuzco, where

> they use terms, and such exquisite modes of expression, although obscure, beyond the boundaries of language. To escape from the vices of these two extremes, one in the middle has been considered suitable, ordinary and easy, observing the translation rule of sense for sense, instead of word for word.
>
> (DCC: 167)

Translation criteria were also established for the Aymara language, again trying to find a balance between an 'exquisite and obscure language spoken by the Indians' and a language lacking refinement.

> Therefore, all the general terms understood by almost all the Aimaraes have been added, also accommodated to the nations in which Aymara is used, that are so many … and to the style of many of the Indians born and raised in Spanish towns, and especially in Potosí.[16]

The Greater catechism and Brief catechism, both of 1584 and approved by Archbishop Toribio de Mogrovejo in 1583, were later complemented by the addition of the Third catechism by sermons (1585), which was made up of a series of sermons in Spanish, also translated into Quechua and Aymara. Learning it was not compulsory like the other two catechisms.[17] There will be more on this Third catechism when we analyze the second, 'disciplinary', part of the TLC corpus.

José de Acosta was the main author of the DCC in its original Spanish version. For the translation into Quechua, those responsible were Juan de Balboa, a Creole from Lima, canon Alonso Martínez, the Jesuit Bartolomé de Santiago, a Creole born in Arequipa, and the secular clergyman Francisco Carrasco. However, Toribio de Mogrovejo and the assembled bishops handed a preliminary version to a group of experts for revision: the Augustinian Juan de Almaraz, the Mercedarians Alonso Díaz and Lorenzo González, the Dominican Pedro Bedón and the Jesuits Blas Valera and Martín de Soto. According to this information, Blas Valera – for a long time regarded as one of the authors of the Quechua version – would have only approved it. As for the Aymara translations, both Carrasco and Santiago took part in them.[18] The translation team had some curious characteristics. First, there was a predominance of secular clerics and second, the most renowned *lenguas* of the time, like Alonso de Barzana, were absent. But Barzana might have been consulted in relation to the criteria for the translations, as in 1582 he was in Lima attending the provincial congregation of the Society of Jesus (Durston 2007: 97–8; Bartra 1967: 360).

According to Alan Durston, the TLC broadened the scope of pastoral Quechua by informing all the texts with an unusual terminological, dialectal and orthographical homogeneity. The main characteristic of the corpus is its absolute preference for loan terms in Spanish, instead of terms in or adapted from Quechua, except for some 'harmless' terms that remained, such as *hucha* for sin, *supay* for devil and *mucha* for worshipping. Durston also observes that the Christian translations into Quechua were much more homogenous and uniform than the pastoral texts in colonial Mexico, as the Andean soil harboured a harsher and more radical Counter-Reformation spirit (Durston 2007: 92–93). However, the 'standard colonial Quechua' was not systematically imposed as a language of everyday use, instead it coexisted with other varieties of Quechua. It was, above all, the language of Christianity; the language in which prayers, catechisms and hymns were recited or sung and the language parish priests were taught to use to preach and administer the sacraments by official instructors and examiners in Lima and Cuzco. Even priests who were native speakers of a particular spoken variety of Quechua still had to be examined in their knowledge of the standard colonial Quechua in order to be awarded a parish (Durston 2007: 109–10).

The doctrinal part of the TLC corpus is followed by a second 'disciplinary' one that comprises a confession manual for parish priests, '*El Confessionario para los Curas de Indios con la Instrucción contra sus Ritos y Exhortacion para Ayudar a Bien Morir: y Summa de Sus Pribilegios y Forma de Impedimentos del Matrimonio*', printed in 1585. From the beginning of the thirteenth century, confession manuals had been conceived of to provide priests with the necessary knowledge – theoretical and practical – for the practice of their ministry (García 1986: 186). In the DCC, the confession manual aims to show the errors of the superstitious rites of the Indians, since it was impossible for them to receive the faith without first knowing their errors (DCC: 199–202). That had been the reason why the previous evangelization in Peru had been superficial, where

> as long as they [the Indians] are not disillusioned of their errors by those who teach doctrine, it is pointless to think that these Indians will receive the faith, even if they are asked to learn and repeat the Christian doctrine once and again.
>
> (DCC: 199)

In short, the main explicit objective of this section is to write an account of 'the most common errors and superstitions of the Indians', as these could only be extirpated if priests were knowledgeable of them (DCC: 200–202). The *confessionario* for the Indians and the relevant questions and answers are followed by a sub-section with 'Questions for the caciques and curacas', aiming to make them confess if they had been taking advantage of the Indians in charge, of the Spaniards, or of the Church and also if they had organized *taquíes* – dances – or *borracheras* – drunkenness – or public feasts where rituals were performed, among other things (DCC: 226–32). Another set of questions is for the *hechiceros* – sorcerers – all followed by an 'Exhortation confession', including a 'reprehension for the idolatrous'. Worshipping the *huacas* was a devilish trick, like everything the Indians' ancestors did. So the exhortation says: 'Don't be foolish. Worship God, who is the creator of all things, and believe in Jesus Christ' (DCC: 245).

The confession manual is followed by an Instruction against the Ceremonies and Rituals of the Indians from When They Were Infidels – *Instrucción contra las Cerimonias y Ritos que usan los Indios Conforme al Tiempo de Su Infidelidad*. The information in this section was wholly taken from Polo de Ondegardo, who is cited explicitly in a section entitled On the Indians' Rites: Errors and Superstitions of the Indians Taken from the Treatise and Enquiry by the Licenciado Polo. This is a reproduction of the homonymous treatise '*Informaciones Acerca de la Religión y Gobierno de los Incas por el Licenciado Polo de Ondegardo (1571) Seguidas de las Instrucciones de los Concilios de Lima*' (DCC: 262–83; Polo de Ondegardo [1571] 1916: 3–43). As mentioned in Chapter Three, Polo's contribution to the extirpation campaigns between 1555 and 1565 had no precedent. He was convinced that rebuttal had to come before repression, and this was only possible with a thorough knowledge of the Indians' rites (Duviols 1977: 124–26). In Acosta's view, Polo was a counter-example to the priests in the Andes who had been responsible for a superficial evangelization and made little effort to know and extirpate the Indians' errors. So the Jesuit introduced

Polo in *De Procuranda* as a 'curious investigator of the Indies and a cautious observer' (De Proc: 511).

As mentioned above, to the Brief and Greater catechisms was added a Third catechism, by sermons, composed a year later, in 1585. This one, though, had not yet been composed when the TLC was held, but 'because of both its importance and the will of the Prelates, it was decided that the same person who had composed the other catechisms should make this one too, to be published with the approval of the archbishop' (DCC: 358; Castillo Arroyo 1966: 46–47). Everything, in addition to its contents, seems to indicate that José de Acosta was the author of this third catechism as well. Last but not least, if this third catechism had not been composed when the council was held, it had probably already been written but not officially approved as part of the DCC (Estenssoro 2003: 256).

This Third catechism is a compendium of sermons in Spanish, translated into Quechua and Aymara. Acosta's imprint can be observed starting with the first 'notice' or *aviso*, which, following Augustine's example, promotes and encourages plain preaching, far from 'sophisticated', to accommodate to the capacity of the faithful – the Indians. This was not only because they were new to the faith, but because of their limited capacity (DCC: 352–53). The purpose was to instil 'the most essential points of our religion' in the rough disciples – *rudos* – who should fix them in their memory so they become familiar. The third *aviso* again places stress on the style required for sermons: plain and simple, with no very long clauses and no beating about the bush – *las clausulas no muy largas, ni de rodeo.* The fourth *aviso*, and the most important, stresses the need to 'persuade' through doctrine, with plain reasons and with examples from the Scripture, but always with the purpose of unveiling the Indians' errors, showing them their falseness and undermining their teachers – the sorcerers – for their ignorance, tricks, and evil (DCC: 355). This was simple to do, as long as their rites and superstitions were known. It also strongly suggests resorting to various kinds of oratorical devices such as exclamations, for the Indians were more motivated by feelings than by reasons. This gives us an idea of the oral dimension of this Third catechism, by sermons, which aims to develop preaching skills in the parish priests, replacing the question-and-answer format for sermons (DCC: 358). In turn, by memorizing the catechisms, these sermons would lead the Indians to actually believe what they were taught. As Estenssoro states, the main purpose of the sermon is to go beyond the limited knowledge contained in a word, fixed by memory, turning it into faith (Estenssoro 2003: 257).

The Third catechism sets a stronger anti-idolatrous tone in the DCC through sermons that explicitly refer to idolatry.[19] We will come back to this theme in the next chapter; suffice it here to mention some general aspects. The sermons that specifically attack Indian idolatry are: the eighteenth, which explicitly focuses on breaking the first of the Ten Commandments – i.e. idolatry, expressed in the worship of both the *huacas* and natural phenomena; sermon nineteen, which encourages reprimanding the devil's ministers, the

TERCERO,
CATECISMO·

Y EXPOSICION DE LA DOCTRI-
NA CHRISTIANA POR

SERMONES.

PARAQUE LOS CURAS, Y OTROS
Ministros prediquen, y enseñen à los Indios,
y à las demàs Personas:

CONFORME A LO QUE SE PROVE-
yò en el Santo CONCILIO PROVINCIAL DE LIMA
el año pasado de 1583.

MANDADO REIMPRIMIR POR EL
CONCILIO PROVINCIAL *del año*

EN LA OFICINA DE LA C.
SAN JACINTO.

Figure 4.2 *Doctrina Christiana, Tercero catecismo* (1584)

hechiceros – sorcerers – and their superstitions and vain rites. This latter sermon, for instance, prohibits the Indians from celebrating the *Intiraymi* – the Inca celebration of the sun, or any veneration of their ancestors, since they worshiped the devil. It suggests, instead

> when you sow and reap maize or potatoes do not dance the *taquíes* nor celebrate *Aymuray*, but thank God who provides you with food. And when rain is needed ... do not invoke thunders nor celebrate the *Yntiraymi* ... but pray to God who is the provider of the fruits on earth.
>
> (DCC: 574–75)

Sermon twenty-three is against drunkenness – *borracheras* – itself a mortal sin, and the principal means to destroy faith and preserve superstition and idolatry.[20] 'Drunkenness brings the man closer to a beast and, even worse than a beast, he is deprived of judgement, which is the light of his soul' (DCC: 629). As for its many damages, drunkenness is harmful because 'it kills the faith in Jesus Christ and nurtures idolatries and devilish sects of the infidels and the devil' (DCC: 637).

Regarding the anti-idolatrous hallmark of the Third catechism, we have to go back – again – to *De Procuranda* to trace its inception. In the fifth book, chapter nine, Acosta manages to bring together two issues, or goals to achieve: a Christian mode of life, led by the Ten Commandments, and the struggle against idolatry. To encourage the Indians to despise the vanity of idols it was not necessary to resort to exquisite reasons, but to use plain and simple reasons that could never be better explained than in the Scriptures, especially the books of Wisdom, Isaiah, and Jeremiah. This biblical imprint is present in the Third catechism as well (DCC: 562).

As for a Christian mode of life, we have seen in the third chapter how the TLC corpus relates to a civilized state [*policía*], and the third catechism is the one that especially focuses on 'civilizing' the Indians. In the section on the commandments, it states that learning the Christian doctrine also contributes to distinguishing men from beasts. The twenty-first sermon states which religious feasts the Indians were obliged to observe, stressing the importance of Mass, for the Indian who does not learn the law of God is like a beast. 'Man, you are not a ram, nor a horse, and the tongue you have is not only to eat, like a horse, but to speak like a man' (DCC: 605).

To conclude, we can see that the DCC imposed Tridentine Catholicism adapted to Andean soil. But it was not exclusively confined to the adaptation of Tridentine Catholicism in Peru. The pre-Hispanic past was now dismissed for its idolatrous essence, thus condemning any possible resemblance with Christianity. A 'colonial orthodoxy' was born, meaning by 'colonial' the exclusion and marginalization of that past, which, in turn, and at the same time, helped shape an identity, in this case an Indigenous Catholicism (Estenssoro 2003: 26–28). As we have seen in these pages, there is also the imprint of Acosta as the theologian who shaped doctrine for the Province of

Peru. Salvation of the Indians through minimum contents of the faith was not only impossible, but also unacceptable. The SLC set a precedent that Acosta acknowledged, but that at a certain point had stopped short of introducing positive theology to frame doctrine and impose it as authoritative and exclusive. According to Acosta, it was not necessary for the Indians to actually comprehend the mysteries of faith, i.e. the supernatural, for they were difficult for most mortals. But they were essential for salvation, which was unquestionable. But here the missionaries and colonial authorities too found a major problem: a lazy clergy unwilling to learn the vernaculars. In this regard, the TLC corpus was not only a doctrine accommodated for the Indians and translated into the most widely-spoken Andean languages. It was also an evangelization tool for the parish priests, who would make good use of the translations to communicate with the Indians. One particular aspect that runs through the various doctrinal texts up to and including the DCC is that, apart from the Indians' limited capacity being a concern for their Christianization, the idle secular clergy was a clear obstacle to it as well. Matienzo included this in his manual, Toledo in many of his documents and Acosta in *De Procuranda* and the DCC too, in the very introductory documents. As we shall see in the next section, the Jesuits in the China mission did not have to deal with an idle secular clergy. They sent their own people, and among their people they sent the best ones, those well trained to learn the vernaculars on their way to the mission.

Last but not least, the DCC was itself both a proof and a result of the presence of the proactive Society of Jesus in Peru. But was it really 'the Society'? As we saw in the first chapter, not all the Jesuits in Peru saw eye to eye. We know that Acosta led the Jesuit faction that sided with the Spanish crown, which in the TLC was headed by archbishop Toribio de Mogrovejo. We know that other Jesuits, maybe not present in the years of the TLC, like Plaza and Luis López, had objected to Toledo's policies and had disagreements with Acosta as well. In this particular regard, it is Acosta's imprint that we see in the TLC corpus, also because he was 'the' theologian of the mission and the right-hand man of the royal and ecclesiastical authorities.

Framing Christian doctrine in the China mission

Michele Ruggieri's True Record of the Lord of Heaven

In their first years in Guandong province, those of their residence in Zhaoqing, the Jesuits introduced themselves as servants of *Tiandi*, from India – *Tian zhuguo* – which for the Chinese represented all the places west of China. Right from the start they referred to the Christian God as *Tiandi* and not *Tianzhu*. As mentioned in Chapter One, both *di* and *zhu* refer to 'lord', together with *tian*, which means heaven.[21] As we know, Ruggieri arrived in China some years earlier than Ricci. In a letter to the General Mercurian from Macao in November 1581 Ruggieri said that these people [the Chinese] do not have cognition of God, and the first and supreme cause is that they attribute everything to heaven, which they call *Tian*; and this world is the most important they have, and they say that it is like their father from whom they receive everything.

(OS II: 402)

It was one of the first Chinese to be baptized, named Cheng, who suggested the combination of *Tianzhu* to the Jesuits. One time that the Jesuits paid him a visit they saw those two characters – without images, Ricci clarifies – on the altar in his house. That is why this name later consolidated as the name for Catholicism in the Chinese language in East Asia. The Jesuits were unaware that *Tianzhu* was a Buddhist honorific title to refer to the Lord of the *devas* – deities in Sanskrit – and also that the Daoists honoured a deity with the same name (FR I: 186, note 1); but more on this in the next chapter.

Soon after his arrival in China and urged to spread the Christian doctrine, Michele Ruggieri started writing the True Record of the Lord of Heaven or *Tianzhu shilu* in Chinese (TZSL). In 1582 Visitor Valignano gave the order to print it as soon as possible. But the first publication from the Jesuits in China was the Ten Commandments which, according to D' Elia, must have been printed before November 1584, when the TZSL was printed. November 30 of that same year a copy of the TZSL was sent to Rome together with translations of the Pater Noster, Hail Mary and the Creed (FR I: 195, note 1). Pasquale D'Elia was very sceptical about Ruggieri having composed the TZSL by himself because when the work was finished on November 12 1581 the Jesuit had spent little more than two years in China – without counting the trips back and forth to Canton in that period (D'Elia 1934: 197).

Ruggieri first composed a text in Latin together with Pedro Gómez in mid-1581; the TZSL has been regarded by some scholars as a Chinese translation of this Latin text, although it is longer and has passages that do not exist in the Chinese version.[22] After his return to Europe, Ruggieri showed the Latin version of TZSL, the *Vera et Brevis Divinarum Rerum Expositio*, to Pope Gregory XIV in Rome in 1591.

The Chinese version was then translated by a catechized young Chinese in Macao who served both as teacher and interpreter. By now, we know that this did not mean that Ruggieri was not devoted to learning the language, as he communicated to Acquaviva in February 1583. Ruggieri stated that for three years he had dedicated himself

to learning the characters and writing some doctrinal texts, like a Catechism, Flos sanctorum, a Confession manual and a Doctrine which, according to the Visitor's will, as well as that of the other fathers, he ordered that I printed it, for a universal knowledge of God to be transmitted to the gentiles and to bring them closer to this holy law.

(OS II: 412)

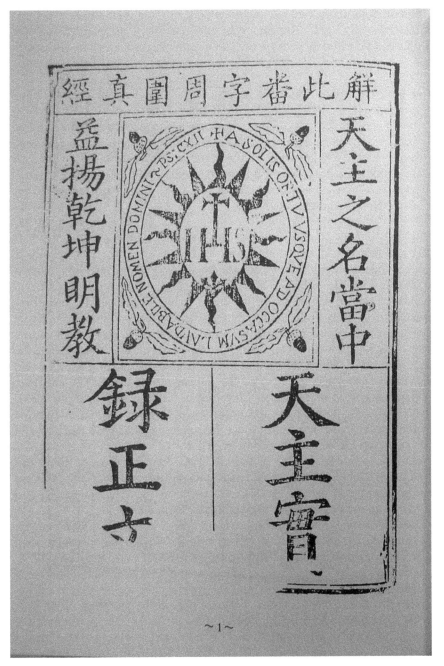

解此書字當周圍真經

天主之名當中

盍揚乾坤明教

錄正士

天主實

~1~

Figure 4.3 Michele Ruggieri's *Tianzhu Shilu* (True Record of the Lord of Heaven; front cover) (1584)
Source: Courtesy of USF Ricci Institute for Chinese-Western Cultural History

As Joseph Shih points out, we only know one of these three small works, i.e. the *Doctrina* or TZSL. Ruggieri does not refer to it as a catechism;[23] it was Ricci who referred to it as such in a letter to Acquaviva in November 1584:

> I have come here from our residence in Zhao Qing for several things suggested to me by Father Michele Ruggieri. The Catechism that we have made and printed in the Chinese language, by the grace of the Lord, has been very well received. In it, by means of dialogue between a Gentile and a Father from Europe, all the things necessary for being a Christian in good order, good letters, and good language are presented. The main sects of China are confuted, and there are the Ten Commandments, the Pater Noster, and the Ave Maria.
>
> (Rienstra 1986: 24–25)

Ricci also mentioned that the *letterati* wanted to know more things about their law than those in the Ten Commandments, so with the help of a literatus baptized in 1584 'the fathers' – Ricci uses the plural – composed the TZSL, in which they refuted some precepts of the sects in China. And, in turn, 'they expounded the Holy Faith, especially those truths that could be more easily understood through the natural light of reason' (FR, I: 197–98). Even though Ricci – maybe unfairly – takes credit for being a co-author of the TZSL, the language used in chapter fourteen of the TZSL resembles that of Ricci's world map, edited just a few days before the publication of the TZSL. This may suggest that Ricci could have been involved in the final version of the TZSL (Shih 1964: 37). These were the years when Ruggieri and Ricci worked together, in the same direction. In fact, between 1583 and 1588 Ruggieri and Ricci composed a Portuguese–Chinese dictionary in which they developed a romanization system. But this dictionary in the Jesuit archives in Rome also contains a Chinese text that is quite a complete summary of Christian doctrine composed by the Jesuits, addressed to the Chinese literati and mandarins in the first years of the Jesuits in Zhaoqing.[24]

The TZSL manuscript circulated among literati in Canton and Zhaoqing, in Guandong province. The first edition was of twelve hundred copies, soon to be followed by a second of three thousand (FR I: 198). Ruggieri's TZSL consists of sixteen chapters, in a question-and-answer format, between a Buddhist monk – *seng* – and an anonymous interlocutor presented as 'someone' – *huo*. The chapters and themes present the following order: first, On the true and only Lord of Heaven; second, Attributes of the Lord of Heaven; third, An explanation of the false claims to knowledge of the Lord of Heaven that men make; fourth, On the Lord of Heaven as the creator and controller of mankind and all the things in the world; fifth, On the angels and Adam; sixth, A dissertation on the immortality of the human soul, which does not perish, unlike that of birds and beasts; seventh, an explanation of the four places where the soul goes; eighth, the three times that the Lord of

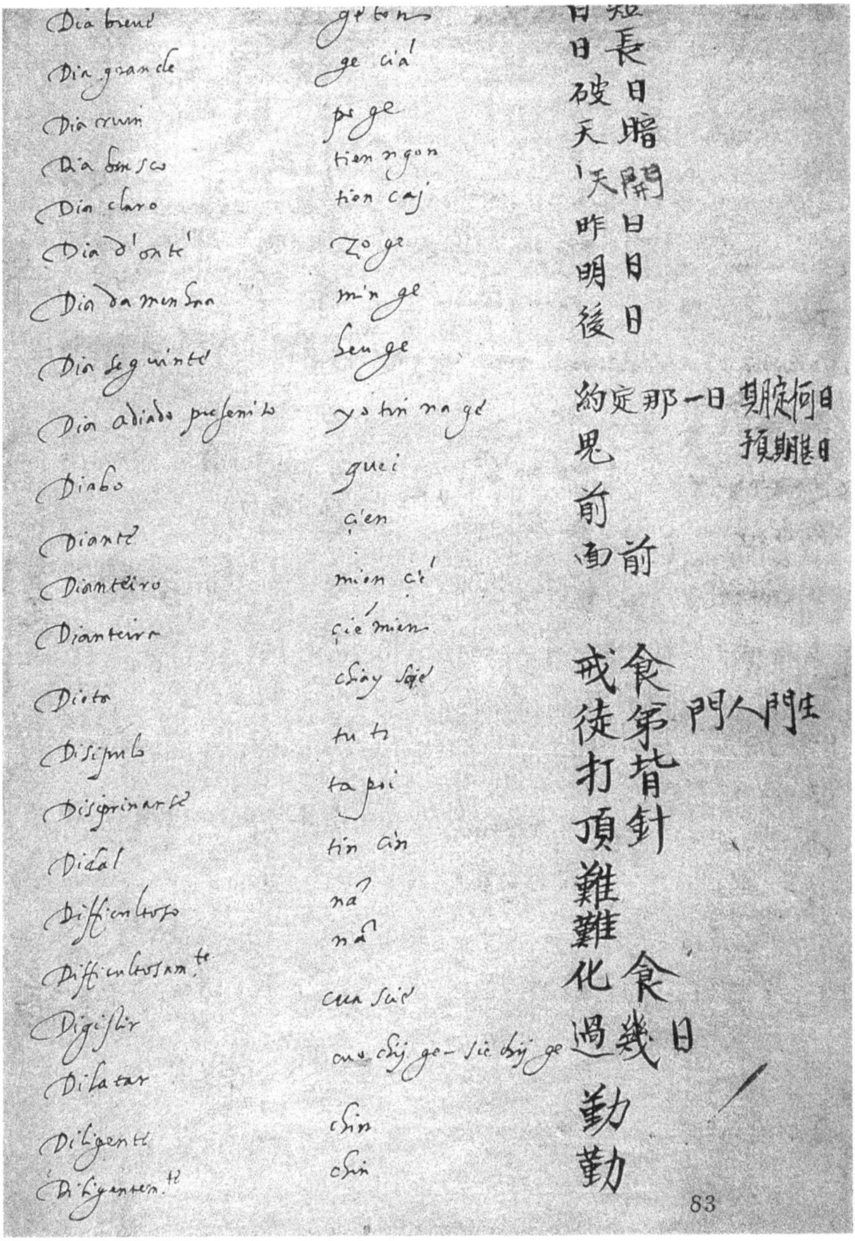

Figure 4.4 Portuguese–Chinese dictionary by Michele Ruggieri and Matteo Ricci (1584)
Source: Courtesy of USF Ricci Institute for Chinese-Western Cultural History

Heaven promulgated his law from ancient times to the present i.e. natural, Mosaic and Christian; ninth, On the third law promulgated by the Lord of Heaven when he descended to this world; tenth, An explanation of the nature of this third law promulgated to men; eleventh, On how men must sincerely believe in the Lord of Heaven; twelfth, On the Ten Commandments; thirteenth, An explanation of the [first three] commandments of the first table – it is in the previous chapter that the division between tables is established, not precisely in the title; fourteenth, An explanation of the [seven] commandments of the second table and their nature; fifteenth, An explanation of how the true way to heaven is the religious life, which consists of the sincere practice of virtue; sixteenth, On how holy water eliminates all past sins (TZSL: 7–8).[25] An appendix with the Ten Commandments in Chinese was added at the end of the TZSL (TZSL: 82–3).[26] Jacques Gernet states that neither of the scholars who are considered knowledgeable of the TZSL, i.e. Leon Wieger SJ and Pasquale D'Elia SJ, makes reference to a second version of it, a manuscript version at the Zikawei Library, probably from 1648, but not later. According to Gernet, the revision of the vocabulary between the two versions is not limited to introducing the Jesuits as bonzes, but also to removing 'involuntary loans' of Daoist terms (Gernet 1979: 410 onward).

It is a well-known fact that Ruggieri's TZSL was a first attempt to present the faith in a Chinese context. And many of the terms that he used, such as *Tianzhu, tiantang* – paradise, *mogui* – devil, *diyu* – hell, among others, were later used by Ricci and other Jesuits and have remained in use until the present (Criveller 1997: 96; Criveller 2008: 211). The doctrinal and textual path followed by Ruggieri and Ricci in China seemed to go in the same direction until Ruggieri's TZSL was replaced by Ricci's TZSY. Analysed from the perspective of internal Jesuit policies, this decision leads to Visitor Valignano. It could therefore be said that Ricci's TZSY comes between two texts, Ruggieri's TZSL and Valignano's *Catechismus Christianae Fidei*, as shown below.

The sources of Ricci's TZSY

One of the aspects some scholars drew attention to when comparing Ruggieri's TZSL and Ricci's TZSY is related to genre. Indeed, as mentioned in the introduction, regarding the distinction between a 'catechism' – a work of apologetics defending Christian teaching against objections – and a 'doctrine' – a positive and systematic exposition of Christian doctrine – some scholars claim that the TZSL is clearly a doctrine and the TZSY a catechism. In summary, the TZSL could be both, a catechism and a *Doctrina Christiana*, and this could indicate that a clear distinction between the two genres was not yet in place (Criveller 1997: 91). Apart from these distinctions, which refer to genres, there is a breach between the two catechisms and that is – simply put – Ricci's interpretation of Confucianism. Indeed, the TZSL, which was intended for circulation among a well-read audience, does not have even one mention of Confucius or, in more general terms, of Confucianism (Gernet 1979: 409; Rule 1986: 7).

This does not mean that the TZSY did not reuse the 'useful' parts of the TZSL. In addition to repeating many passages from the TZSL, the TZSY further develops its first eight chapters, which are both more general and more philosophical than the last eight chapters of the TZSL. Indeed, some of the first chapters of the TZSL are practically reproduced verbatim in Ricci's TZSY, e.g. chapter three, chapter four and chapter six (Gernet 1979: 413–14). There are only minimal differences regarding certain terms used.[27]

One of the key terms present throughout the TZSY is the Chinese concept of 'orthodoxy' – *zheng*. As already mentioned, it is of a different order to the monopolistic, all-inclusive Mediterranean type of orthodoxy, of which Christianity – in its seventeenth-century, Roman Catholic, post-Tridentine form – was an outstanding example. *Zheng* is, first and foremost, a moral and political orthodoxy. However, it also has an important religious dimension. Confucian values reflect the qualities of the cosmos itself; the conception of a morally positive universe directed by the Mandate of Heaven had important ideological and ritual consequences; in fact it formed the basis of the Confucian state religion. Finally, the concept of *zheng* also comprises an individual component: the Confucian ideal of 'self-cultivation', closely related to virtue (Zürcher 1997: 616–22). In sum, Ricci's TZSY was the first piece of writing by a Jesuit in China that clearly proclaimed its teachings to be 'on the orthodox side', in a Confucian register, inaugurating a strict and exclusive division between orthodoxy and heterodoxy. This is, indeed, something completely absent in Ruggieri's TZSL. The orthodoxy Ricci is forging, grounded on the Confucian orthodoxy, apparently needs a more vehement tone; and this is another difference to Ruggieri's TZSL. In the TZSL, the characters involved in the dialogue are more anonymous and less eager to debate. This contrasts markedly with the two scholars in Ricci's TZSY and its more contentious atmosphere.

Valignano's greatest rival in Japan, Francisco Cabral, had composed a catechism – which has not survived – with the help of a very well-learned convert *bonze*, named Kenzen João, together with his interpreter, Brother Juan de Torres de Yamaguchi. When Valignano arrived in Japan this was the catechism in use. Cabral had worked on it from 1571 to 1578 and in it he confuted Buddhist sects and transmitted the philosophical foundation of *Christianitas*. There is no record of why Valignano considered this catechism had to be replaced, nor of the criteria for its replacement.[28] The full title of Valignano's catechism is *Catechismus Christianae Fidei, in quo Veritas Nostrae Religionis Ostenditur, et Sectae Japonenses Confutatur, Editus à Patre Alexandro Valignano/Societatis Iesu*. It was printed in Lisbon at the beginning of 1586 under General Acquaviva's instruction and without the author's knowledge. As a summary of Catholic doctrine, in its Japanese version the catechism was of importance for the native preachers and for the native Church in general. Valignano received the help of native converts, especially the brothers – the *irmãos* – and the bonzes numbered among the converts, for Valignano's knowledge of Japanese was only superficial. Thanks to this cooperation the Jesuit grasped the essentials of contemporary Japanese Buddhism, although without delving into its different branches. The Jesuit Luis Frois, the European most well informed on Shintoism and Buddhism, had also collaborated [29]

Valignano's catechism, especially the first part, which is divided into eight chapters or conferences, would have a major influence on Ricci's TZSY, as we shall see later. At the beginning of the first *concio* – conference – Valignano presents God – *Deus* – as the creator of all things and ruler of man's destiny. Francis Xavier had started to use the Latin *Deus* in Japan, after what was regarded a critical failure, i.e. Xavier's using the term *Dainichi* – the abbreviated form for the Shingon Buddha, Dainichi Nyorai – for the Christian God. In Valignano's catechism, the scholastic argumentation for the existence of God runs parallel with the rejection of false teachings and the clarification of the erroneous points of the 'ridiculous and absurd' sect of *Fotoque* and its fabrications. *Fotoque* refers to the Japanese *Hotoke*, the Buddha himself, but throughout the catechism we also find other names for Buddha, like Cami and Amida (Catechismus: f.6). The second *concio* starts by showing the source of the errors of the Buddhists, i.e. the 'first Principle' as the creator of things in this world, followed by a positive exposition of the Christian notion of God: one creator God, who not only created the world but also preserves it in being, and guides it; his divine attributes are also explained. This positive exposition of the Christian notion of God is followed by three points of discrepancy between the principle of the supreme being and the 'pantheism' of the Buddhist 'sects' in Japan, which do not properly explain the origin of things. The first argument is that there are two constituent principles, matter and form, and an efficient principle – an extrinsic cause – that brings both together. God is the supreme efficient cause; it is he who causes a thing to exist, but he is not one of its constituent principles, i.e. matter or form. Second, the Buddhists' error arises from ignoring the fact that one thing can be in another in different ways, e.g. as matter and form are in a natural object. However, God is in all things as their efficient cause but, as such, he does not constitute a part of the substance of the thing produced. In sum, according to Valignano, the error of the Buddhists was to believe that the first principle is in all things, just like matter and form can be. A third cause of error, in his opinion, is that Buddhists failed to distinguish the ways in which being is communicated: namely, by the form giving being to the whole composite, and whereby being is communicated by the efficient cause. In short, the point that Valignano emphasizes is that the efficient cause gives life to things without being part of them. These arguments were echoed by Ricci, as shown below.

Valignano discusses the immortality of the soul in great detail, providing sets of proofs that stem from its immaterial nature. In the fourth *concio*, he harshly criticizes certain precepts like the transmigration of souls, and *Cami* and *Hotoke* as bestowers of blessings in this life and rewarders in the next, among others (Schütte 1985: I, part II, 79–80). Valignano refutes the Buddhist precept regarding the attainment of perfect knowledge and thus of divinization in this life, meaning that all men can be Buddha. Then Valignano remarks that Buddha – *Xaca*, *Amida*, as well as *Cami* and *Hotoke* – are historical figures: they were born, had ancestors, families of their own and descendents, and they died. Here lies one of the reasons why men fell away from an original monotheism. First, they transferred the attributes of supreme rule and power – proper to God alone – to things or persons in whom they observed those qualities to a heightened degree. Second, according to Valignano, they misinterpreted the cult of images: powerful rulers prompted by personal ambition had statues or other representations of themselves set up and honoured as though they were present in them. As a third cause, Valignano mentions sheer diabolical deception. The devil – represented in Japanese as *tengu* – lay concealed in statues and figures, gave out oracular answers from them and caused figures to move in various directions; so the people believed that a divinity lay concealed in these works of their own creation. Then, avaricious men set themselves up as bonzes of these possessed figures and led people astray with their deceitful stories. In the fifth conference, Valignano attacks both the idolatrous crime of the Japanese sects of worshipping *Cami*, *Fotoque* and demons and the 'unnatural vices' widely spread by the bonzes (Catechismus: f. 45). Among the latter he mentions the killing of animals being forbidden by the 'sects' – something that Ricci would also attack in his TZSY – in contrast with regarding suicide as 'virtuous', among other things. In the sixth conference Valignano focuses on proving that the Christian law is the only one in harmony with reason. Then, he introduces the mysteries of faith – *supranaturalia mysteria* – and the divine revelation that cannot be known through natural reason (Catechismus: f. 55). In the seventh conference, he expounds the mystery of the Trinity; then he introduces Lucifer, Adam and Eve and the expulsion from the garden of Eden. In the eighth *concio*, Valignano continues expounding Christian dogma, now introducing the Virgin Mary and the Incarnation of Jesus Christ. This closes the first book of the catechism, the one on which Ricci's TZSY is based, while the second book furthers Christian dogma. In sum, at the end of the last conference the author concludes that all that is contained in Christian law with regard to man's behaviour in this life and to the rewards and punishments in the next is God's word and accords with reason, while the Japanese sects are all false (Catechismus: Liber Secundus, f. 24). As mentioned in the first part, Ricci started to compose the TZSY at Valignano's command in 1593. According to Nicolas Standaert, who poses some key questions about the role Japan played in the China mission, the influence of the visitor can be observed in the similarities between Valignano's catechism and Ricci's TZSY i.e. the division into eight chapters, and the rational-scholastic approach being among the most telling, as we shall see below (Standaert 2009: 61–62; Shih 1964: 21).

Ricci's True Meaning of the Lord of Heaven: an 'orthodox' teaching is born

Before the TZSY – and also at Valignano's command – Ricci had engaged in translating the Four Books into Latin in the 1590s, which gave him insight into the useful terminology and concepts he could employ to transmit doctrine, especially to the literati, whom he regarded as exclusively Confucian. At the end of 1593 Duarte de Sande wrote to Acquaviva saying that, even though Ruggieri's TZSL had been well received by the literati and had circulated in Japan and Korea, Valignano wanted another catechism to be written which was to be more apologetic and more severe in refuting idolatry. Soon afterward, in December of that same year Ricci put Valignano's mandate into effect and sat down to the task of writing the TZSY, as he stated in his *storia*, writing in the third person, showing a clear intention to replace Ruggieri's TZSL:

> At that time, Father Ricci wrote a Catechism on the things of our Holy Law [the TZSY], more extensive than the previous one which, besides being brief, was made according to the condition of the Fathers at that moment and according to how they were called, similar to Buddhist monks, whereby orders were given to break the wooden blocks. As for us, we had not used that book [Ruggieri's TZSL] for a long time nor was it given to anybody. Henceforth they used this other new one, transcribing it in all the houses, until it was printed.
>
> (FR I: 379)[30]

Thus the more thorough catechism aimed to displace the TZSL, which embodied that particular stage of the mission in which the Jesuits adopted a Buddhist persona that now some of them – especially Ricci – wanted to leave behind. At the end of 1595 Ricci started to rewrite the reusable parts and chapters of the TZSL. The most obvious case is the way he addresses the two characters involved in the dialogue. Instead of *he shang* or *seng*, both Chinese terms referring to a Buddhist monk, we find *shi*, a literatus, one from the West, a *xi shi* – Ricci himself – and one Chinese, a *zhong shi*. Ricci clearly states that this catechism, the TZSY, does not focus on the mysteries of faith, but covers

> some of the main ones, especially those that, one way or another, can be proved through natural reasons and comprehended with the same natural light, so that it can be used by both Christians and Gentiles and understood in faraway parts of the world, out of our reach, in order to open the paths to mysteries that depend on faith and revealed science. This is equivalent to saying that the universe has a Lord who is the creator of all things and their keeper; that man has an immortal soul and that God will demand reward or punishment for his good and wrongful deeds in another life; that the transmigration of the soul into the body of

men and also animals is false … . And all this was proved not only on grounds of the many reasons and arguments provided by our holy doctors, but with the authority of the ancient books written by the Father, which gave this work great credit and authority.

(FR II: 292–95)

By 1596 Ricci had finished the catechism and was fully dedicated to its revision. Apart from the copies he made for the closer literati, he sent a copy to the bishop in Japan, Luis Cerqueira, based in Macao. De Sande and Valignano examined the text and underlined all those points that needed corrections – not to the Chinese terminology but to the contents. For various reasons, such as the death of the superior de Sande, Ricci received the revised version when he arrived in Peking in 1601, when the permission from the Inquisition in Goa had just arrived. In sum, Ricci composed his TZSY at Visitor Valignano's command, with the same scholastic approach, and embodying a more aggressive rebuttal of the 'idolatrous sects', especially Buddhism, as the visitor wanted. Ricci's TZSY was the first catechism to circulate among a broader network of literati from different cities, some of them with a strong literary tradition such as Nanchang, Nanjing and the imperial capital, Peking. As Ricci said to his fellow Jesuit in Siena, Girolamo Costa, in a letter of October 1594, his catechism 'all about natural reasons' was meant 'to circulate throughout China once it is printed' (OS II: 122).

Let us now focus on the way Ricci expounded Christian doctrine to be understood through the light of natural reason. The True Meaning of the Lord of Heaven, divided into eight chapters, opens with an introduction, written in the first person. Ricci introduces himself as a traveller who has been all around the world and in the course of his journeys has discovered that there are doctrines that poison people's minds. His friends have encouraged him to reveal them and hence the dialogues found in the book. In fact, the TZSY is, to a great extent, the outcome of all the scholarly debates Ricci held with the Chinese literati in their circles in Nanchang, Nanjing and Beijing, such as a discussion with the well-learned Buddhist San Huai that he thoroughly described in his *storia* (FR II: 72 onward) and in one of his later works, *Jiren Shipian*. This catechism, written in the form of a dialogue between a scholar from the West and a Chinese scholar, reflects Ricci's own experiences, being the dialogue form not only familiar in catechisms but also a cherished genre in Ming China. In this introduction the Jesuit states that there can be only one doctrine claiming to achieve peace and sound government in the universe. All men of virtue believe in a superior being to whom worship shall be rendered. The doctrine of the Lord of Heaven is mysterious and difficult to learn, but men have to learn it.

The first chapter is a 'Discussion about the Creation of Heaven, Earth and All Things Created by the Lord of Heaven, and How He Controls Them'. Ricci presents the doctrine of the Lord of Heaven as a true and universal teaching – *gong jiao* – with a subsequent explanation of the principles – *li* – that it is based on. The Lord of Heaven is the creator of heaven, earth and all things; he is the origin of all things, and has no beginning and no end. He created the category of all things and exerts control over his creation. The Lord of Heaven is an active and ultimate cause, not formal or material. Ricci offers an explanation based on the four causes, following Aristotle's Metaphysics: active – *zuo zhe*, formal – *mo zhe*, material – *zhi zhe*, and ultimate – *wei zhe* (TZSY I: 390, III–IV). The second chapter is entitled 'An Explanation of Men's Misconceptions Concerning the Lord of Heaven'. Here, Ricci begins with his harsh attacks against Buddhism and Daoism, always to be confuted exclusively 'through reason, not hate'; Confucianism is the 'religion' closest to the teachings of the Lord of Heaven, which rejects both Buddhism and Daoism. Among the main tenets of the first two, impugnation is against the Daoist concept of 'non-action' – *wu wei*, and of 'emptiness' – *kong*, according to the Buddhists, both regarded by Ricci as 'absurd' teachings – *la miu*. A still shy Chinese scholar asks about the Great Ultimate, the *Taiji*, as the scholars of his country talk about it. The scholar from the West argues that the Great Ultimate is not the creator of heaven and earth, the sole creator of which is the Lord of Heaven, and that is why there is no mention of the *Taiji* in the Chinese canonical papers, which do mention the Lord on High or *Shang di*. In the TZSY Ricci uses both, *Tian zhu* and *Shang di*, indistinctly. The Lord of Heaven created different categories – *li* – of things, and Ricci explains this through the Aristotelian concepts of 'substance' – *zi li zhe* – and 'accident' – *yi lai zhe* (TZSY II: 406, II–VII). The Jesuit includes a diagram, a medieval *arbor Porphyrii* – it has an arboreal structure – of the different types of accidents, as a visual help to the reader (TZSY: 462; Lackner 1996: 209–10). Ricci argues that substance does not depend on other things for its existence, and the Great Ultimate falls into the category of accident, for it is dependant; therefore it cannot be the creator of all things. Here we can see a resemblance to Valignano's *Catechismus Christianae Fidei* and the refutation of the first principle as the origin of things. But, as a good disciple of the visitor, Ricci adapted his doctrine to Chinese soil, so here he is not arguing against Japanese Buddhism, but is attacking Song Neo-Confucianism, specifically making reference to the Neo-Confucian thinker Zhou Dunyi (1017–73). In his Explanation of the Diagram of the Great Ultimate, *Taiji tushuo*, Zhou Dunyi explains the *Taiji* as the cosmic origin that can explain how all things came to be what they are and how they relate to each other. Zhu Xi wrote a commentary on this text and, although he disagreed with Zhou on certain aspects, Zhu Xi maintains the idea that *Taiji* is the ultimate principle of the universe. Ricci's contention is that *Taiji* is principle, and principle belongs to the category of accident, so it cannot create all things like the Lord on High. That is why – Ricci argues – ceremonies and sacrifices to Heaven and Earth are meant for the service of the Lord on High – and not for *Taiji*.

The third chapter is 'A dissertation on the human soul, which does not perish, unlike those of birds and beasts'. A long monologue by the Chinese scholar ends by mentioning how many schools or teachings in China in those days were all believed to be orthodox. Then Ricci claims that this earthly world is not the world of men but of birds and beasts, since mankind's real home is in heaven, in the hereafter. But the Chinese scholar immediately relates the notions of heaven – *tian tang* – and hell – *di yu* – to Buddhism. Of course, Ricci vehemently dismisses any possible resemblance to the transmigration of souls of the Buddhists and provides arguments concerning the human soul, which does not perish. In Christian doctrine, the doctrine of the immortality of the soul buttresses the foundations of heaven and hell, for without immortal souls eternal bliss and endless pain become pointless. Ricci invokes and explains in detail Aristotle's concept of the soul, more specifically the hierarchy of souls: the vegetative – *sheng hun*, the sensitive – *jue hun* and the rational soul – *ling hun*, which in Ruggieri's TZSL we find as *hun ling* (TZSY III: 429, IX; 430, I–VII). The latter does not depend on the body and is exclusive to men. The human soul is not destroyed because it is spirit and not formed of any of the four elements. To prove the immortality of the soul in a Confucian register, Ricci refers to the rituals dedicated to ancestors according to the Chinese virtue of filial piety – *xiao* – for even though 'our ancestors cannot see nor hear these rituals, they still take place'. Filial piety has maintained its paramount position among Chinese ethical principles, at the core of all other virtues. The relationships between father and son, and husband and wife, and between brothers, are all based upon the central concept of filial piety.

The fourth chapter is 'A discussion about spirits and the human soul and an explanation of why all the things in this world cannot be regarded as an organic unity'. According to the Western scholar, in the ancient Chinese canonical writings the offerings to ghosts and spirits – *gui shen* – by the Son of Heaven – the Emperor – and noblemen proved that in the olden days the Chinese already believed in the immortality of the soul. For instance, in the Annals of Spring and Autumn the ghost of the Earl of Cheng appeared after his death, which proves that the human soul is not extinguished. The Chinese scholar states that the soul after death is regarded as material energy – *qi, yin* and *yang* being the two kinds of *qi*. Therefore, if the human soul in the West is like the *qi*, then there is not much difference from the Chinese beliefs. Here, Ricci reacts and makes a distinction between spirit and material energy – *qi*, which only provides objects with a physical form but is not spirit, and which does not form part of matter. The Chinese scholar introduces the Neo-Confucian category of organic unity, innocently suggesting that in ancient times it was believed that the nature of things in this world was organically whole. In this way, the Lord of Heaven/Lord on High is in all and everything, thus forming a unity with all things. Again, Ricci feels compelled to rebut the assimilation of the Lord of Heaven with his creation as an organic whole by establishing a comparison with the devil, Lucifer, who proclaimed himself equal to the Lord of Heaven. Consequently, what the Chinese scholar says assimilating the creator with his creation sounds just like the devil's arrogance. Overall, Ricci's contention with and rebuttal of an organic unity takes up countless columns of the TZSY to the point of becoming redundant and exasperating. It is a long-winded attack that serves as a springboard for Ricci's attacks – once more – against Buddhism in the following chapter.[31]

The fifth chapter is entitled 'A discussion about the false teachings of reincarnation in the Six Directions and the taking of life, and an explanation of correct and proper fasting'. Ricci argues that reincarnation is originally a Pythagorean theory. Indeed, *Sakyamuni* – Ricci always refers to Buddha as *Sakyamuni* – took many concepts from Pythagoras that he later twisted and added to Buddhism, like the transmigration of the soul, and established a new teaching in India, adding the Six Directions, i.e. east, west, north, south, above and below (TZSY V: 492, III–IX; 493, I–IV)). In turn – and this is the reason why the Chinese did not know of the teachings of the Lord of Heaven – when the emperor sent an ambassador to obtain the sacred texts of the Lord of Heaven, the ambassador headed in the wrong direction, to India, bringing Buddhist sutras instead. In Ricci's view, the transmigration of souls is nothing but a devilish trick, for the devil – *mo gui* – deceives people into following him and attaches himself to the bodies of beasts. This view of idolatry on Chinese soil was also included in the Latin version of the TZSY which was sent to Rome for approval, the *Deo Verax Disputatio*, defined as a *catechismus sinicus* (Ricci [1603] 1985: 460–72). Basically, Ricci had to convince the Chinese of the immortality of the soul by attacking the Buddhists, for in the transmigration of the soul he saw a strong contestant. Belief in reincarnation leads Buddhists to advocate no killing, since any animal could be the reincarnations of one's parents. We shall come back to this theme in the next chapter.

Another issue that Ricci addressed is fasting; fasting is good in itself, as long as it is not related to the Buddhist prohibition of the killing of animals. Fasting is necessary to cultivate virtue, which is man's main task on earth. One of the first reasons for fasting Ricci provides is an indirect reference to Moses' tablets. Even virtuous men could offend the Lord of Heaven in the past, by not complying with the truths that he ordered sages to carve and record on the tablets.[32] Those who violate these truths and thus offend the Lord on High/Lord of Heaven cannot bear happiness because of their shame. However, by reducing his intake of food and drink to the minimum – as one of the ways to self-inflict suffering – a man purges himself (TZSY V: 512, VI–VIII). Another reason for fasting is that it is also related to the mind, not just the body. When the body is restricted by reason, desires are subjected to reason. This is a world of suffering, says Ricci, which does not mean that the Lord of Heaven deprives men of happiness, but it is the result of the cultivation of virtue and not a light physical happiness.

The sixth chapter is entitled 'An explanation of why will does not perish. A discussion of why good and evil are rewarded in heaven or punished in hell after death'. For the Chinese scholar, good or bad deeds cannot have ulterior motives, otherwise they would be motivated by profit; he grounds his contention on Mencius's concept of profit – *li*. Ricci refutes him by saying, first, that Confucianism promoted ulterior motives, while the theory that men act free of intentions comes from other heterodox schools. For instance, in the Great Learning, the *Da xue*, sincerity is the ulterior motive for the ordering of the economy, the state, the family and the kingdom. The origin of good and evil, explains Ricci, is clearly the will or intention. The Chinese scholar is very reluctant to believe in ulterior motives throughout the chapter. In his view, if there is will, or intention, it is related to virtue, which means that the beauty of good does not necessarily have a reward and nor is there punishment for evil. The Chinese scholar also suggests that it is more realistic to focus on things in this world instead of the hereafter, but Ricci dismisses this reflection as superficial – *lou*.

One of the problems the Jesuit sees in this regard is that, being too concerned about style, Confucians have misinterpreted the canonical books in which there are many references to heaven, because they overlooked them. Ancient Chinese texts refer to heaven as a place to rise up to; and if there is a heaven there is a hell. It is in this chapter that Ricci introduces and briefly explains the notion and purpose of purgatory.

Chapter seven is 'A Discussion Concerning the Goodness of Human Nature and an Explanation on the Orthodox Teaching of Those Who Follow the Lord of Heaven'. It is each man's individual actions that determine whether human nature is good or not, through the interaction with feelings and passions. Ricci distinguishes two kinds of goodness: an innate goodness – *liang shan*, the virtue provided by the Lord of Heaven, and an acquired goodness – *xi shan*, which is the result of the exercise or practice of good works and one's own efforts. He who does good cultivates the merit of virtue. And, among the Chinese virtues, humanity – *ren* – is the most important. Interpreting the Chinese virtue of humanity in his own terms, the Jesuit equates humanity to Christian charity: love the Lord of Heaven and others as you love yourself.

Ricci – and previously Ruggieri in his TZSL – states that a family can have only one head, and it is a crime to have two; a kingdom can only have one king, and it is a crime to have two, and the universe must have only one master. Accordingly, there cannot be two coexisting truths. If the religion of the Lord of Heaven is the true one, the other one is not, and if that one is the true one, the Lord of Heaven's is not. Buddhism and Daoism do not venerate the Lord of Heaven but themselves, and one could say that they were self-summoned, for they were not summoned by the Lord of Heaven. Ricci complains about the fact that even though Confucians in China wish to eliminate Buddhism and Daoism, together with the worship of idols – literally 'images' –, 'we just see they themselves building more temples' (TZSY VII: 592, VI–IX). What is more, there is an even worse teaching than Buddhism and Daoism. If in the past there used to be three 'religions' in China, now there is this monstrosity – according to Ricci – of the Three teachings, the *San jiao*. The Jesuit points out the differences among the three religions, for Buddhism places stress on 'emptiness', Daoism on 'non-action' and Confucianism on 'sincerity' and 'being', the latter being a complete opposite to the former two, and opposites do not find harmony. Those who follow the Three teachings are following no religion, because they do not believe in one single religion (TZSY VII: 601, III–IX).

The last chapter, chapter eight, is 'A summary of western customs. A discussion about the meaning of celibacy for those who preach the Way, and an explanation of why the lord of heaven was born in the west'.[33] Ricci argues that in the West everybody is dedicated to cultivating the Way – the *Dao*, understood as the true religion – and those who rule preserve its orthodox transmission. There is another authority, the pope, who makes sure that false and heterodox teachings do not have the upper hand. As for celibacy, some societies, like the Society of Jesus, include celibate members who travel to transmit the principles of the Way and eradicate heterodox teachings. As an argument in favour of celibacy, Ricci says that his mission cannot be weakened by earthly pleasures, like the pleasures of sexuality. His Chinese interlocutor's counter-argument is grounded on filial piety. But Ricci responds that virtue is not defined simply by descendants: it is necessary to first determine the father-son relationship. There are three types of fathers in this world: the first is the Lord of Heaven, the second is the sovereign and the third is the father of the family. The Lord of Heaven is the creator of heaven, earth and all things, and humanity is not filial if it does not venerate Him. When man disobeyed the Lord of Heaven, many disasters occurred as a consequence. Here Ricci introduces one of the mysteries of faith: the Incarnation of Jesus – *yesu*. Out of compassion, the Lord of Heaven descended to earth and was incarnated as a man, Jesus, and spread his teachings on earth for thirty-three years. Ricci explains, again, that if the Chinese had not heard of his teachings it is because when an emperor in the Han dynasty heard about them, the ambassadors he sent on a mission to find those canonical writings took the road to India by mistake and adopted the Buddhist sutras instead. In the end Ricci succeeds in convincing the Chinese scholar to be a follower of the Lord of Heaven; and he wants to go through the door that leads to the Way, so he must first receive the holy water – *sheng shui*.

Now that we know more about the core themes of each chapter of Ricci's TZSY, let us underline some general aspects of this catechism. We have already made reference to the extent of Valignano's influence on Ricci's TZSY. One of the aspects mentioned was scholastic argumentation and dialectical reasoning. Ricci followed these guidelines in China and managed – with the help of his friends – to find the most adequate terms, at the risk of oversimplifying certain Chinese concepts. In this regard, Ricci's argumentation on the existence of God derives from Aristotelian metaphysics – let us remember that in Aristotle's metaphysics knowledge is knowledge of the cause. So Ricci introduced the four causes in Chinese, and causality too, translated as *suoyiran*, to explain why things are what they are.[34] He also introduced the terms 'substance' and 'accident' to prove the existence of one God, creator and keeper of all things. In general terms, Ricci's TZSY is a proof of his struggle to find concepts to transmit his ideas, often forcing them into tight categories. We find an example in the term 'reason', 'principle' or 'intellect' – *li*. *Li* is far from being a clear-cut Chinese concept. The notion of *li* – a key term in Neo-Confucian thought – generally means the immanent principle of things. However that may be, Ricci's TZSY found its own Confucian tone, in turn feeding on other Jesuit doctrinal texts, like Ruggieri's TZSY and Valignano's *Catechismus*.

In both mission spaces, Jesuits Acosta and Ricci managed to redirect doctrine to be conceived as authoritative and exclusive; indeed, both of them defined and set the doctrinal guidelines, with their DCC and TZSY respectively, from the moment they were published onward. In Peru, Acosta was fully supported by the colonial authorities who decided that the DCC catechisms were the only ones approved to circulate throughout the Viceroyalty of Peru. In China, Ricci was fully supported by Visitor Valignano to circulate the TZSY, in turn replacing Ruggieri's TZSL. The good reception that the TZSY found in the literati circles ran parallel to what became an internal affair among these Jesuits. This did not mean that Ricci's interpretations and translations would not later be criticized in the seventeenth century; this already happened in the case of the superior who succeeded him, Niccolò Longobardo, as shown in Chapter Five. However that may be, the point is that both catechisms – the DCC and the TZSY – became major demarcation lines, leaving a past – more or less recent – behind. Where Acosta and Ricci part ways is in the main tools they used to transmit doctrine. In the case of Ricci, natural reason – *la ragione naturale* as he would say in his native tongue – was the cornerstone of expounding the teachings of the Lord of Heaven. But, for Acosta, natural reason was completely out of the question, and explicit faith in Christ became the path to salvation, through simple unsophisticated reasons, accommodated to the Indians' capacity. Last but not least, as a general overview of the two catechisms and what they had in common, the authoritative doctrine in them does not – does not intend to – ignore the local context. Whether they adapted to it or just impugned its nature, the catechisms were not intended to be abstract doctrines, meaning by 'abstract' an 'exported' orthodoxy from Europe expected to be imposed while ignoring the question of 'where'. In this sense, we could say that both the DCC and Ricci's TZSY are what we could consider *ad hoc* doctrines. The next chapter focuses on 'doctrinal intersections' between the DCC and the TZSY; on precisely how these catechisms adapted the core shared Christian truths.

Notes

1 These texts have been thoroughly analysed by Juan Carlos Estenssoro (see Estenssoro 2003) and Alan Durston (Durston 2007).
2 Constitutions 38 and 39 are dedicated to the *Instrucción*.
3 In this version – in constitution 39 – there is a mention of the mysteries of the Trinity and the Incarnation; see also Estenssoro (2003: 58–59).
4 For these similarities see Estenssoro (2003: 583–86); Alan Durston (2007: 69).

5 Estenssoro underlines the silenced doctrinal themes: the Trinity, mention of Christ, the Church – although the Virgin is mentioned very briefly – along with an explanation of the immortality of the soul based on a comparison between men and beasts, using expressions borrowed from the *Instrucción* of 1551 and the *Plática*.

6 From the ninety-eighth constitution onwards.

7 Viceroy Toledo to the King, Los Reyes, 8 de Febrero de 1570. The *yanaconas* were individuals who had left their *ayllus* – Andean communities – and worked at a variety of tasks for the Inca and after the conquest they assisted the Spaniards as servants, in *encomiendas* or in military forces.

8 Constitutions 76 to 78 inclusive, under the title *De Parochis* (Vargas Ugarte: 1951: 193–95).

9 In the late 1570s Toledo established a Quechua Chair with wide-raging powers at the University of San Marcos.

10 Even though references and mention of this problem are scattered throughout *De Procuranda*, the fourth book deals specifically with this problem, especially from chapters three to nine, in which Acosta insists on this problematic aspect of evangelization in the Andes.

11 In the third chapter of the second action of the TLC constitution 'On the composition and edition of a catechism', the exclusiveness of this catechism had to be guaranteed under pain of excommunication if priests did not comply with it, a penalty also applicable to the Quechua and Aymara translations (Lisi 1990: 125).

12 The order does not follow that of the Roman catechism: the Sign of the Cross, the Pater Noster, the Hail Mary, the Creed – following the scholastic division into fourteen articles instead of the twelve articles in the Roman catechism – the Salve Regina, the articles of faith – fourteen: seven articles concerning the Godhead and seven articles on the human nature of Christ – the Commandments of the law of God, the commandments of the Holy Church, the Sacraments, the works of mercy – seven corporeal and seven spiritual – the theological and cardinal virtues, the capital sins, the enemies of the soul, the four *novissimos* and a general confession.

13 The themes are introduced in this order: introduction to the Christian doctrine, the Symbol, the sacraments, the commandments of the law of God, the commandments of the Church, works of mercy and the Pater Noster.

14 Acosta claims that catechisms at that time did not include the mystery of the Church because they followed the articles of faith divided into the seven articles referring to the divinity of Christ and the seven referring to his humanity, instead of considering the order of the Creed. See Lopetegui (1942: 529) and J.G. Durán (1982: 245 onward).

15 The full title is *Annotaciones, o Scolios, sobre la traduccion de la Doctrina christiana y Catecismo en las lenguas Quichua y Aymara. Con la declaracion de las phrases, y vocablos que tienen alguna dificultad, los quales se hallará por su ordé de Alfabeto.*

16 In the *Annotaciones Generales de la Lengua Aymara* these are the nations mentioned: '*Aymaraes, Cachis, Canas, Contes, Collas, Lupazas, Pacajas, Charcas, Carangas, Quillazas, y otras naciones* and other nations' (DCC: 175).

17 The title is complemented with the addition, *For Priests and other Ministers to preach and teach the Indians and the rest of the people. In Accordance with the Provisions of the Provincial Council of Lima'* (DCC: 333).

18 Javier Castillo Arroyo claims there are no doubts about the Quechua translation team, thanks to a document at the Archivo Eclesiástico de Lima that proves its composition. See J. Castillo Arroyo (1966: 44). Alan Durston followed the same source in the Archivo del Cabildo Metropolitano de Lima, so he draws the same

conclusions regarding the four translators and the six others who approved the translations. See A. Durston (2007: 97).

19 Pierre Duviols stresses this strong anti-idolatrous tone of the *Tercero cathecismo,* ascribing it to the Society of Jesus and responding to one of the Society's wishes: to provide the materials that would prepare the terrain for the extirpation of idolatry. Duviols make special reference to sermons XVIII, XIX and XX. However, they do not correspond with the numbers of the sermons in the edition consulted for this book, Luciano Pereña (ed.)(1985), *Doctrina Christiana y Catecismo para Instruccion de Indios,* Facsimile of the trilingual text, Corpus Hispanorum de Pace, Volumen XXVI-2, Madrid, Consejo Superior de Investigaciones Cientificas, which here I cite as DCC.

20 DCC, *Tercero catecismo, por sermones,* Sermón XVIII: 537–48; Sermón XIX: 564– 81; and Sermón XXIII: 624–42.

21 Michael Puett interprets the origin of *Di* as a spirit – not ancestral or natural – in the Shang Dynasty. According to Puett, one of the Shang cult's concerns was to anthropomorphize the spirit world, i.e. to make the deceased into proper ancestors and to have the ancestors guide the nature spirits and *Di* (Puett 2002: 47 onward).

22 Joseph Shih agrees with D'Elia that, when comparing the Latin version – the *Vera Expositio* – and the Chinese text – the TZSL – the former must be the original Latin version of the Chinese catechism. Shih is in discussion with P.Tacchi Venturi, Louis Pfister and H.Bernand-Maitre, who believe that the Latin text is a translation of the Chinese text. See Shih (1964: 21). The Latin version can be found in Tacchi Venturi (OS, II: 498–540).

23 Shih also states that in the Roman archives of the Society of Jesus, the Portuguese– Chinese dictionary written by Ruggieri and Ricci contains several other documents, for instance a Chinese dialogue in Roman characters by Ruggieri, entitled *Pin-cian uen-ta ssi-gni* and a Discourse in Chinese characters, that D'Elia entitles 'Catechetical Conversations', and which he attributes to Ricci. But Shih states that the author is Ruggieri rather than Ricci (Shih 1964: 14).

24 D'Elia has translated this text. This Christian doctrine is about the existence of God, his attributes, the creation, the worship of the one true God, rewards and punishments in the hereafter, Adam and Eve, original sin, the Incarnation, Jesus, his passion and crucifixion, his resurrection and ascension, and the Apostles and their preaching of the Gospel throughout the world (D' Elia 1935).

25 D'Elia analyzes certain aspects of Ruggieri's Latin text and the TZSL, providing an index by chapters of the Latin version. The latter does not coincide exactly with the TZSL (D'Elia 1934).

26 D'Elia provides a translation of the Ten Commandments into Italian (1934: 195).

27 There are minor differences, e.g. in the third chapter of Ruggieri's TZSL, 'An explanation of the false claims to knowledge of the Lord of Heaven that men make' we find *mao ren,* that here I translate as 'false claim', and in Ricci's TZSY there is the idea of 'misconceptions' – *cuo ren.*

28 See Alejandro Valignano S.I. [1583] (1954) In the Introduction, there are fragments of Cabral's catechism in Portuguese (taken from a letter to Tawara Chikahiro), contrasted with that by Valignano in Latin in folio 14 of the second book of his *Catechismus,* and the similarities are noticeable (Sumario: 139–42).

29 Some passages of Valignano's *Catechismus Christianae Fidei,* which will be analyzed below, are taken from the nineteenth chapter of his *Historia del Principio y progresso de la Compañia de Jesús en la Indias Orientales* (1583) and, in turn, this chapter draws on the three preliminary chapters of the *Sumario de las Cosas de Japón* (Sumario: 178–85).

30 Ricci is referring to the printing blocks where the characters are engraved for future printing.
31 One of the Mahayana Buddhism precepts is that all natural phenomena participate in the same essence or substance.
32 The translators of the TZSY into English, Douglas Lancashire and Peter Hu Kuo-chen SJ point out this reference to the Ten Commandments (Ricci [1603] 1985: 303).
33 *Dao* does not refer to Daoism. It is a term usually found in ancient literature, which means a correct, orthodox, way of proceeding. And this is the meaning Ricci adopts.
34 Analyzing translation as a means of cultural transmission, Nicolas Standaert points out how translation work entailed creating not only new terminology but also a new style. Regarding this particular term, the new mathematical discourse aimed to show 'that through which things are the way they are' (*suo yi ran*), providing not only methods (*fa*), but also explanations (*yi*) (Standaert: 2001: 100). Joachim Kurtz suggests that Ricci's translation of '*suo yi ran*' links an Aristotelian term to a notion of long tradition in Confucian natural and moral philosophy, thus implicitly demanding equal dignity (Kurtz 2011: 31).

5 Christian truths in the Andean and Chinese settings

Both the *Doctrina christiana y Catecismo* (DCC) and the *Tianzhu Shiyi* (TZSY) represent and embody a doctrine set out as dominant and authoritative enough to dismiss the catechisms that preceded them in the respective mission contexts of Peru and China. Both being catechisms, they approach core Christian truths: the existence of God – the Lord of Heaven in China – the creator of all things in the universe; that he is the only God of all men, who are endowed with a corruptible body and an immortal soul and who can either be rewarded in heaven or punished in hell.

This chapter focuses on how these core Christian principles are interwoven according to the specificity of the mission space in which they were introduced. In both spaces the missionaries had to make complex belief systems comprehensible by resorting to a familiar – and limited – canon of European concepts. In the China mission, the Jesuits soon found opponents who objected to their views and interpretation of Chinese thought. In fact, even the Jesuits themselves did not see eye to eye when it came to translating religion according to Confucian tenets. In Peru, the Spanish had consistently disparaged the Indians' views of the world and tried to impose their own. The Andean population had to adapt, but adaptation never meant the abandonment of the their religious practices. Apart from exploring the interweaving of the Christian tenets, this chapter approaches the obstructed dialogues and miscommunications in the mission spaces.

Dios, Viracocha, Tianzhu, Shang di: different names for one creator God

From the alleged creator Viracocha to the idolatrous huacas in Peru

As we know, the Europeans brought to the New World with them the belief that, as rational beings created in the image of God, human beings were able to recognize his existence through reason, together with a natural inclination to love God as the supreme being. This idea of a supreme being, omniscient and more powerful than men, soon found a name in a local deity in Peru: *Viracocha*. According to pre-Columbian Andean myths which the first chroniclers reproduced, *Viracocha* was responsible for a dualist organization of the Andean space in an upper half, *hanan*, and a lower half, *urin*. Each of these spaces was defined as a *suyu*, and was in turn subdivided in halves, resulting in the four parts of the – Andean – world: *Chinchaysuyu, Collasuyu, Antisuyu* and *Cuntisuyu*. Each half, upper and lower, was represented by a deity. According to the first chroniclers, *Viracocha* was a celestial deity whose domain belonged to the upper part of the world. Moreover, according to this dualist notion of opposition and complementarity, while *Viracocha* was a heavenly male deity with solar features, there was a female earth deity known as *Pachamama* who matched *Viracocha* in the upper half. However, neither *Viracocha* nor *Pachamama* were exclusive names for the deities respectively identified with heaven and earth. This was notable particularly in the case of *Viracocha*, who also had local denominations like *Pachacamac* – especially along the Peruvian coast – or *Tunapa*, both of which referred to a deity with similar characteristics. *Viracocha* was part of a cyclic mythical tradition in the Andes referring to a set of accounts in which the *Viracocha* heroes, with different assignments, played a key role. It was one of the mythical cycles in the pre-Columbian tradition, and coexisted with others such as the non-Cuzco Andean myths of *Huarochirí* (Urbano 1981: XVIII–XIX). The anonymous Huarochirí Manuscript, written in the first decade of the seventeenth century, is the only colonial Quechua text of clear indigenous authorship. It is a book-length account of the religious lore of the Huarochirí province of the central Peruvian highlands, which alternates between narratives of the deeds of the local deities – *huacas* – and ethnographic descriptions of ritual practices, collected by the secular cleric Francisco de Ávila. Instead of the historical revelation brought by the Spanish, in the Andes we find a cyclical sequence in which there is no elimination of 'defeated' deities in successive cycles. Even though their status or influence might vary in the sacred realm, these vanquished deities continued to be active (Pease 1999: 136–41). In this regard, as Henrique Urbano claims, the introduction of the Judeo-Christian mythical discourse altered both the conditions for the production of pre-Columbian mythical discourses and the foundations of their logic (1981: XVIII–XXII).

Among the first chroniclers, Juan de Betanzos states that *Viracocha* was the proper Quechua term for 'god', which suggests that his catechetical texts in Quechua from the 1540s employed this name (Durston 2007: 210). Acosta recounts that *Viracocha* was acknowledged as the supreme Lord and maker of all things in Peru. This explains why those who preached the Gospel to the Indians

> had hardly any difficulty in convincing them that there is a supreme God and Lord of all things and that this is the God of Christians and the true God. However, it has greatly surprised me that they did not have their own word to name God ... whereby those who preach or write for the Indians use our word in Spanish, *Dios*, accommodating

the pronunciation and sentences of the Indian languages, which are very diverse.

(HNyM: 141–42)

In turn, the Anonymous Jesuit (see Chapter 3) begins his treatise *De las Costumbres Antiguas de los Naturales del Piru* – On the Ancient Customs of the Natives of Peru – by claiming that *Illa Tecce* – eternal light – is the maker of the world, heaven and earth, the sun and the moon, to which the 'moderns' added the name *Viracocha*, meaning 'Immense God of Peru' (Anónima (1968) 153). As mentioned in the first part of the book, we have access to the Jesuit Blas Valera's view through Garcilaso's *Comentarios Reales de los Incas*, and Garcilaso states that 'Father Blas Valera, interpreting the significance of this name – *Viracocha* – called it *Numen*, which means "God's will and power"':

> besides worshiping the Sun as a visible God, to whom they offered sacrifices and celebrations, the Inca kings and the *amautas* [the philosophers] traced the true God our Lord through natural light, the creator of heaven and earth whom they called *Pachacamac*. It is a compound name: *Pacha*, the word for universe, and *Cámac*, the past participle of the verb *cama*, 'to animate', which means *anima* [soul]. *Pachacamac* means 'the one who animates the universe'.

(Garcilaso [1609] 1945: 66)

According to Garcilaso – and Valera – a problematic issue was that the Indians did not know how to explain these things using their own terms, while the Spanish, who were by no means straightforward in their questioning about these things, in turn preconceived them as devilish. This attitude was also the result of the Spaniards' ignorance of the general language of the Incas – Quechua. Therefore, states Garcilaso, they named God *Ticsi Viracocha*, which 'I do not know what it means, and neither do they'. Garcilaso insists that the Incas worshiped *Pachacamac* as the supreme God and lord, and he refers to *Viracocha* as a spirit that came as a vision to a prince and heir of the Incas, introducing himself as the son of the Sun (Garcilaso [1609] 1945: 67–71). For Andean historians like Guaman Poma de Ayala, who both reconsidered and revised the Andean religion of the Incas, *Viracocha* was not only the creator of the world and all things in it, but was also the single ancestor of a lineage. Guaman Poma established parallel Andean and European chronologies connected by the conquest. In the first Andean age, *uari Viracocha runa*, the cult of the most ancient deity in Cuzco–*Viracocha* – represented the moment of the greatest knowledge of the biblical God. These origins and the biblical ancestry, together with apostolic preaching, became the prototype of 'true' original Christianity (Pease 1981: 24–29). At the very beginning of his chronological narration of Andean history, Guaman Poma denies the validity of the titles concerning the right of the Spanish to spread the gospel. The chronicler invalidates them by attributing the presence of the historical cross of Carabuco to a visit by St. Bartholomew, apostle of Christ. He explicitly makes the point that this visit established Christianity in Peru prior to the arrival of the Spanish (Adorno 2000: 27).

Scholars like Urbano and Duviols have pointed out that the Spaniards needed to make of *Viracocha* an omnipotent and omniscient creator 'god'. Duviols offers a first explanation within the theological framework of the sixteenth-century missionaries, i.e. that the Spanish needed to believe that the Indians had come to a notion of the existence of a supreme being, maker of all things in the world, also called the 'first cause' by the Europeans. This belief not only became a convenient argument to use against the Andean *huacas*, but the notion that the Indians had of a 'first cause' also indicated that they were halfway toward cognition of the 'true' God. All that was left to the Spaniards was the task of showing the Indians the revelation of 'the true and only God, creator of all things'. In sum, right from the beginning some Spaniards manipulated the name *Viracocha* into one sole character and one sole function, that of 'creator and maker of all things'. Duviols uses the example of José de Acosta to show the Jesuits' serious mistake of considering that *Pachacamac* was not an autonomous deity, but just an epithet of *Viracocha*, like *Pachayachachic* (Duviols 1977: 53–54):

> Even though darkness of infidelity dims the understanding of those nations, in many things the light of truth and reason still has an influence on them; so they usually acknowledge and confess to a supreme lord, maker of all things, which in Peru they call *Viracocha*, and add a name of excellency, like *Pachacamac* or *Pachayachachic*, creator of heaven and earth, or *Usapu* … . Him they worship, and this was the principal that they venerated looking up into the sky.
>
> (HNyM: 145)

Indeed, discovering who the Andean creator 'god' was represented a difficult task for men obsessed with accuracy. The names attributed to 'god' in the Andes changed and resisted any kind of tight definition, posing this conundrum: Is there one or many *Viracocha*? (Bernand and Gruzinski 1992: 95). As Estenssoro points out, be it as a result of translation or periphrasis, a name or an attribute, or an indigenous or Spanish initiative, three pre-Hispanic names, *Viracocha*, *Pachacamac* and *Tunupa* soon became related to 'God', Christ or any of the apostles. The Spaniards acknowledged their status as deities and were unable to reduce them to idols because, even though they might have been regarded as 'false gods', the fact that creation was ascribed to them prevented the worship of them from being seen as idolatrous. In New Spain – modern Mexico – the Christian God was designated primarily by the Spanish term *Dios*, but the Náhuatl word *teotl* was used as a generic term for 'god' and thus it could be applied to 'the one true God'. The translation of *teotl* as *dios* – god – during the whole colonial period contributed to creating both an assimilation and an opposition between the 'ancient gods' and the 'true one'. Unlike in New Spain, where the generic term for 'god' was expressed with the Nahuatl term *teotl*, in Peru the term '*huaca*' soon became identified with 'idol' and, what is more, the deities, the *huacas*, were defined and perpetuated as 'idols' (Estenssoro 2003: 94–96). Idolatry in Peru manifested itself – according to Acosta in his *Historia Natural y Moral* – above all in the *huacas* – regional Andean deities – generally places or objects linked to an ancestor or protector (see chapter 3, p. 96 note 16) – which Acosta, like many other Spaniards, usually defined as *adoratorios*, i.e. places of worship (HNyM: 140). Acosta's influence – via Polo de Ondegardo – is clearly reflected in the DCC, where natural phenomena and their idolatry were the greatest competitors of the unique creator God. This was a form of idolatry that Acosta attributes exclusively to Peru and was regarded by the Jesuit as less pernicious than the idolatry of the Mexicans, for their idolatry was expressed in idols alone, without including natural phenomena (HNyM: 143–44). Acosta never regarded *Viracocha* as a real threat, like the *huacas*. However, when the Jesuit follows Polo de Ondegardo more closely, *Viracocha* is a *huaca*, the principal one worshiped by the Incas. Indeed, in his *Historia*, Acosta classifies the different types of idolatry under the title 'On the First Genre of Idolatry of Natural and Universal Things' – *Del Primer Género de Idolatría de Cosas Naturales y Universales* – basing himself on Polo's report.[1] Here, *Viracocha* and the sun are introduced as *huacas* – or *adoratorios* – followed by a third *huaca*, thunder:

> After *Viracocha* or the supreme, the sun is the one most worshiped among the infidels, along with other things that in celestial or elemental nature are known as the moon, bright stars, the sea, the earth. The Incas, masters of Peru, after *Viracocha* and the sun, placed thunder as the third *guaca* – or *adoratorio* – most worshiped, which they called by three names: *Chuqilla*, *Catuilla* and *Intillapa*, featuring it as a man in heaven with a slingshot … . This was a *huaca* for all the Indians in Peru, to which they offered various sacrifices.
>
> (HNyM: 142–43)

Thus, it can be inferred that these nuances in Acosta's statements regarding *Viracocha* also depend on the sources the Jesuit is considering. As mentioned above, in this part of the *Historia Natural y Moral*, Acosta is following Polo de Ondegardo literally, especially the chapter in Polo's treatise 'On *Huacas* and Idols' (Polo [1571] 1916: 5). The same references can be found in the DCC, in the section entitled 'Indian Rites. Errors and Superstitions of the Indians Taken from the Treatises and Inquiries Made by the Licenciado Polo de Ondegardo' (DDC: 265).

One main goal of the DCC is to uphold monotheism as opposed to the worship of natural phenomena. Acosta acknowledges the Book of Wisdom in this regard, for one can take from it 'wonderful and effective arguments to convince people about the great deception of heathen idolaters, who would rather serve and worship the creature than the Creator' (HNyM: 144). In the Brief catechism – *Catecismo Breve* –, the stress is placed on natural phenomena:

> P: The Sun, the Moon, the Stars, the Bright Star, Lightning, are they not God?
>   R. None of that is God, but creatures made by God who made heaven and earth and everything in them for man's own good.
>
> (DCC: 47)

However, the focus on breaching the first commandment changes throughout the DCC. In the Greater catechism – *Catecismo Mayor* –, he who breaks the commandment to honour God is 'He who worships any creature or has idols or *guacas*, or gives credit to false sects and heresies, or dreams and omens, which are vanity and deceit of the Devil' (DCC: 135–36). Finally, this issue of the worship of natural phenomena is repeated in the Third catechism, by sermons, and addresses the eventual chaos and disorder brought by belief in more than one god:

> Do not believe, my children, that one God rules in heaven, one on earth, one in the sea and another in livestock … neither is there one God for the *Viracochas* and another one for the Indians. Thus it was said by your ancestors … . Don't you realize that, in the world of men, when there are many lords there is war and trouble and things go wrong? … because each wants to have a hold over the other.
>
> (DCC: 405)

Tianzhu and Shang di: the Chinese names for 'God'

In the Andes, the Spaniards believed they had found in the local deity *Viracocha* proof of the Andeans acknowledging a supreme being, which made the task easier of showing the Indians the revelation of the true and only God. In turn, the Jesuits in China appropriated the name *Tianzhu*, the Lord of Heaven, who became the Chinese version of the Christian God. Indeed, the China mission was no exception to the need of Europeans to introduce the notion of a unique God, an omniscient and omnipresent creator. Michele Ruggieri and Matteo Ricci were the first to take on this task. Taking advice from a Chinese convert, the Jesuits chose the word *Tianzhu* as a local term for the Christian God, with the difference that Ricci alternated between *Tianzhu* and *Shangdi* – the Lord on High – in his TZSY, while Ruggieri stuck to *Tianzhu* exclusively. As one of the 'unconscious' borrowings – quoting Jacques Gernet – by the Jesuits, *Tianzhu* is the Chinese translation of *Devapanti*, representing a deity of second order in the Buddhist pantheon.

Tianzhu, of whom there were millions, rule the worlds of the cosmos and are, by definition transitory (Dehergne 1983: 23; Gernet 1979: 409). Both Ricci and Ruggieri tried to prove the universality of the doctrine of the Lord of Heaven, the sole creator of all things, who was accessible to all men through natural reason, and they insisted on this aspect in a chapter in both their catechisms about men's misconceptions – or false cognition, as in Ruggieri's TZSL – concerning the Lord of Heaven. To a European audience, Ricci explained that, because the Chinese language does not have a name corresponding to *Dio* – God, in his native Italian – and because *Dio* cannot be pronounced in Chinese because it lacks the letter 'd', they started to name God *Tianzhu*, which means Lord of Heaven. Furthermore, Ricci claims

> this serves their purpose very well, because, as the Chinese worship Heaven as the supreme numen, and many of them think that it is material, with the same name that we gave to God is explicitly expressed how superior our God is to what they have as supreme numen [Heaven], for God is its Master.
>
> (FR I:193)

Ricci thus tried to assimilate the Christian God with the Lord of Heaven or the Lord on High – *Shang di* – the latter being present in the Chinese classics. In fact, his proposal of a return to an ancient Confucianism free of the influence of 'false doctrines' like Buddhism and Daoism fed on the Chinese canonical books and the references to the Lord on High that they contain, which Ricci often exchanged with the Lord of Heaven. As Ricci states in his TZSY, 'our Lord of Heaven is called the Lord on High in Chinese'; he takes this idea further in saying that 'our Lord of Heaven is the Lord on High of the – Chinese – ancient canonical texts. In short, the Lord of Heaven and the Lord on High differ only in name (TZSY II: 415, I–V; 416, VI–VII). Some years later in his *Tuiyan zhengdao lun*, the Jesuit Alfonso Vagnone (1566–1640) would follow Ricci's steps by using many quotations from the Chinese Classics to prove that *Shangdi* is equal to *Tianzhu* (Standaert 1985: 25).

One of the first attributes of the Lord of Heaven in the Jesuit version was creation *ex nihilo*, an aspect of the divine that Ruggieri and Ricci introduced. Of course, this was an alien notion to Chinese thought, according to which the world as an organic order is not perceived outside of men, and the man who finds his place in it cannot perceive himself outside the world (Cheng 2002: 50). Indeed, if ancestor worship in pre-modern China developed from the worship of a supreme deity – ancestor *par excellence* – it was not conceived of as an all-powerful creator force or first principle *ex nihilo*. In short, the idea of a once-and-for-all *ex-nihilo* creation that the Jesuits tried to impose from the very start was completely alien to traditional Chinese thought in all its major variants.[2] Thus, this particular aspect became an almost unbridgeable gap between traditional Chinese thought and the creationist standpoint of the Jesuits (Zürcher 1995: 140–44).

However, the Lord of Heaven soon found a 'local competitor' in the Great Ultimate, the *Taiji*, which was highly predominant in Neo-Confucian thought from thinker Zhou Dunyi (1017–73) onwards, and Ricci tried his best to dismiss it. In a letter to General Acquaviva, Ricci explains the concept of *Taiji*, as a new doctrine:

> In this book [TZSY] rather than attacking what they [the Chinese] say, we prefer to twist it around so it will fit the idea of God. That way, it will not seem that we are following the ideas of the Chinese but that they follow ours. And since many of the men of letters ruling in China would be offended if we attacked this principle [*Taiji*], we have tried to question their explanation of the principle rather than the principle itself.
>
> (FR II: 297–98, note 1; Gernet 1985: 27)[3]

According to Erik Zürcher, Ricci might have been toying with the idea of reinterpreting the Great Ultimate in such a way that it could be used as an equivalent of the Christian creator God. This can be observed in the Latin summary of his TZSY, in which he concludes his discussion of *Taikieus – Taiji* – with the following remark: 'If [the Chinese] understood *Taiji* to be the first principle, substantial, endowed with intelligence and infinite, we would truly recognize it to be God, and nothing else' (Zürcher 1995: 162–63; Ricci [1603] (1985), Introduction and Notes by Lancashire and Hu 1985: 483).[4]

Christian creationism would eventually be rejected by some Buddhist authors of the late Ming period. Buddhist monks, and in particular the prominent scholar-monks who in this period played an important role as leaders of a Buddhist revival, had every reason to oppose Christianity. This was in part because the Jesuits were their direct competitors in the struggle for high-class patronage and also because they must have been irritated by the Jesuits' extremely negative attitude toward both Buddhism and the Buddhist clergy, not to mention their almost complete ignorance of Buddhist doctrine (Zürcher 1995: 153–54). Among their anti-Christian arguments, the primary one referred to the identity of the Christian creator God. In the Buddhist worldview, rebirth as a god is merely the highest of the five – or six – karmic destinations; it is the result of the acquisition of a considerable amount of karmic merit. However, unlike Buddhas, Buddhist gods are in no way transcendental. They enjoy their divine status for a certain period, after which they exhaust their merit and are reborn at a lower level, according to a multi-layered hierarchy extending from the lowest heaven to the upper 'limit of existence'. Zhu Hong (1535–1615), one of the eminent Buddhist monks that Zürcher analyses in an account of an early reaction – 1613 – to Christian teachings, identified the Christian Lord of Heaven with the god Sakra, who is the head of the Trayastrimsa heaven. Sakra is a rather low-ranking potentate in the celestial hierarchy, for his domain still belongs to this world. In short, he is only a minor deity (Zürcher 1995: 153; Gernet 1985: 294). Buddhist criticisms of the Jesuit mission during the late Ming period were anthologized in the Collected Refutations of Heterodoxy or *Pixie ji*. In the introduction to this work, the Chinese Buddhist monk Ouyi Zhixu (1599–1655) regarded it as regrettable that no one had seriously engaged the Jesuits' writings in order to refute them systematically. Zhixu had read four of the Jesuit publications and responded to them in detail. A first part of Zhixu's treatise is a 'Preliminary Investigation' inspired by his reading of a piece attributed to the Chinese convert Xu Guanqi entitled Short Explanation of the Sacred Images or *Tianzhu shengxiang lueshuo* (Handbook: 615). It is followed by a second part, 'Further Investigation', that focuses on three other Jesuit works: Ricci's TZSY, João Soeiro's Brief Account of the Religion of the Lord of Heaven or *Tianzhu Shenjiao Yueyan*, and Giulio Aleni's Recorded scholarly discussions from Fuzhou or *Sanshan lunxue ji*. As mentioned above, Zhixu lamented that no one had so far refuted the Jesuits' writings, which is why 'the disciples of Ricci and Aleni have become numerous, and the wind of heterodoxy grows hotter' (Jones 2009: 352). One of the – many – things that Zhixu criticizes in the TZSY is Ricci's belief in only one cosmos and, therefore, only one Lord in it. In Buddhist cosmology there are multiple worlds and so there can be multiple lords, even though each world can have only one lord. Secondly, Zhixu sees Ricci as positing a pre-existent Lord who is self-sufficient and creates all things without being affected by them. To this, Zhixu opposes the Buddhist doctrine of interdependence, in which lines of causality move in all directions at once. The Lord of Heaven could not be what he is independently of creation and therefore creatures create him as well as vice versa (Jones 2009: 365). There can be no doubt that the Jesuits were able to convince Chinese converts of the story of creation, which was alien to Chinese thought. Nevertheless, outside the circle of believers the reaction to the Jesuit message ranged from pointed criticism to outright rejection (Zürcher 1995: 163). Moreover, some objections to Ricci's translations and interpretations also came from some of the Jesuits who followed him in China. Niccolò Longobardo (1559–1654), who succeeded Ricci as the Superior of the China Mission, objected to Ricci's exposition of one creator God in the Chinese version. In Longobardo's view, the Christian God was not *Tianzhu*. He acknowledges that 'Matteo Ricci has been the first to openly state that the ancient Chinese knew the true God, *Shang di*, that is, the Lord on High' (Longobardi 1701: 56).[5] But Longobardo begs to differ, and actually thinks the contrary, for

> according to the principles of ancient Chinese Philosophy, neither the ancient nor the modern have ever known a first efficient cause who created *ex nihilo* all things by his own will and power; but they had cognition of only a first material and bodily principle, unlike that of faith.
>
> (Longobardi 1701: 56)

In short, the man Ricci had designated as his successor as superior of the mission, Niccolò Longobardo, began to have scruples about aspects of Ricci's interpretation of Confucianism (Rule 1986: 74). Moreover, after Ricci's death, misgivings about the use of these terms arose among the Jesuits in Japan, who found in Longobardo an advocate of their views. They had a common base with the China mission in Macao and had made use of some of the Chinese works of their colleagues in China; and it was then that they became disturbed at certain policies in this mission. They felt that the use of Chinese terms for the Christian God was dangerous and that the distinctiveness and integrity of the Christian message was compromised by an identification, even partial and critical, with Confucianism. At the instigation of João Rodrigues, the foremost expert on Japanese language and culture among the missionaries, the Society's superiors in East Asia opened an inquiry into the Chinese terms employed to signify Christian concepts. Between 1613 and 1615 Rodrigues had travelled through China, visiting the mission's residences and conversing with Chinese converts. In short, the most important point at issue in Rodrigues' objections to the way Matteo Ricci and his successors had promoted Christianity in the Ming empire rested on their use of what was regarded as dubious doctrinal terminology.

The terms that caused the most problems were *Tian* – heaven; *Shangdi* – Lord on High; *Tianzhu* – Lord of Heaven; *Tianshen* – angels; and *Linghun* – rational soul (Brockey 2007: 84 onward). This became a controversy, or controversial discussion, within the Society of Jesus. Later on, Franciscans and Dominicans in China would object to the Jesuits' methods; they argued that the native Chinese terminology for God and the Chinese rites regarding ancestors and Confucius did violate the teachings of Christianity. The controversy about whether to choose, as in Japan, a Latin transliteration to name the Christian God or a Chinese term lasted within the Society of Jesus until the early 1630s and ended with the decision to use Chinese names.

On Jesus Christ

The previous chapter made reference to how Acosta in Peru, on the one hand, and Michele Ruggieri and Matteo Ricci in China, on the other, introduced Jesus Christ in their respective catechisms.

In Peru, it was vitally necessary to teach the Indians and all infidels the mystery of Christ. In fact, according to Acosta, 'to exclude a lineage [the Indians] from this general rule of men is a serious mistake, not to speak of heresy, as some important authors – i.e. Domingo de Soto – state without any doubt' (De Proc: 552). In Peru, knowledge of Jesus Christ was directly related to salvation. Acosta was here solving one of the major conundrums following the conquest. How could Christ have been the saviour of the indigenous people of the Americas? How could they be saved through his redemptive grace without even hearing his name? (O' Collins 1995: 208–09). Acosta's discussion is also with the Spanish theologians. His insistence on salvation through explicit faith in Jesus Christ was not only related to the inquisitorial trial of Francisco de la Cruz in Peru, but it was also at the same time connected with a theological debate that took place in the Council of Trent and in which Acosta continued to participate from Peru. As we know, the conquest of a 'New world' had created a real quandary – that of the salvation of the infidels – and theologians had to provide solutions for it. That the infidels could be saved without the knowledge of God and through the practice of moral law was one of the first solutions. However, it required making certain adjustments to avoid the risk of mistaking these ideas with Pelagianism, which denied the need for the grace of God and held that man could be saved on his own. A need for an equivalent of faith, a knowledge of God independent of evangelical preaching but supernatural in itself, was then required. Some called this an implicit faith, comprising the only two truths that St Paul demanded for salvation, i.e. that there is only one God and that he is a rewarder. This implicit faith excluded knowledge of the mysteries of the Trinity and Jesus Christ, and theologians like Domingo de Soto and Andrés de Vega, among others, believed it to be sufficient for the salvation of the Indians (Mateos 1945: 582–87). Soto had taken part in the Council of Trent from its outset and had composed and dedicated to it *De Natura et Gratia* in 1547, in which he outlined a theory of the salvation of the Indians. He accepted – albeit temporarily – that salvation was most likely possible without explicit faith in Christ, i.e. without the supernatural but just through the knowledge and practice of natural law. In writing *De Procuranda*, Acosta was not only arguing with Domingo de Soto, but also with Melchor Cano, Andrés Vega and Juan Gallo, who also stated – with some variations – that salvation without faith in Christ was possible. Cano strongly refuted the idea that the salvation of the infidels was possible by natural reason: a real and strict faith was necessary. However, regarding the mysteries of Christ, it sufficed that this faith be implicit. In his chapters on this subject, Acosta does not mention these names explicitly, but he let his reference to their ideas be understood (Lopetegui 1942: 273–83).

At this point we might wonder how a native Quechua speaker could understand or interpret Jesus Christ. Jan Szeminski has analyzed the Quechua text of the 'articles of faith' comprised in the *Doctrina* of the DCC to find answers to this question (DCC: 27–31). Jesus was identified with Pachacamac, as a 'Lord of the lower world'; Pachacamac was always located in the inner-lower world. When Jesus descended, the event created a *pachacuti*, that is, the end of an era and the beginning of a new one. So this proves his unique power in both the lower world and the future. His death associated with a *pachacuti* can be found in the works of two Indian chroniclers, Guaman Poma de Ayala and Juan de Santa Cruz Pachacuti (Szeminski 1992: 191–94).

The TLC's strong emphasis on explicit faith in Jesus Christ as the pathway to salvation is reflected in Guaman Poma's *Nueva Corónica*, and the chronicler gives credit to the Society of Jesus for introducing Christians to faith in Jesus Christ, the gospel and the Passion of Christ (Guaman Poma de Ayala [1615] 1980: 603).

In China, Michele Ruggieri was the first to announce the passion of Christ to the Chinese. By preaching salvation through the incarnation and the passion of Christ, Ruggieri encouraged kerygmatic preaching.[6] Like Ruggieri, Ricci announces the incarnation of God, and Christ is at the centre of missionary preaching, but Ricci presents Christ as a master rather than a saviour. In short, both Ruggieri and Ricci agree on the importance of the incarnation as one of the main themes of missionary preaching but, unlike Ricci's TZSY, Ruggieri stresses the soteriological aspects, i.e. Christ is the Saviour and Redeemer (Shih 1964: 52). Let us remember the summary of Christian doctrine that Ruggieri and Ricci composed together and included in their Portuguese–Chinese dictionary, which was addressed to the Chinese literati and mandarins in the Jesuits' first years in Zhaoqing. Here, they make reference to the incarnation, the passion and crucifixion of Christ, and his resurrection and ascension (D'Elia 1935: 44–45). In the TZSY, Ricci refers to the incarnation in the eighth and last chapter. He introduces Christ after mentioning the existence of man before the Fall, when the world was free of disease and death, when it was a place of eternal happiness. This is why he himself had to descend to save the world, and hence his name Jesus Christ – transliterated into Chinese as *Ye su*. He established and taught his own teachings for 33 years (TZSY VIII: 628, V–IX; 629, I). In the Compendium of Christian Doctrine, or *Tianzhu Jiaoyao*, dedicated to the catechumens, there is a thorough explanation of the passion of Christ (TZJY: 187–90). And in both the TZSY and TZJY the incarnation is dated according to the Chinese Imperial timeline, that is, in the second year after Emperor *Ai* of Han adopted the title *Yuanshou* 1603 years before. His descent into the world is proven by the testimonies of the 'saints' – *sheng* – a title that, according to Ricci, is used more strictly in the West than in China (TZSY VIII: 629, III; TZJY: 120). The Chinese concept of 'saintliness' is associated with that of sovereignty, in which there is a fusion between the cosmic and the ethical, the religious and the political. Saints – *shengren* – might be considered to be those exceptional individuals who have known how to perfect their nature and thus identify themselves with the order of the world and apply themselves to accomplishing saintliness. The title *sheng* was attributed to the emperors and the ruling dynasty. It could also be applied to Confucius himself, who was considered to be a sovereign without a kingdom. In short, both Ruggieri and Ricci, as well as the missionaries who followed them, borrowed the word *sheng* to translate 'saint' (Gernet 1985: 158).

Jesus Christ and Confucius have been compared as models, one for the West and the other for the East. However, unlike Jesus Christ, what made Confucius a model to his disciples is his constant search for perfection (Ching 1977: 79–80). In contrast, at least in general terms, it is the historical nature of divine revelation – first to the Jews on Mount Sinai and then to the rest of mankind – in Jesus Christ that marks an essential difference between the idea of the Christian God and Confucianism. Jesus Christ is a historical figure; his whole life represents this historical revelation. Even though there is a soteriological dimension to the Confucian notion of wisdom through which the wise man is conceived of as a person aware of having a mission to save the world from moral and socio-political degeneracy, the uniqueness of the historical dimension of salvation is absent (Ching 1977: 143 onward).

Ricci, however, does not make this comparison, but just makes it clear that Christ is above any king, any teacher, saint or scholar. In sum, according to Criveller, the TZSY's Christology may be incomplete, but certainly not manipulated (1997: 112). The Jesuit Giulio Aleni (1582–1649) – who regarded Ricci as his teacher – was the first missionary to introduce a detailed account of the life of Jesus, together with theological considerations about the mystery of Christ, in China.[7] However, before Aleni, Diego de Pantoja had composed a piece on the Symbol, probably between 1608 and 1610, which was collected and published after his death as a posthumous collection of his writings, the *Pangzi Yiquan*. In a part of this collection Pantoja explains the passion and death of Jesus Christ and his descent into hell, and there is a long summary about the mysteries of the incarnation, passion, resurrection and ascension (Criveller 2003: 441 onward; Criveller 1997: 120–21).

But the figure of Christ – especially the passion – raised controversies among the Chinese. In the subsequent anti-Christian Writings, the figure of Christ was to be associated with that of a criminal. Gernet cites an extract from the proclamation after the arrest of the heterodox associations at the time of the Christian 'persecution' in Nanjing in 1616–17. The facts it mentions with respect to Christ are the same as those Ricci cites in the TZSY:

> these barbarians have published a Brief Version of the Doctrine of the Lord of Heaven, where they clearly state that the Lord of Heaven was born on one particular year during the reign of Emperor Ai of the Han dynasty, that his name is Jesus and that his mother was called *Yalima* [*Maliya*, for Mary]. So he is only a barbarian of the Western seas. They also say he died at the hands of evil officers, nailed to a structure in the shape of the number ten. Therefore he is only a barbarian condemned to death. How can a barbarian that dies executed be named the Lord of Heaven?
>
> (Gernet 1985: 56–57)[8]

In summary, in the missions in Peru and China the Jesuits had to 'find' and 'translate' their God on local soil. 'God' was *Dios* in Spanish, without any other possible translation in Quechua, and *Viracocha* could be no contestant. Meanwhile, Indian idolatry was expressed through the *huacas*, which were almost ubiquitous. In the China mission on the other hand, Ricci was among the first to find a 'local competitor' in the Great Ultimate, the *Taiji*, but felt comfortable with the names for the Christian God – *Tianzhu* and *Shang di* – that he and Ruggieri had been using so far. Problems regarding translating 'God' would come later.

On the immortality of the Soul

The immortality of the soul – sustained by Neoplatonic theology and placed at the heart of the Aristotelian tradition – was declared philosophically provable by the Lateran Council in 1513 and soon became another challenge for the Jesuits to impose in the missions. One way or another, they found ways to express and transmit the idea that the individual was made up of a corruptible body and an immortal soul. Interestingly, in both the Peru and China missions the immortality of the soul as a Christian principle was entangled with a local belief in a continuing exchange between the living and the dead. In the Andes, the belief that the dead are active in the world of the living explains the cult of ancestors. The ancestors' sphere of influence affected practically every aspect of human activity. In the rituals conducted in their honour, their kin invoked them to ensure the fertility of the earth and an adequate supply of the goods needed for subsistence; ancestors prayed for the health and well-being of their descendants, who asked for their ancestors' intercession to ensure the political fortunes of the group that fell under their tutelage (Ramos 2010: 10–11). In China, the exchange between the living and the dead was expressed concretely in the transfer of food, money and goods to the deceased. In return, the living expected to receive certain material benefits, including luck, wealth and progeny.

In the Christian world there is no exchange between the living and the dead; the latter are not believed to be able to receive anything from the living. There is instead a relationship between the living and God and the dead and God. This is very much linked to specific notions about heaven and the underworld. Indeed, upon the death of the body, the soul goes to heaven or hell, or in most cases to purgatory, and the aim of ritual is to help the salvation of the soul (Standaert 2008: 35–37).

In the Andes, the chronicler Pedro de Cieza de Leon is well known for his record of the various beliefs with respect to the afterlife. Indeed, Cieza dedicated a remarkable number of pages to descriptions of the funeral customs of the different Andean people that he was able to observe during his travels; for example, the widespread custom of burying deceased noblemen with their wives, possessions and food, so that in the afterlife they could enjoy the same status and pleasures as they enjoyed in their life on earth (Bernand and Gruzinski 1992: 30; MacCormack 1993: 89). Cieza concluded that the Andeans shared similar beliefs to the Europeans, i.e. that there is an afterlife which in many ways is similar to life in this world. The sources that describe pre-Hispanic funerary rituals for the most part focus on the Incas. The bodies of the Inca rulers were embalmed by means of a careful treatment that, according to these same authors, conserved an appearance very much as in life. They were dressed in clothing and insignias designating their rank and were placed not in tombs but in temples or their own homes, where their kin could provide them with the care and attention that benefitted their status (Ramos 2010: 21). Following the Book of Wisdom in the Old Testament, Acosta traces the origin of idolatry in a father with an image – a portrait in this case – of his beloved dead son. Thus, the portrait of a mortal human being would be worshipped by the father, as if it were 'God'. 'Our Indians' says Acosta, followed these same steps and reached the highest of idolatries. Indeed, the Indians in Peru knew how to preserve the bodies of dead Inca kings and lords without any kind of odours and without decay for more than two hundred years. However, the Indians were not satisfied with preserving the bodies of the dead, so they also made statues. And every king would have an idol or statue of himself when alive, made of stone, to be worshipped during his life as well (HNyM: 146–47). Before Acosta, Polo de Ondegardo's inquiries had revealed the importance of tombs and temples to the native population. Moreover, the sacking of shrines had shown the conquistadors, colonists and missionaries how the bodies of the dead were laid out. In the *Instrucción contra las Cerimonias. Y Ritos que Usan los Indios Conforme al Tiempo de Su Infidelidad* included in the DCC, in the third chapter, 'De los Difuntos' – On the Departed – it says that the Indians 'shared the belief that the souls lived in the afterlife and that good people had glory and evil ones had sorrow'. Therefore, 'they put great diligence in preserving the bodies and supporting them and honouring them after death' (DCC: 266). It was reported to be a common practice among the Indians 'to secretly unearth the bodies of the deceased from the churches … to bury them in *huacas*, or the hills or the *pampas*, or in theirs or the deceased's homes, to give them food and drink' (DCC: 256). In general terms, for the Spanish – as Acosta puts it – the Indians in Peru believed that the soul was not extinguished in the afterlife and that the good would find glory and the evil punishments, 'so it was not difficult to persuade them with regard to these aspects' (HNyM: 147).

The immortality of the soul is dealt with in the first sermon of the Third catechism. In this sermon, Indians are expected to follow the same reasoning as the Spanish, since if their ancestors 'were deceived and erred in many things, they knew well that there is another life, and that the souls that come out of the bodies are not extinguished, but live in the afterlife' (DCC: 364–65). Among the last sermons, the thirtieth begins by introducing the general topic of death, which comes equally to all human beings, so men live in a constant state of preparation (DCC: 734). After stressing the importance of adequate preparation for death, the sermon warns that if any stain should remain on the soul as a result of its not having fully expiated its sins – something few people could be certain to have done – the soul will then be sent to purgatory, where it is purified with fire in order to meet the conditions for finally entering heaven. The living have to help the dead with prayers, good works and especially masses. All of these things, the sermon explains, together with offerings of wheat, rams and wax given in the name of the deceased, are received by God 'as if the deceased themselves had made these offerings; through charity and the love of God all Christians are one, and therefore they may help each other' (DCC: 743–44). In this way, the Church expressed the compromise it had reached with the custom of leaving offerings in tombs (Ramos 2010: 85–86).

The Spanish found various solutions to the problem of how to both translate and express the term 'soul'. By now, we know that from the *Plática* by Santo Tomás to the TLC corpus the tendency in the earlier texts to use neologisms gradually decreased until Spanish loan words gained the upper hand. Initially, a variety of Quechua terms to designate the Christian soul were employed by the Spanish. In the *Plática* by Saint Tomás, 'soul' – *alma* – is glossed as both *songo* – heart – and *camaquem*, and in the Spanish–Quechua section of his dictionary, there is another term, *çamaynim* – breath – not present in the *Plática* (Taylor 2003a: 24). According to Alan Durston, the most interesting of these terms is *camaquem*, the agentivized form of the verb *cama*, which originally referred to the activity of animating or strengthening living beings. In native cosmology it was considered certain that the world and everything in it, including human beings, were animated by a vital force that made it possible for things to be what they were, or to realize their potential. This vital force, *camac* or *camaquem*, was identified by some observers as a possible equivalent of the Christian soul, although they also identified it with the principle that had brought everything into being. However, the fact that *camac* was also attributed to animals and objects led some Churchmen and functionaries to state that Andeans did not recognize the fundamental difference between themselves and animals. They noted that the Indians attributed faculties to things that, from a Christian point of view, were exclusively reserved to animated beings, in addition to assigning an extraordinary, even sacred, character to a variety of objects and natural phenomena (Durston 2007: 213–14). At the time of the TLC, the search for a Quechua term for 'soul' was abandoned, and the term *ánima* was imposed. Indeed, the TLC imposed the Latin form *ánima* – instead of the Spanish *alma* – as the only legitimate term to express this Christian concept. Nevertheless, the Latinism *ánima* was also frequently used in Spanish (Taylor 2003a: 23; Durston 2007: 213–14).

Apart from being a pathway to hell, as it was a clear manifestation of idolatry, drunkenness – *borracheras* – was harshly attacked throughout the TLC corpus. The twenty-third sermon warns the Indians against *borracheras*, as it is like 'killing your soul', and it is a mortal sin because 'it takes away from you what God endows you with: human judgement and reason; so you turn into a horse, or even worse' (DCC: 627).

In Chinese thought, no radical dualism separated body from soul, unlike the central concern that governed European notions of life and death. One of the primary goals of Chinese funeral rites, in fact, was to keep the corpse and spirit together during the initial stages of death; separation prior to the ritualized expulsion from the community was thought to bring disaster (Standaert 2008: 35). To prove the immortality of the soul, the Jesuits had first to be able to express and explain the relationship between immanence versus transcendence, which was certainly a major challenge for them as it was alien to Chinese thought. Nevertheless, both Ruggieri and Ricci had to face the challenge. As we saw in Chapter Four, they introduced the three Aristotelian souls, resorting to the word *hun*, which – according to Jacques Gernet – denoted the more volatile of the two souls attributed to men by the Chinese, *hun* and *po*. *Hun* is inseparable from vital energy – *qi* – and will sooner or later vanish with death, as will *po*, which is the greater of the two souls. But neither have anything in common with the Christian distinction between eternal soul and mortal body. In fact, the concept of *hun* did not play any important role in the philosophical ideas of the Chinese and was so lacking in substantiality that sometimes the missionaries took recourse to a transcription from the Latin, in the form *yanima*. After Ricci's death, some missionaries opted for yet another term, *xing* understood as 'human nature'. (Gernet 1985: 146). The Chinese believed in a universe composed of one sole substance, *qi*, and Ricci did not hesitate to attack and reject this notion, as the Jesuits regarded it as 'material energy' instead of spiritual – another distinction that did not exist in China. Far from representing an abstract notion, *qi* is perceived by the Chinese in the innermost part of a being and in its body (Cheng 2002: 35–36). All the principles that control the body are reduced to the presence and action of *qi*, the vital energy that is also the ultimate constitution of the body as such (Zhang 2000: 368). However, the omnipresent *qi* was not the only competitor the Jesuit found when transmitting the immortality of the soul to the Chinese. As mentioned in Chapter Three, Ricci also found that the Buddhist transmigration of souls could rival the Christian immortal soul. Ricci dedicated two chapters of the TZSY to this subject.

Rewards and punishments in the afterlife

The introduction by the missionaries of the Christian principle of the immortality of the soul was intimately linked to the rewards and punishments in the afterlife. As already mentioned, in the 'New World' the Spanish had to decide whether the Indians could be saved or not. Many years later, as one of the main theologians in the Peru mission, Acosta's view regarding the salvation of the Indians was quite optimistic; his optimism was grounded on his understanding of their intrinsic good nature. For Acosta, the Indians were saved when the word of God reached the New World, a divine rescue that weakened the devil's power, thus protecting the Indians' nature (Sánchez 2002: 18–24). Indeed, both in *De Procuranda* and the DCC, Acosta draws the line between nature and grace, which does not mean that nature is the devil's domain, as nominalists would claim.[9] After establishing missions from the Lima College as a starting point, Acosta narrates that he visited a village, where he stayed for some days to preach and hear the Indians' confessions. He claims that 'even though these people do not seem very enlightened, or maybe they did not understand the general language – Quechua – I still found traces of predestined people' (EM: 267). As mentioned in the previous chapter, with Acosta's imprint, the DCC clearly states that salvation is possible if men believe in Jesus Christ; explicit faith in Christ as the means to achieve salvation is at the core of the DCC. In the Greater catechism, the conditions for being saved are explained slightly more thoroughly than in the Brief catechism and the *Plática*:

> P: What is necessary to please God and achieve salvation?
> R: To believe in Jesus Christ, son of God and Our Lord, by confessing his Holy name and abiding by his law, by placing one's hopes in Him. That is what a good Christian does.
> P. Who believes in Jesus Christ?
> R. He who firmly believes in the mysteries revealed to us by his Holy Word and contained in the Symbol or Creed.
> P. Who confesses his Holy name?
> R. He who is baptised and receives the other Sacraments.
>
> (DCC: 72–73)

It is important to stress here that Acosta redefines salvation in the realm of the supernatural, and there is no other possible way. Thus divine grace becomes indispensable for earning salvation and Jesus Christ shows the path to recovering grace after having lost it with original sin (DCC: 88). In turn, idolatry is the path to hell where the devil, the *Supay*, dwells. A doomed man is 'He who adores any creature, or has idols or *huacas*, or believes in false sects and heresies or dreams and omens, which are vanity and a ruse of the Devil' (DCC: 135–37). In the DCC, explicit faith in Christ as a *sine qua non* for reaching salvation plays a leading part throughout the pages of the whole corpus; and the devil, the *Supay*, awaits in hell those who do not believe in Jesus Christ, worship the *huacas*, break the commandments, do not confess and do not do penance. Regarding the *Supay*, Gerald Taylor has posed a key question: Why, among the various spirits in the Andes, did the Church choose the *Supay* to embody Satan, the enemy of God and the human race? First, it seems evident that the devil the Spaniards saw did not necessarily coincide with the same concept of 'spirit' of the ancient Andeans. And, second the spanish chroniclers themselves did not initially have the same view of *supay*. For instance, according to Santo Tomás, a *supay* can be either an evil or good angel, as well as a goblin. But the positive aspects faded away in the late sixteenth century, and *supay* gradually became a synonym of evil goblin, ghost or spirit of the doomed (Taylor 1980).

In China, there were mixed opinions about heaven and hell after death, and they did not belong to the realm of Confucianism. The idea the Chinese had of heaven – *Tian* – was understood as a cosmic power which rewarded good and punished evil. A good deed produced a proportionate good reaction, and an evil one a bad reaction; and all this happened in this world (Standaert 1994: 85). It was Chinese Buddhism that harboured notions of a punitive underworld, salvation, and merit-making. The first Jesuits in China had translated the notions of heaven and hell into Chinese with the Buddhist words *diyu* and *tiantang*, respectively. The term Ricci uses for hell is *di yu*,

PLATICA 'BRE-
VE EN QVE SE CONTIENE
LA SVMMA DE LO QVE HA
de faber el que fe haze
Chriftiano.

YEME HIIO MIO CON attencion , y dezirte he breueméte lo que te conuiene faber para faluarte.
Primeramente fabras, q̃ ay vn Dios que es feñòr de todo, hazedor del Cielo y dela tierra y de todas las cofas, y no ay mas q̃ vn

QVICHVA.

S Onco camalla vyari-
huay churi, huc yfcay
fimıllapı, quifpincayqui
pacyachácayquicta villa
fcayq. Caytarac ñaupac-
lla yachay. HucllamDios
llapayma hayca cacpa a-
pun. Cay Diosmi hanac-
pachacta, caypachacta,
llapaymaymana, haycay
manactahuampas camar
cá, pacarichircá. Pay ça-
Pallá

AYMARA.

A Squi chuyma ifapita
yocày. Maya paya a-
rònquihua quifpiñama-
tàqui yatiñama yaticha-
máma. Acara nàyra yáti-
ma. Mayniquipi DIOS
taque cuna càuquina à-
pupa. Aca DIOS alca
haracpàcha, acapàcha,
taque cuna càuquifa ca-
miri, luriripi. Hupa ça-
pa

Figure 5.1 Doctrina Christiana y Catecismo, Platica breve, Lima (1590)
Source: Courtesy of Lilly Library, Bloomington, Indiana University

which literally means 'prison on earth' and it is different from the Western transcendental notion of hell. In the Buddhist tradition, the idea of salvation is to pass through the courts of *di yu* to eventually be reborn. *Di yu* is a place of retribution, where one pays for one's misdeeds. Even though Buddhism has an equivalent that comes quite close to the notion of hell, China lacked the idea of the devil as master of that domain. Evil is solely the responsibility of he who commits it, and that is what is at stake in the prison on earth (Goodrich 1981: 67–68). Nevertheless, the Buddhist equivalent of hell did not stop Ricci from his strategy of criticizing Buddhism and approaching Confucianism. In his collection of moralistic sayings, the *Jiren Shipian* [1608] (1965) (hereafter cited as JRSP), which has been translated as *Ten Paradoxes of an Exceptional Man*, Ricci offers more arguments against Buddhist reincarnation, especially in the eighth chapter. He claims that

> if people doomed to hell knew that they can come back to this world, the suffering in hell would not be the most serious they can ever experience; therefore, hell will not be a means for the Lord of Heaven to punish vices.
> (JRSP VIII: 241, V–IX)

The Chinese convert – and former devoted Buddhist – Yang Tingyun, was of the idea that the two concepts of heaven and hell had been stolen from the West and actually denied that the notions belonged to Buddhism (Yang Tingyun [1621] 1965: 513–15; Standaert 1994: 88). Moreover, Ricci also had to confront one of the beliefs in the Confucian tradition, i.e. that men are naturally predisposed to good, which clearly opposed the notion of the Christian man as a sinner who can only be redeemed and saved through his good deeds. Indeed, Chinese optimism, as Gernet points out, opposed the Christian pessimism that recognizes no good or virtue in man without effort (1985:163). And as Ricci concluded in his *Jiren Shipian*, 'virtue will always be rewarded after death' (JRSP VIII: 251, VIII–IX).

Based on insights acquired in discussions held with the rulers of the different kingdoms in China, Confucius's disciple Meng zi (380–289 BC) – latinized as Mencius – sustained that the best way of ruling was to put into practice the virtue of humanity – *ren*.[10] What in Confucius was only intuition, in Mencius became a categorical claim about the goodness of human nature in a moral sense, part of cosmic harmony (Cheng 2002: 139 onward). Therefore, Ricci introduced the notion of free will, or intention – *yi*, to explain that men are free to choose between doing good or evil. In short, the source of good or evil lies in the intention, and there cannot be good or evil without motivation. Right from the first chapter of his TZSY, Ricci resorted to the Confucian books to depict the virtuous man, the nobleman – the *jun zi* – as opposed to the petty man – the *xiao ren* – the first being fully dedicated to the cultivation of virtue as the most important accomplishment in this world.[11] Ricci had used this pair of opposites, *jun zi* and *xiao ren*, from his first treatise in Chinese, On Friendship or *Jiaoyou lun*, onward. In this early work, he portrays the nobleman as the virtuous friend, disinterested in worldly pleasures, unlike the petty man or *xiao ren*. In the TZSY, Ricci states that the choice to do good is what differentiates the gentleman:

We can avoid the effort to do good, but it is only when we do it that we can be called noblemen. When the Lord of Heaven endowed men with their nature, they were able to do good as well as evil … . Therefore, since men can take or abandon goodness, not only is the merit of goodness increased, but that merit is of men's own … . This merit is not that of honor and rank, but the true merit of virtue. Even though human nature is basically good, one cannot say that all men in this world are good. Only the virtuous men are good.

(TZSY VII: 567, V–IX; 568, III–V)

Ricci establishes three motives for doing good deeds, although they are not at the same level. The lowest is to go to heaven and to avoid going to hell; the second is to return favours to the Lord of Heaven; and the third and highest is to agree with and obey the Lord of Heaven's will (TZSY VI: 539, VII–IX; 540, I). The wicked, says Ricci, avoid doing evil for fear of being punished and the good for love of virtue. Even so, people need to be shown the torments and punishments in hell:

If we want people to only seek protection in virtue and we only show them the beauty of moral behaviour, they will never see it for themselves because they are full of selfish desires … . We will only describe to them the sufferings of hell to frighten them and the glories of heaven to motivate them; in time, they will listen.

(TZSY VI: 540, V–IX)

In summary, a lifetime is too short to cultivate virtue so heaven is nothing but the glorious place where those who cultivated humanity and righteousness in the past and in the present – in this world – reunite. However, the Chinese literati objected to this. In the first place, the theory of reward in heaven and punishment in hell would encourage people to act exclusively motivated by personal gain. Whereas a noble man imbued with Confucian learning, instead, does good regardless of what is to come in the afterlife. Many of them also found it unfair that heaven should be reserved for Christians, while other good people would be excluded from it. In short, this theory would not encourage the common man to do good. Last but not least, according to the Chinese literati – portrayed by Ricci as Confucians – the Jesuits attached little value to earthly existence (Standaert 1994: 90). A core element of their objection was filial piety, to which Ricci never gave importance. Filial piety is the reciprocity relationship *par excellence*: it is a son's natural response to his parent's love in the general context of family harmony and brotherhood between generations. The Chinese scholar with whom Ricci debates in the TZSY insists on the virtue of filial piety in this world rather than a reward in an afterlife. But Ricci had to turn a blind eye to it, not only to shift the Chinese's attention towards the transcendental dimension, but also because love for the Lord of Heaven came first. As filial piety was expressed in this world, and not in the world beyond, Ricci gave no importance to it.

This chapter has examined how the DCC in Peru and the TZSY in China outlined the path to salvation. In the DCC, salvation is only possible through explicit faith in Christ. Conversely, one is led along the pathway to hell by the devil in the Andes, *Supay*. However, for the Spanish, the possibility of Indians falling into *Supay*'s clutches was not the greatest concern. In the seventeenth century there was a permanent fluctuation of opinions among churchmen on the most effective means of eradicating Andean idolatry and in this respect the *huacas* were much more threatening than the *Supay*. In the case of the TZSY, its orthodoxy is associated with Confucian orthodoxy – *zheng* – proved through reason – *li*. The doctrine of the Lord of Heaven provides the cultivation of virtue with a transcendental dimension, rendering salvation possible. As previously mentioned, Ricci's TZSY was the first piece of writing by a Jesuit in China that clearly proclaimed that its teachings were 'on the orthodox side'. Indeed, Ricci introduces a strict and exclusive division between orthodoxy and heterodoxy, which involves his interpretation of Confucianism. However, in the Chinese context 'the orthodox Way' meant much more than a purely religious awareness of heaven as the highest authority in the universe. The practice of orthodoxy – orthopraxy – contributes to the realization of a whole set of ideals regarding harmonious social relations, hierarchical order, correct ritual behaviour, benevolent rule and, as a result of all this, a stable government and general prosperity (Zürcher 1993: 76; 91–92).

   In Peru, Acosta did not stop short of shaping doctrine according to supernatural theology to redefine the conditions for salvation through explicit faith in Jesus Christ. This was so, even if the mystery of Christ was too complex for the Indians. Acosta could afford to bluntly and openly impose these conditions, for the Jesuits and churchmen in Peru – unlike the Jesuits in China – did not have to convince anyone. The Jesuits in China, on the other hand, composed different kinds of doctrinal texts for their audience, without hiding their true intentions as missionaries. Indeed, they found ways to transmit the mysteries of faith in different registers depending on the hearers. Reason, and not hate, as Ricci says in his TZSY, was an alternative to mere impugnation, but this did not mean that he could not be vehement and unfairly critical himself. Finally and not less important, all the decisions made by the Jesuits in China would be eventually questioned, whether by the Chinese themselves, their fellow Jesuits or, in the seventeenth century, the mendicant orders and Rome. The extent to which Ricci's decisions regarding precise Chinese vocabulary to transmit Christian terminology and precepts did not pass unnoticed has been shown. However, in Peru, Acosta – among other Spaniards – would not be questioned for his – sometimes imprecise – interpretations of *Viracocha*, at least not until scholars in the late twentieth century reviewed his works.

Notes

1 The second type of idolatry of human invention can be subdivided into two different forms: one that consists in worshiping idols, which differs from that which worships *what was and is something*, such as idolatry of the dead. In the fourth chapter of the *HNyM*, Acosta refers to this as a 'type of idolatry with the deceased', following the Book of Wisdom. He points out that the Incas, not content with idolizing the bodies of the deceased, went even further and made statues of them.

2 In this regard, Nicolas Standaert points out that, even though the idea of creation by a personal being was a notion foreign to the Chinese, it was present in popular traditions such as that of the Eternal Venerable Mother (*wusheng lao mu*), whose cult was brought to full development by the sectarian Precious Scrolls (*baojuan*) in the late Ming and Early Qing periods. See Nicolas Standaert, *Yang Tingyun, Confucian and Christian in Late Ming China. His Life and Thought* (1988. Leiden: Brill) p. 110.

3 From a letter in Latin sent by Ricci to Acquaviva in 1604, found by D'Elia at the Biblioteca Casanatense de Roma (ms. N. 2136) (FR II: 297–98, note 1).

4 '*Et in fine si Taikieum intelligerent esse primum principium substantiale, intelligens, et infinitum; illud asserimus quidem ess Deum et nihil aliud.*'

5 Longobardo's views were comprised in a collection of treatises with the Portuguese title *Resposta Breve sobre as Controversias do Xámti, Tienxin, Limhoên, e Outros Nomes e Termos Sinicos: per Se Determinar quaes delles Podem ou Nao Poden Usarse nesta Xrandade. Dirigida aos Padres das Residencias da China, pera a Verem, a Depois, Emviare como u Seu Parecer sobre Ella ao Nosso Padre Visitador em Macao*. Amidst the Rites Controversy in the last decade of the seventeenth century, Louis Champion de Cicé (1648–1737) (MEP – Mission Etrángeres de Paris), Vicar Apostolic of Siam and Japan, translated the treatise into French, under the title of *Anciens Traitez de Divers Auteurs sur les Ceremonias de la Chine* of 1701. In this translation Longobardo appears as Longobardi.

6 Kerygmatic preaching is direct teaching addressed to the hearer, with substantial knowledge regarding the good news of Christ's salvation, death and resurrection as basic grounds of the Christian faith.

7 The first twelve years of Aleni's mission were focused on natural revelation and, according to Gianni Criveller, in a second period that lasted twenty-five years Aleni incorporated positive revelation based on dogmatic Christology. Aleni's catechism, *The Origin of All Things* or *Wanwu zhenyuan* continues the apologetic method followed by Ricci, using natural revelation as a shared starting point, in dialogue with the Chinese literati to whom the book is addressed. Nevertheless, Aleni carefully avoids reducing the Christian God to the natural concept of a Supreme Being who can be known via man's simple search for the origin of all things.

8 The number ten in Chinese is similar to a cross.

9 This is the opinion of Fernando Cervantes, who makes reference to an alleged nominalist separation of nature and grace made by Acosta instead of a Thomistic stand of an intrinsic goodness of nature independent of the effects of grace (Cervantes 1994: 20 onward).

10 In pre-Confucian texts, *ren*, 'humanity' also translated as 'benevolence' referred to the particular virtue of kindness, especially the kindness of a ruler to his subjects. And Confucius made of *ren* a general virtue; the man of *ren* is the perfect man, the nobleman – *jun zi* (Chan 1963:16).

11 In its origins, the term *jun zi* referred to noblemen in the pre-Confucian Classics. But with Confucius – especially in the Analects – these terms gained another meaning, in which the quality of a man is not determined by birth, but now also has moral value, to the extent that it has acquired a stronger moral than social significance (Cheng 2002: 60).

Conclusions

Let us remember the letter from Saint Ignatius of Loyola, quoted in the Introduction of this book, and his advice to Diego Laínez to avoid any particular inclination towards certain places – missions – instead of others. It has, however, been shown throughout this book why the Jesuits indeed felt inclinations and how they expressed their preferences when it came to leaving Europe for the missions overseas. The Society's expansionism aroused expectations, and those expectations in turn led to appraisals of the mission spaces that the same Society of Jesus created in the search for its own universalism.

This has also been the story of two men. Before being sent to Peru, Acosta claimed he felt 'a certain disgust to think that what is over there – the Portuguese Indies – is more than what is over here'. Be this true or not, he became the main theologian in the Peru mission and, as such, he shaped evangelization in Peru, in part through a fictional dialogue with the theologians in Spain, reflected in De *Procuranda Indorum Salute* and crystallized in the DCC. Matteo Ricci spent almost half his life in the Middle Kingdom, where he died. From his letters and works, and indeed his TZSY, it is not difficult to gather how absorbed Ricci was by and in that 'other world of China', an expression he used in a letter to Acquaviva from Macao before entering China in February 1583 (OS II: 35). One subtle thread running through this book has been the different sides of China present in Acosta's works. Before Ruggieri and Ricci established a residence in Zhaoqing, inspired by Francis Xavier's apostolate, Acosta established in *De Procuranda* different evangelization methods for the missions, seeing the *Indias Orientales* as the only place where apostolic preaching was possible. Eleven years after finishing *De Procuranda* in Mexico on his way to Spain, he held to the same idea when refuting Sánchez's plans for a war against China in two memos.

Acosta came back to Europe in the late 1580s, when China was beginning to be portrayed in missionaries' chronicles. However, it had not yet become an object of intellectual curiosity in Europe when Acosta's *Historia Natural y Moral de las Indias* (1590) elaborated on the few works circulating, in particular a compilation of letters from Jesuits, including those by Michele Ruggieri and Matteo Ricci. Indeed, Acosta seems to have gleaned fresh information regarding the China mission from this collection and included certain aspects of it in his *Historia Natural y Moral de las Indias*. In chapter five of the sixth book, 'On the Kind of Letters and Books used by the Chinese', Acosta states that:

> as countless as things are, the letters or figures the Chinese – *los chinas* – use to depict them are also countless.... he who reads or writes in China, as the mandarins do, must know eighty-five thousand figures or letters; and those whose reading skills are perfect, a hundred and twenty or so thousand. It is prodigious, and would be hard to believe were it not for the fact that fathers of our Society are currently learning their language and writing.... This is the reason why in China the literati are so esteemed.... And it is why only they are mandarins and take the offices of governors, judges and captains.
>
> (HNyM: 186)

Ricci defined Chinese 'letters' – *letras* – as 'such a gentile yet difficult invention', according to which 'as many things as are in this world, so many are the letters, so different from one another', as he explained in a letter in Spanish to the royal representative in the Philippines, Juan Bautista Román (OS II: 45). Acosta's remark on Chinese 'letters' echoes Ricci's observation that there is 'one letter' for 'each thing'. And he – again, based on Ricci – underscores the political role of the literati in China and how esteemed they are. Acosta encountered other non-alphabetic writing systems in Peru, such as *quipus*. These systems proved effective means of indoctrination and for the confession of the Indians, as shown in Acosta's statements, although – over time – any use of them other than the religious was to be prohibited. In short, the dark side of this 'permission' to still use these systems for religious purposes amounted to a rejection of them as forms of knowledge. According to Acosta, if there was a difference, a real difference, from the Greeks and Romans, it was not the Indians' rites and customs; in fact, it was foolish – *necio* – to hate them as inhuman and devilish, considering that the Greeks and the Romans had similar rites and customs, and even worse. Instead, the difference lay in the ancient gentiles' natural knowledge, which exceeded that of the Indians. In sum, the Indians lacked supernatural light, philosophy and natural doctrine (HNyM: 139). And here lies one of the major divergences between the Peru and China missions for a man like Acosta. Unlike the Chinese, the Indians were excluded from the 'lettered city'. Meanwhile, Ricci assimilated the Chinese with the philosopher-kings of Plato's Republic, not as a Western speculation, but as a fact. In sum, both Ricci and Acosta made of China an ideal space for the realization of projects, the Society of Jesus' own universal projects, which found limits in the Peru mission, those of – quoting Walter Mignolo – coloniality (Mignolo 2000). This was a space that indeed fed a universal project, without being part of it; it became a telling proof of how 'colonial' could not be part of 'universal'.

If we think of a tension of distance and proximity between the two missions in Peru and China, there was proximity between them as they were both subjected to how Europeans saw the different religious worlds through their own lens, adjusting the unfamiliar to the familiar, resorting to a limited canon of European concepts and views. Indeed, missions came closer when the missionaries, wherever they were, attempted to make complex belief systems comprehensible to themselves. However, in this tension, the distance – the abyss – was marked by coercion, and this would grow greater in the seventeenth century. In Peru, a consistently disparaging view of that Andean world, justified by its 'idolatrous' and 'superstitious' nature, led to vehement extirpation of idolatry campaigns in the seventeenth century. Official support quickly grew for a systematic and forceful initiative to solve what was regarded as a widespread problem. The extirpation amounted to a series of inquisitorial investigations held in a succession of parishes. Specially commissioned and empowered visitors, the *visitadores de idolatria*, invited individual confessions of guilt and denunciations of other religious offenders. The Jesuit Pablo José de Arriaga's *Extirpación de la Idolatría en el Perú* [1621] (1968) – On the Extirpation of Idolatry in Peru – offers a detailed guide to a *visita* procedure. The Jesuits supervised the instruction and detention of those regarded as the principal religious offenders from the beginning of their campaigns in the second decade of the seventeenth century. However, the Society of Jesus withdrew from official participation in the idolatry campaigns in the 1650s. This withdrawal could be related to disagreement hinging on the measure of force and coercion that should accompany the continuing evangelization of the Indians (Mills 1994: 88–94).

Acosta never dismissed coercion as a means of achieving certain goals; it was justified by the Indians' condition as subjects of 'Christian princes'. In *De Procuranda*, this tension between persuasion and coercion is always ambiguous; but that ambiguity does not darken the search for a balance between the two. This book has stressed Acosta's ambiguity over various aspects of pre-Hispanic religions and culture. Although he was very close to Viceroy Toledo and the colonial authorities and accommodated to their conditions for establishing the mission in Peru, he set his own tone regarding the Hispanicization of the Indians. Moreover, his appraisals of the Indians' idolatry do not lead to the conclusion that he was obsessed with its extirpation. Arriaga, instead, could be regarded as a more obedient apprentice of Viceroy Toledo. Meanwhile, in China and Europe, the Jesuits' views and methods were questioned during what became the 'Chinese rites and terms-controversy'. But, by and large, controversies in the China mission challenged the Jesuits to ponder and reflect once again on their methods and translation policies, as well as on the decisions initially made. The struggle for accuracy continued.

Glossary of Chinese terms

Ai 哀
bai fo xiang 拜佛像
Bailudong shuyuan 白鹿洞書院
Baojuan 寶卷
bu ru 補儒
Celiang Fayi 測量法義
Chen rui 陳瑞
Cheng Yi 程頤
Da Xue 大學
dao 道
Daiyi pian 代疑篇
Dao Xue 道學
di yu 地獄
Donglin shuyuan 東林書院
Donglin xuepai 東林學派
Ershiwu yan 二十五言
Fen shu 焚書
Feng Yingjing 馮應京
gelao 閣老
gong jiao 公教
Guandong 廣東
gui shen 鬼神
he shang 和尚
huo 或
Jian an 建安
Jiaoyou lun 交友論
Jiren Shipian 畸人十篇
jue hun 覺魂
jinshi 進士
jun zi 君子
kong 空
la miu 剌謬
Le an 樂安
liang shan 良善
li 理
Li Madou 利瑪竇

Li zhi 李贄
Li zhizao 李之藻
ling hun 靈魂
lou 陋
Lu Xiangshan 陸象山
Majia 馬家
Ma Tang 馬堂
mo gui 魔鬼
mo zhe 模者
nian qi jing 念其經
Ouyi Zhixu 蕅益智旭
Pangzi Yiquan 龐子遺詮
Pi xie ji 闢邪集
po 魄
qi 氣
Qiuyou pian 逑友篇
Qu Taisu 瞿太素
ren 仁
ru jia 儒家
ru zhe 儒者
San Huai 三淮
San Jiao 三教
San shan lunxue ji 三山論學記
San zi jing 三字經
seng 僧
shan ren 山人
Shang di 上帝
Shen Que 沈㴶
sheng 聖
sheng hun 生魂
sheng shui 聖水
Shenjing yuelu 聖經約錄
shi 士
Si shu 四書
suoyiran 所以然
Taiji 太極
Taiji tushuo 太極圖說
Taizhou 泰州
Tian 天
Tiandi 天帝
Tianshen 天神
Tianxue 天學
Tianzhu guo 天竺國
Tianzhu shilu 天主實錄
Tianzhu shiyi 天主實義

Tianzhu shengxiang lueshuo 天主聖像略說
tian tang 天堂
Tian zhu 天主
Tianzhu Jiaoyao 天主教要
Tianzhu shenjiao yueyan 天主聖教約言
Tuiyan zhengdao lun 推驗正道論
Wanli 萬曆
Wang Pan 王泮
Wanwu Zhenyuan 萬物真原
Wang Yangming 王陽明
wei zhe 為者
wokou 倭寇
Wusheng lao mu 無生老母
wu jing 五經
wu wei 無為
Xiguo Jifa 西國記法
xiang 像
xiao 孝
xiao ren 小人
xie 邪
xinxue 心學
xing 性
xi shan 習善
xi shi 西士
Xu Guangqi 徐光啟
yang 陽
Yang Tingyun 杨廷筠
Yesu 耶穌
yi lai zhe 依賴者
yin 陰
Yi ti 一體
Yuanshou 元壽
Zhang Huang 章潢
Zheng 正
Zheng dao 正道
Zhengde 正德
zhi zhe 質者
zhong shi 中士
Zhou Dunyi 周敦頤
Zhu Hong 袾宏
Zhu Xi 朱熹
zi li zhe 自立者
zuo zhe 作者

Bibliography

Manuscript collections

ARSI, *Fondo Gesuitico*
ARSI, *Prov. Japonica-Sinica*
ARSI, *Prov. Toletana*
ARSI, *Assistentia Hispaniae*
Lilly Library (LL)

Primary sources

Acosta, José de. [1590] (1940) *Historia Natural y Moral de las Indias, en que Se Tratan las Cosas Notables del Cielo, y Elementos, Metales, Plantas y Animales de Ellas: y Ritos y Ceremonias, Leyes y Gobierno y Guerras de los Indios.* Mexico: FCE Edición preparada por Edmundo O'Gorman.
——[1588] (1954a) *De Procuranda Indorum Salute*, in *Obras del P. José de Acosta de la Compañía de Jesús. Estudio Preliminar y edición del P. Francisco Mateos de la Misma Compañía.* Madrid: Biblioteca de Autores Españoles.
——[1590] (1954b) *Historia Natural y Moral de las Indias* in *Obras del P. José de Acosta de la Compañía de Jesús. Estudio Preliminar y Edición del P. Francisco Mateos de la Misma Compañía.* Madrid: Biblioteca de Autores Españoles.
——(1954c) *Escritos Menores*, in *Obras del P. José de Acosta de la Compañía de Jesús. Estudio Preliminar y Edición del P. Francisco Mateos de la Misma Compañía.* Madrid: Biblioteca de Autores Españoles.
Anónima, Jesuita. (1968) *Relación de las Costumbres Antiguas de los Naturales del Piru*, in Esteve Barba, Francisco (ed.) *Crónicas Peruanas de Interés Indígena. Edición y Estudio Preliminar de Francisco Esteve Barba.* Madrid: Biblioteca de Autores Españoles CCIX.
Anonymous. [1605] (2002), *Tianzhu jiaoyao* 天主教要 Jap-Sin I, 57a, in Standaert, Nicolas, 鐘鳴旦 and Dudink, Adrian, 杜鼎克 (eds) *Yesuhui Luoma dang'anguan Ming Qing Tianzhujiao Wenxian*, 耶穌會羅馬檔案館, 明清天主教文獻, *Chinese Christian Texts from the Roman Archives of the Society of Jesus.* Taipei: Taipei Ricci Institute, Vol. I: 307–74.
Arriaga, Pablo José de. [1621] (1968) *Extirpación de la Idolatría del Pirú*, in Esteve Barba, Francisco (ed.) *Crónicas Peruanas de Interés Indígena.* Madrid: Biblioteca de Autores Españoles CCIX.

Cartas de Japao & China. (1598) *Cartas que os Padres e Irmãos da Companhia de Iesus Escreverao dos Reynos de Iapão & China aos da Mesa Companhia da India & Europa des do Anno de 1549 atè o de 1580*, [Early Jesuit Missionary Letters from Japan and China] 2 vols. Evora: Manoel de Lyra, Vol I.

Colín, Francisco. [1904] (1663) *Labor Evangelica de los Obreros de la Compañía de Jesús en las Islas* Filipinas *por el P. Francisco Colín de la Misma Compañía, Nueva Edición Ilustrada con Copia de Notas y Documentos por el Padre Pablo Pastells, SJ*. Barcelona: Heinrich y Compañía; Madrid: Ioseph Fernandez de Buendia.

D'Elia, Pasquale. (1942–49) *Fonti Ricciane. Edite e Commentate da Pasquale M. D' Elia, SI sotto il Patrocinio della Reale Accademia D'Italia. Storia dell' Introduzione del Cristianesimo in Cina*. Roma: La Librería dello Stato, Vol. I–III.

Doctrina Christiana en Letra y Lengua China, Compuesta por los Padres Ministros de los Sangleyes de la Orden de Santo Domingo. (1593) Primer libro impreso en Filipinas. Facsimile del ejemplar existente en la Biblioteca Vaticana, con un ensayo histórico-bibliográfico por Fr. J. Gayo Aragón, OP, y observaciones filológicas y traducción española de Fr. Anotinio Doménguez, OP.

Egaña, Antonio, SI (ed.). (1954) *Monumenta Peruana I* (1565–75), Roma: Monumenta Missionum Societatis Iesu Vol. VII.

——(1958) *Monumenta Peruana II* (1576–80), Roma: Monumenta Missionum Societatis Iesu Vol. XIII.

——(1961) *Monumenta Peruana III* (1581–85), Roma: Monumenta Missionum-Societatis Iesu, Vol. XVIII.

Garcilaso de la Vega, el Inca. (1945) *Comentarios reales de los Incas*, Edición al cuidado de Angel Rosenblat del Instituto de filología de la Universidad de Buenos Aires. Prólogo de Ricardo Rojas. Buenos Aires: Emecé, 2 vols.

González de Mendoza, Juan. [1585] (1944) *Historia de las Cosas Mas Notables, Ritos y Costumbres del Gran Reyno de la China …* . Edición, prólogo y notas por el P. Felix García, OSA. Madrid: M. Aguilar Editor.

Guaman Poma de Ayala, Felipe. [1615] (1980–88) *El Primer Nueva Corónica y Buen Gobierno*, Edición crítica de Murra, John V., and Adorno, Rolena, Siglo XXI. México: Instituto de Estudios Peruanos, 3 volumes.

Levillier, Roberto. (1921) *Gobernantes del Perú. Cartas y Papeles, Siglo XVI*, Documentos del Archivo de Indias, Vol. III. Madrid: Imprenta de Juan Pueyo.

——(1924) *Gobernantes del Perú. Cartas y Papeles, siglo XVI*, Documentos del Archivo de Indias, Vol. IV. Madrid: Imprenta de Juan Pueyo.

Li Zhi. [1590] (1975) *Fen Shu* 焚書. *Xu Fen Shu* 續焚書. Beijing: Zhonghua shuju.

Longobardi, Nicolò. (1701), *Traité sur Quelques Points de la Religion des Chinois*. Paris: Jacques Josse.

Loureiro, Rui Manuel. (1992) Um Tratado sobre o Reino da China. Dos Padres Duarte Sande e Alessandro Valignano (Macau, 1590). Introduçao, versao portuguesa e notas de Rui Manuel Loureiro. Macau: Instituto Cultural de Macau.

Loyola, Ignacio de. (1753) *Carta del Bienaventurado PS Ignacio de Loyola, á los Padres, y Hermanos de la Compañía de Jesú*s. La Reimprime para Mayor Gloria de Dios, y Augmento en la Perfeccion de los Religiosos de su Filiacion, el Paternal Afecto del Illmo. Sr. Arzobispo, Obispo de la Puebla de los Angeles. Reimpressa en la Puebla, y por su original en Mexico, por la viuda de Joseph Bernardo de Hogal.

Matienzo, Juan de. [(1567] (1967) *Gobierno del Perú, Edition et Etude Préliminaire par Guillermo Lohmann Villena*. Lima: Institut Français d'Etudes Andines.

Pereña, Luciano (ed.). [1584] (1985) *Doctrina Christiana y Catecismo para Instrucción de Indios. Facsimil de texto trilingüe. Volumen XXVI–2*. Madrid: Consejo Superior de Invenstigaciones Científicas.

Polo de Ondegardo, Juan. (1916) *Informaciones acerca de la Religión y Gobierno de los Incas por el Licenciado Polo de Ondegardo (1571) seguidas de las Instrucciones de los Concilios de Lima*. Lima: Imprenta y Librería Sanmarti y Ca.

Ricci, Matteo. (1942–49) *Storia dell'Introduzione del Cristianesimo in Cina*, nuovamente edita ed ampiamente commentata col sussidio di molti fonti inedite e delle fonti cinesi da Pasquale M. D'Elia, SI. Roma: La Libreria dello Stato.

——(1596) (1965), *Xiguo Jifa* 西國記法. Taibei: Taiwan xuesheng shuju 臺灣學生書局.

——[1603] (1965) *Tianzhu Shiyi* 天主實義, in Li Zhizao, 李之藻 *Tianzhu Chuhan*. Taibei: Taiwan xuesheng shuju 臺灣學生書局.

——[1608] (1965). *Jiren Shipian* 畸人十 篇, in Li Zhizao 李之藻 *Tianzhu Chuhan*. Taibei: Taiwan xuesheng shuju 臺灣學生書局.

——[1603] (1985) *The True Meaning of the Lord of Heaven (T'ien-chu Shih-i)*, translated, with Introduction and Notes by Douglas Lancashire and Peter Hu Kuo-chen, SJ, A Chinese-English Edition by Edward J. Malatesta, SJ. St. Louis: The Institute of Jesuit Sources.

——(1999) *Lettere della Cina*. Italy: Ancona.

——(2000) *Della Entrata della Compagnia di Giesú e Christianitá nella Cina*. Macerata: Quodlibet.

——(2005) *Dell'Amicizia*. Macerata: Quodlibet.

——[1595] (2009) *On Friendship. One Hundred Maxims for a Chinese Prince*, translated by Timothy Billings. New York: Columbia University Press.

Ruggieri, Michele/Luo Mingjian 羅明堅. [1584] (2002) *Tianzhu Shilu* 天主實錄, Jap-Sin, I, 189, in Standaert Nicolas, 鐘鳴旦 and Dudink, Adrian, 杜鼎克 (eds) *Yesuhui Luoma dang'anguan Ming Qing Tianzhujiao Wenxian*, 耶穌會羅馬檔案 館, 明清天主教文獻, *Chinese Christian Texts from the Roman Archives of the Society of Jesus*, Vol. I: 1–86. Taipei: Taipei Ricci Institute.

Santo Tomás, Domingo de. [1560] (1951) *Grammatica o Arte de la Lengua General de los Indios de los Reynos del Peru, Reproducción Facsimilar Publicada, con un Prólogo, por Raúl Porras Barrenechea*, Ediciones del Instituto de la Facultad de Letras en el IV Centenario de la Universidad Nacional Mayor de San Marcos. Lima: Ediciones del Instituto de Historia de Lima.

——[1560] (1951) *Lexicon o Vocabulario de la Lengua General del Peru*. Valladolid: Francisco Fernandez de Cordova; edición facsimilar, Lima: Universidad Nacional Mayor de San Marcos.

Tacchi Venturi, Pietro, SJ. (1911–13) *Opere Storiche del P. Matteo Ricci SI, Edite a Cura del Comitato per le Onoranze azionali con Prolegomeni Note e Tavole dal P. Pietro Tacchi Ventura SI*, 2 vols. Macerata: Stab. Tip. Giorgetti.

Valignano, Alessandro, SI. [1583] (1954) *Sumario de las Cosas de Japón (1583). Adiciones del Sumario de Japón (1592)*, edited by José Luis Alvarez Taladriz, Vol. I, Monumenta Nipponica Monographs (No. 9). Tokyo: Sophia University.

——[1586] (1972) *Catechismus Christianae Fidei in quo Veritas Nostrae Religions Ostenditur, et Sectae Japonenses Confutan-tur*, facsimile edition. Tokyo.

Vargas Ugarte, Ruben, SJ. (1951) *Concilios Limenses (1551–1772)*, Vol I. Lima.

——(1952) *Concilios Limenses (1551–1772)*, Vol II, Lima.

Witek, John, SJ and Sebes, Joseph, SJ (eds). (2002) *Monumenta Sinica I (1546–1562)*. Rome: Institutum Historicum Societatis Iesu.

Yang Tingyun, [1621] (1965) *Daiyi Pian* 代疑篇. in *Tianzhujiao Dongchuan Wenxian* 天主教東傳文獻, 影印梵諦岡圖書館藏本巴黎國立圖書館藏手寫本, Taipei: Taiwan xuesheng shuju 臺灣學生書局.

Zubillaga, Félix, SI. [1567](1943) Métodos Misionales de la Primera Instrucción de San Francisco de Borja para la América Española. Archivum Historicum Societatis Iesu, XII.

——(ed)(1956) *Monumenta Mexicana*, Vol. I (1570–80). Roma: Monumenta Historica Societatis Iesu.

——(1959) *Monumenta Mexicana*, Vol. II (1581–85). Roma: Monumenta Historica Societatis Iesu.

Secondary sources

Abril Castelló, Vidal. (1992) *Francisco de la Cruz, Inquisición, Actas I: Anatomía y Biopsia del Dios y del Derecho Judeo-Cristiano-Musulmán de la Conquista de América.* Madrid: Centro de Estudios Históricos, Consejo Superior de Investigaciones Científicas.

Adorno, Rolena. (1987) 'La "Ciudad Letrada" y los Discursos Colonials', *Hispamérica*, Vol. 16, No. 48: 3–24.

——(2000) *Guáman Poma: Writing and Resistance in Colonial Peru.* Texas: University of Texas Press.

Albó, Xavier, SJ. (1966) 'Jesuitas y Culturas Indígenas. Perú 1568–1606. Su Actitud. Métodos y Criterios de Aculturación (Primera Parte)', *América Indígena*, Instituto Indigenista Interamericano, México, Vol. XXVI, No 3: 262–79.

Alden, Dauril. (1996) *The Making of an Enterprise. The Society of Jesús in Portugal, its Empire, and Beyond, 1540–1750.* Stanford, CA: Stanford University Press.

Andrien, Kenneth. (2001) *Andean Worlds. Indigenous History, Culture and Consciousness under Spanish Rule, 1532–1825*, Albuquerque: University of Mexico Press.

Aparicio, Severo, OP. (1972) 'Influjo de Trento en los Concilios Limenses', *Missionalia Hispanica*, Madrid, Vol. XXIX, No 85: 215–39.

Archivum Romanum Societatis Iesu, ARSI. (1992) *Glossario Gesuitico, Guida all' Inteligenza dei Documenti.* Rome: Archivum Romanum Societatis Iesu.

Armas Medina, Fernando de. (1952) 'Evolución Histórica de las Doctrinas de Indios', *Anuario de Estudios Americanos*, Sevilla, Vol. IX: 101–29.

Assadourian, Carlos Sempat. (1988) 'La Renta de la Encomienda en la Década de 1550: Piedad Cristiana y Deconstrucción', *Revista de Indias*, Vol. XLVIII: 182–83, 109–14.

Astrain, Antonio, SJ. (1909) *Historia de la Compañía de Jesús en la asistencia de España*, Vol. III, Mercurian-Aquaviva (Primera parte), 1573–1615. Madrid: Administración de Razón y Fe.

——(1913) *Historia de la Compañía de Jesús en la Asistencia de España*, Vol., Aquaviva (Segunda parte) 1581–1615. Madrid: Administración de Razón y Fe.

——(1914) *Historia de la Compañía de Jesús en la Asistencia de España*, Vol. II, Laínez-Borja, 1556–72. Madrid: Administración de Razón y Fe.

Bartra, Enrique. 1967. 'Los autores del Catecismo del Tercer Concilio Limense', *Mercurio Peruano*, 52/470: 359–72.

Bataillon, Marcel. (1977) *Erasmo y el Erasmismo, Nota Previa de Francisco Rico*, Barcelona: Crítica.

Bernand, Carmen and Gruzinski, Serge. (1992) *De la Idolatría. Una Arqueología de las Ciencias Religiosas.* México: Fondo de Cultura Económica.

Bernard, R.P. Henri. (1937) *Le Père Matthieu Ricci et la Société Chinoise de Son Temps (1552–1610)*. Tientsin: Hautes Études.

Bettray, Johannes, SVD. (1955) *Die Akkommodationsmethode des P. Matteo Ricci SI in China*. Rome: Università Gregoriana.

Boone, Elizabeth Hill and Mignolo, Walter (eds). (1996) *Writing without Words: Alternative Literacies in Mesoamerica and the Andes*. USA: Duke University Press.

Borges, Pedro, OFM. (1960) *Métodos Misionales en la Cristianización de América*. Madrid: Consejo Superior de Investigaciones Científicas.

Boxer, Charles (ed.). (1948) *Fidalgos in the Far East, 1550–1770. Fact and Fancy in the History of Macao*. The Hague: Martines Hijhoff.

——(1967) *South China in the Sixteenth Century. Being the Narratives of: Galeote Pereira, Fr. Gaspar da Cruz, OP, Fr. Martín de Rada, OESA (1550–75)*. Liechtenstein: Nelden.

Brading, David. (1986) 'The Incas and the Renaissance: The Royal Commentaries of Inca Garcilaso de la Vega', *Journal of Latin America Studies*, Vol. 18, No. 1: 1–23.

——(1991) *The First America. The Spanish Monarchy, Creole Patriots, and the Liberal State 1492–1867*. Cambridge: Cambridge University Press.

Braga, J.M. (1963) 'The Beginning of Printing at Macao, Separata de Studia', *Revista Semestral*, No. 12, Julho: 29–137.

Brockey, Liam. (2000) 'Largos Caminhos e Vastos Mares. Jesuit Missionaries and the Journey to China in the Sixteenth and Seventeenth Centuries', *Bulletin of Portuguese/Japanese Studies*, Universidade Nova de Lisboa, Portugal, December, Vol. 1: 45–72.

——(2007) *Journey to the East. The Jesuit Mission to China, 1579–1724*, USA: The Belknap Press of Harvard University Press.

Broggio, Paolo. (2004) *Evangelizzare il Mondo. Le Misioni della Compagnia di Gesù tra Europa e America (Secoli XVI–XVII)*. Prefazione di Francesca Cantù, Rome: Carocci.

Broggio, P., Cantú, F., Fabre, P.A. and Romano, A. (eds). *I Gesuiti ai Tempi di Claudio Acquaviva, Strategie Politiche, Religiose e Culturali tra Cinque e Seicento*, Brescia, Italiy: Morcelliana.

Brooks, Timothy. (1993a) *Praying for Power: Buddhism and the Formation of Gentry Society in Late-Ming China*. USA: Harvard Yenching Institute Monograph.

——(1993b) 'Rethinking Syncretism: The Unity of the Three Teachings and Their Joint Worship in Late-Imperial China', *Journal of Chinese Religions*, Fall, No. 21: 13–44.

Burgaletta, Claudio, SJ. (1999) *José de Acosta SJ (1540–1600). His Life and Thought*. Chicago: Loyola Press.

Burke, Peter. (2006) 'The Jesuits and the Art of Translation in Early Modern Europe', in O'Malley, John, SJ, Bailey, Alexander Gauvin, Harris, Steven and Kennedy, Frank, SJ *The Jesuits II. Cultures, Sciences and the Arts, 1540–1773*. Toronto: University of Toronto Press: 24–31.

Burke, Peter and Po-Chia Hsia, Ronnie. (2007) *Cultural Translation in Early Modern Europe*. Cambridge: Cambridge University Press.

Castagna, Paulo. (1999) 'The Use of Music by the Jesuits in the Conversion of the Indigenous Peoples in Brazil', in O'Malley, John, SJ, Bailey, Alexander Gauvin, Harris, Steven and Kennedy, Frank, SJ *The Jesuits. Cultures, Sciences and the Arts, 1540–1773*. Toronto: University of Toronto Press: 641–58.

Castelnau L'Estoile, Charlotte de. (2007) 'Élection et Vocation. Le Choix de la Mission dans la Province Jésuite du Portugal à la Fin du XVIe Siècle', in Fabre, Pierre-Antoine and Vincent, Bernard (eds) *Missions Religieuses Modernes 'Notre Lieu est le Monde'*. Rome: Ecole Française de Rome: 21–43.

Castillo Arroyo, Javier. (1966) *CatecismosPperuanos en el Siglo XVI*. Mexico: Centro Intercultural de documentación (CIDOC).

Catto, Michela. (2003) *Un Panopticon Catechistico. L' Arciconfraternita della Dottrina Cristiana a Roma in Età Moderna*. Rome: Edizione di Storia e Letteratura.

Catto, Michela, Mongini, Guido and Mostaccio, Silvia. (2010) *Evangelizzazione e Globalizzazione. Le Misione Gesuitiche nell' Età Moderna tra Storia e Storiografia*. Italy: Societa' Editrice Dante Alighieri.

Certeau, Michel de. (2006a) *La Escritura de la Historia*, México: Universidad Iberoamericana.

——(2006b) *El Lugar del Otro. Historia Religiosa y Mística*. Buenos Aires: Katz.

Cervantes, Fernando. (1994) *The Devil and the New World. The Impact of Diabolism in New Spain*, UK: Yale University Press.

Chan, Albert, SJ. (1993) 'Michele Ruggieri SJ – (1543–1607) and His Chinese Poems', *Monumenta Serica*, 41: 139–57.

——(1996) 'Two Chinese Poems Written by Hsu Wei (1521–1593) on Michele Ruggieri, SJ (1543–1607)', *Monumenta Serica*, 44: 317–37.

Chan, Wing-Tsit (ed.). (1963) *A Sourcebook in Chinese Philosophy*. Princeton, NJ: Princeton University Press.

Cheng, Anne. (2002) *Historia del PensamientoCchino*. Barcelona: Ediciones Bellaterra.

Ching, Julia. (1977) *Confucianism and Christianity. A Comparative Study*. Tokyo: Kodhansa International – The Institute of Oriental Religions, Sophia University.

Clossey, Luke. (2008) *Salvation and Globalization in the Early Jesuit Missions*. New York: Cambridge University Press.

Coello, Alexandre. (2008) 'La Reducción de Santiago del Cercado y la Compañía de Jesús (1568–80)', in Dalla Corte, Gabriela *et al.* (eds) *Poder Local, Poder Global en América Latina*. Barcelona: Publicacions i Edicions de la Universitat de Barcelona, 53–67.

Colombo, Emanuele. (2010) 'Gesuitomania. Studi Ricente sulle Misione Gesuitiche', in Catto, Michela, Mongini, Guido and Mostaccio, Silvia (eds) *Evangelizzazione e Globalizzazione. Le Misione Gesuitiche nell' Età Moderna tra Storia e Storiografia*. Italy: Societa' Editrice Dante Alighieri.

Corsi, Elisabetta (ed.). (2008a) *Órdenes Religiosas entre América y Asia. Ideas para una Historia Misionera de los Espacios Coloniales*, Centro de Estudios de Asia y África. México: El Colegio de México.

——(2008b) 'El Debate Actual sobre el Relativismo y la Producción de Saberes en las Misiones Católicas durante la Primera Edad Moderna: ¿Una Lección para el Presente?' in Corsi, Elisabetta (ed.) *Órdenes Religiosas entre América y Asia. Ideas para una Historia Misionera de los Espacios Coloniales*, Centro de Estudios de Asia y África. México: El Colegio de México: 17–54.

——(ed.). (2008c) 'Del Aristoteles Latinus al Aristoteles Sinicus. Fragmentos de un Proyecto Inconcluso', in *Órdenes Religiosas entre América y Asia. Ideas para una Historia Misionera de los Espacios Coloniales*, Centro de Estudios de Asia y África. México: El Colegio de México: 171–186.

——(2008d) '¿Obreros de la Viña o "Savants?" Los Misioneros de la Compañía de Jesús en China: Entre Evangelización y Mediación Cultural', *Estudios de Asia y Africa*, México: Colegio de México, Sep.–Dec., Vol. 43, No. 3 (137): 545–66.

Criveller, Gianni. (1997) *Preaching Christ in Late Ming China: The Jesuits' Presentation of Christ from Matteo Ricci to Giulio Aleni*. Taipei: Taipei Ricci Institute.

——(2003) 'Christ Introduced to Late Ming China by Giulio Aleni, SJ (1582–1649)' in Roman Malek SVD (ed.) *The Chinese Faces of Jesus Chris*t, Sankt Augustin, Vol. II: 437–60.

——(2008) 'Géneros Literarios y Misión Jesuita en China al Final del Período Ming', in Perla Chinchilla and Antonella Romano (eds) *Escrituras de la Modernidad. Los jesuitas entre cultura retórica y cultura científica*. México: Universidad Iberoamericana.

Cummins, Tom. (1998) *Let Me See! Reading Is For Them: Colonial Andean Images and Objects 'Como Es Costumbre Tener los Caciques Señores'*. Washington, DC: Dumbarton Oaks Research Library and Collection: 91–148.

Dehergne, Joseph. (1983) *Un Problème Ardu: Le nom de Dieu en Chinois, in Actes du IIIe Colloque International de Sinologie, Appréciation par l' Europe de la Tradition Chinoise à Partir du XVIIe Siècle*, 11–14 September 1980. Paris: Les Belles Lettres: 13–46.

D'Elia, Pasquale. (1934). Quadro Storico Sinologico del Primo Libro di Dottrina Cristiana in Cinese, *AHSI, III*: 193–222.

——(1935) 'Il Domma Cattolico Integralmente Presentato da Matteo Ricci ai Letterati della Cina. Secondo un Documento Cinese Inedito di 350 Anni Fa', *La Civiltà cattolica*, Anno 86, Vol. II: 35–43.

Delumeau, Jean. (1973) *El Catolicismo de Lutero a Voltaire*. Barcelona: Editorial Labor.

——(2002) *El Miedo en Occidente (Siglos XIV–XVIII). Una Ciudad Sitiada*. Madrid: Taurus.

Demoustier, Adrien (1996) 'L'Originalité des "Exercises Spirituels"', in Giard, Luce and de Vaucelles, Louis (eds) *Les Jésuites à Lâge Baroque (1540–1640)*. Grenoble: Jèrome Millon: 23–35.

Donnelly, John Patrick. (1988) *Antonio Possevino's Plan for World Evangelization*, *The Catholic Historical Review*, Apr., Vol. 74, No. 2: 179–98.

Dudink, Adrian. (2002) Tianshu jiaoyao, The Catechism (1605). Published by Matteo Ricci, *Sino–Western Cultural Relations Journal*, 24: 38–50.

Dudink, Adrian (1995) *Christianity in Late Ming China (Five Studies)*, Doctoral dissertation.

Dunne, George, SJ. (1962) *Generation of Giants. The Story of the Jesuits in the Last Decades of the Ming Dynasty*. London: Burns & Oates.

Durán, Juan Guillermo. (1982) *El Catecismo del III Concilio Provincial de Lima y Sus Complementos Pastorales (1584–1585)*. Buenos Aires: Publicaciones de la Facultad de Teología de la Pontificia Universidad Católica Argentina.

Durston, Alan. (2007) *Pastoral Quechua. The History of Christian Translation in Colonial Peru, 1550–1610*. Notre Dame, IN: University of Notre Dame Press.

——(2008) 'Native-Language Literacy in Colonial Peru: The Question of Mundane Quechua Writing Revisited'. *Hispanic American Historical Review*, 88:1.

Duviols, Pierre. (1977) *La Destrucción de las Religiones Andinas (Conquista y Colonia)*. Universidad Nacional Autónoma de México.

——(1977) 'Los Nombres Quecha de Viracocha, Supuesto "Dios" Creador de los Evangelizadores, Allpanchis', *Revista del Instituto de Pastoral Andina*, 10: 53–64.

Elliott, John. (1984) *El Viejo Mundo y el Nuevo Mundo, 1492–1650*, Madrid: Alianza.

Elman, Benjamin. (2000) *A Cultural History of Civil Examinations in Late Imperial China*, California: University of California Press.

Estenssoro, Juan Carlos (2003) *Del Paganismo a la Santidad. La Incorporación de los Indios del Perú al Catolicismo, 1532–1750*. Lima: Instituto Francés de Estudios Andinos.

Fabre, Pierre-Antoine. (2008) 'Ensayo de Geopolítica de las Corrientes Espirituales. Alonso Sánchez entre Madrid, Nueva España, Filipinas, las Costas de China y Roma, 1579–93' in E. Corsi (ed.) *Órdenes Religiosas entre América y Asia. Ideas para una Historia Misionera de los Espacios Coloniales*. México: El Colegio de México, Centro de Estudios de Asia y África: 85–104.

Fabre, Pierre-Antoine and Vincent, Bernard (eds). (2007) *Missions Religiouses Modernes 'Notre Lieu est le monde'*. Ecole Française de Rome.

Fois, Mario, SJ. (1982) Il Collegio Romano ai tempi degli studi del P. Matteo Ricci, in *Atti del Convegno Internazionale de Studi Ricciani*, Macerata–Rome, 22–25 Ottobre. Macerata: Centro Studi Ricciani: 203–28.

Foss, Theodore N. (1982*)* 'La Cartografía di Matteo Ricci*', in Atti del Convegno Internazionale di Studi Ricciani*, Macerata-Roma, 22–25. Macerata: Centro Studi Ricciani: 177–97.

Fulop Miller, René. (1929) *El Poder y Secreto de los Jesuitas*. Madrid: Biblioteca Nueva.

García, Antonio. (1986) *La Reforma del Concilio Tercero de Lima, in Doctrina Cristiana y Catecismo para Instrucción de los Indios, Corpus Hispanorum de Pace*. Elaborado bajo la dirección de Luciano Pereña, Madrid: Consejo de Investigaciones Científicas.

Gernet, Jacques. (1979) 'Sur les Différentes Versions du Premier Catéchisme en Chinois de 1584', in *Studia Sino-Mongolica*. Festchrift für Herbert Franke, Münchener Ostasiatische Studien. Band 25, Wiesbaden: Franz Steiner Verlag GMBH: 407–16.

——(1985) *China and the Christian Impact. A Conflict of Cultures*. Cambridge: Cambridge University Press.

González de la Rosa, M. (1907) 'El Padre Valera, Primer Historiador Peruano. Sus Plagiarios y el Hallazgo de Sus Tres Obras', *Revista Histórica*, Lima, II: 180–99.

Goodrich, Swann Anne. (1981) *The Peking Temple of Eighteen Hells and Chinese Conceptions of Hell*. St Augustin: Monumenta Serica Series.

Goodman, Howard L. and Grafton, Anthony. (1991) *Ricci, the Chinese, and the Toolkits of Textualists, Asia Major*, Third Series 3/2: 95–148.

Griffiths, Nicholas. (1998) *La Cruz y la Serpiente. La Represión y el Resurgimiento Religioso en el Perú Colonial*. Peru: Pontificia Universidad Católica del Perú, Fondo Editorial.

Gruzinski, Serge. (1999) 'Las Imágenes, los Imaginarios y la Occidentalización', in Carmagnani, M. e*t al.* (ed.) *Para una Historia de América. I. Las Estructuras*. México: Fondo de Cultura Económica.

——(2001) 'Les Mondes Melés de la Monarchie Catolique et Autres "Connected Historie"s', *Annales. Histoire, Sciences Sociales*, 56e Anée, Jan–Feb., No. 1: 85–117.

Gruzinski, Serge and Wachtel, Nathan. (1997) '*Cultural Interbreedings: Constituting the Majority as a Minority'*, *Comparative Studies in Society and History*, Vol. 39, No. 2: 231–50.

Hyland, Sabine. (2006) *The Jesuit and The Incas. The Extraordinary life of Padre Blas Valera, SJ*. Michigan:The University of Michigan Press.

Huang, Martin (ed.). (2007), *Male Friendship in Ming China*. Leiden: Brill.

Huang Wenshu, 黃文樹. (1995) 李贄於利瑪竇的友誼及其 [友論] 之比較, 玄奘佛學研究,民國 95 年 07 月第 127–52頁.

——(1998) 明後學於利瑪竇的交往及其函義, 漢學研究第27卷第3期 (民國98年9月).

Jami, Catherine and Delahaye, Hubert (eds). (1991) 'L'Histoire des Mathématiques vue par les Lettrés Chinois (XVIIe et XVIIIe Siecles): Tradition Chinoise et Contribution Europénne', in *L'Europe en Chine, Interactions Scientifiques, Religieuses et Culturelles aux XVIIe et XVIIIe Siecles*, Memoires de L'Institut des Hautes Études Chinoises, Actes du Colloque de la Fondation Hugot, vus et établis par Catherine Jami et Hubert Delahaye: 147–67.

Jones, Charles B. (2009) *Pi Xie ji* 闢邪集: *Collected Refutations of Heterodoxy by Ouyi Zhixu (*漢益智旭, *1599–1655), Pacific World*, Journal of the Institute of Buddhist Studies, Third Series, Fall, Number 11: 351–407.

Kurtz, Joachim. (2011) 'The Discovery of Chinese Logic', in Makeham, John (ed.) *Modern Chinese Philosophy*, Vol. I. Leiden: Brill.

Lackner, Michael. (1996) 'Jesuit Memoria, Chinese Xinfa: Some Preliminary Remarks on the Organisation of Memory', in Masini, Federico, Battaglini, Marina and Jesuit Historical Institute (eds) *Western Humanistic Culture Presented to China by Jesuit Missionaries (XVII–XVIII Centuries)*. Rome: Institutum Historicum SI: 201–19.

Lam, Joseph C. (2007) 'Music and Male Bonding in China', in Huang, Martin (ed.) *Male Friendship in Ming China*. Leiden: Brill: 70–110.

Lisi, Francesco. (1990) *El Tercer Concilio Limense y la Aculturación de los Indígenas Sudamericanos. Estudio Crítico con Edición, Traducción y Comentario de las Actas del Concilio Provincial Celebrado en Lima entre 1582 y 1583*. Salamanca: Acta Salmaticencia.

Lopetegui, León, SJ. (1942) *El Padre José de Acosta SI y las Misiones*. Madrid: Consejo Superior de Investigaciones Científicas Instituto Gonzalo Fernández de Oviedo.

——(1947) 'Paso por España del P. Alejandro Valignano. Visitador de las Misiones del Asia Oriental de la Compañía de Jesús. Reclutamiento Misional', *Studia Missionalia*, Vol. 3: 1–42.

——(1961) Influjos de Fr. Domingo de Soto, OP en el Pensamiento del P. José de Acosta. Madrid: Universidad Pontificia Comillas: 57–62.

Lopez-Gay, Jesús, SJ. (1972) 'Las Corrientes Espirituales de la Misión del Japón en la Segunda Mitad del Siglo XVI (II Part)', *Missionalia Hispanica*, Vol. XXIX, No. 85: 61–101.

Lubac, Henry de. (1986) *Christian Faith. The Structure of the Apostles' Creed*. London, Geoffrey Chapman.

Lundbaek, Knud. (1979) 'The First Translation from a Confucian Classic in Europe', *China Mission Studies (1550–1800) Bulletin*, I: 2–15.

MacCormack, Sabine. (1985) 'The Heart has its Reasons: Predicaments of Missionary Christianity in Early Colonial Peru', *The Hispanic American Historical Review*, Vol. 65, Aug., No. 3: 443–66.

——(1993) *Religion in the Andes: Vision and Imagination in Early Colonial Peru*. USA: Princeton University Press.

Maldavsky, Aliocha. (2007) 'Administrer les Vocations. Les Indipetae et l'Organisation des Expéditions aux Indies Occidentales au Début du XVII siècle', in Fabre, Pierre-Antoine and Vincent, Bernard (eds) *Missions Religiouses Modernes 'Notre Lieu est le monde'*. Rome: Ecole Française de Rome: 45–70.

Martzloff, Jean-Claude. (1995) 'Clavius Traduit en Chinois', in Giard, Luce (ed.) *Les Jésuites à la Renaissance. Systeme Educatif et Production du Savoir*. Paris, PUF: 309–22.

Maryks, Robert. (2010) *The Jesuit Order as a Synagogue of Jews*. Leiden: Brill.

Marzal, Manuel. (1993) *Historia de la Antropología Indigenista: México y Perú*. México: Editorial Autónoma Metropolitana.

Mateos, Francisco, SJ. (1945) 'Ecos de América en Trento', *Revista de Indias*, Madrid: 559–605.

——(1947) 'Los Dos Concilios Limenses de Jerónimo de Loaysa', *Missionalia Hispanica*, Madrid, Vol. IV, No. 12: 479–524.

——(1949) '*Una Carta Inédita de Alonso de Barzana*', *Missionalia Hispanica*, Madrid, Vol. VI: 143–55.

——(1950) 'Constituciones para Indios del Primer Concilio Limense (1552)' *Missionalia Hispanica*, Madrid, Vol. VII, No. 19.

——(1954) 'Personalidad y Escritos del P. Jose de Acosta', in Acosta, José de *Obras del P. José de Acosta de la Compañía de Jesús. Estudio Preliminar y Edición del P. Francisco ateos de la Misma Compañía*. Madrid: Biblioteca de Autores Españoles: VII–XLIX.

Menegon, Eugenio. (2005) 'The "Teachings of the Lord of Heaven" in Fujian Between Two Worlds and Two Times', in Struve, Lynn A. (ed.) *Time, Temporality, and Imperial Transition. East Asia from Ming to Qing*. USA: University of Hawaii Press.

——(2009) *Ancestors, Virgins and Friars. Christianity as a Local Religion in Late Imperial China*, Harvard-Yenching Institute Monograph Series 69. Cambridge, MA and London: Harvard University Asia Center.

Mignolo, Walter. (1995) 'Occidentalización, Imperialismo, Globalización: Herencias Coloniales y Teorías Postcoloniales', in *Revista Iberoamericana*, Vol. LXI, Jan–June, No. 170–71: 27–41.

——(2000) *Local Histories/Global Designs: Coloniality, Subaltern Knowledges, and Border Thinking*, Princeton, NJ: Princeton University Press.

Millán, José Martínez. (2007) 'La Transformazione della Monarchia Hispana alla Fine del XVI Secolo. Dal Modelo Católico Castigliano al Paradigma Universale Católico-Romano', in Broggio, P. *et al.* (eds) *I Gesuiti ai Tempi di Claudio Acquaviva, Strategie Politiche, Religiose e Culturali tra Cinque e Seicento*. Brescia, Italy: 19–52.

Mills, Kenneth (1994). 'The Limits of Religious Coercion in Mid-Colonial Peru', *Past & Present*, Nov., No. 145: 84–121.

Mills, Kenneth and Grafton, Anthony. (2003) *Conversion: Old Worlds and New, Studies in Comparative History*. Rochester, NY: University of Rochester Press.

Mungello, David. (1985) *Curious Land. A Jesuit Accommodation and the Origin of Sinology* Honolulu: University of Hawai Press.

——(ed.). (1994) *The Chinese Rites Controversy: Its History and Meaning*, Monumenta Serica Monograph Series, XXXIII, Sankt Augustin. Nettetal: Steyler Verlag.

Nadal, Hieronymi. (1962) *Commentarii de Instituto Societatis Iesu (Epistolae et Monumenta P. Hieronymi Nadal, Tomus V)*, edidit Michael Nicolau SI. Roma: Monumenta Historia Societatis Iesu, 90: 54.

Needham, Joseph. (1965) *Science and Civilization in China*, Vols I–V. Cambridge: Cambridge University Press.

Nylan, Michael. (2001) *The Five 'Confucian' Classics*. New Haven and London: Yale University Press.

O'Collins, Gerald, SJ. (1995) *Christology. A Biblical, Historical, and Systematic Study of Jesus Christ*. New York: Oxford University Press.

Ollé, Manel. (2008) 'The Jesuit Portrayals of China Between 1583–1590', *Bulletin of Portuguese/Japanese Studies*, Universidad Nova de Lisboa, Portugal, Vol 16: 45–57.

O'Malley, John, SJ. (1993) *The First Jesuits*. Cambridge: Cambridge University Press.

O'Neill, Charles Edwards. (1997) 'Florida and the 'New' Missiology of the 1560s', in Gagliano, J. and Ronan, Charles SJ (eds) *Jesuit Encounters in the New World: Jesuit Chroniclers, Geographers, Educators and Missionaries in the Americas, 1549–1767*. Rome: Institutum Historicum SI.

Pagden, Anthony. (1988) *La Caída del Hombre. El Indio Americano y los Orígenes de la Etnología Comparativa*. Madrid: Alianza.

Pease, Franklin. (1981) 'Felipe Guarnan Poma de Ayala: Mitos Andinos e Historia Occidental', *Cahiers du Monde Hispanique et Luso-Brésilien*, No. 37: 19–36.

——(1999) 'La Religión Incaica', in M.Carmagnani *et al.* (ed.), *Para una Historia de América. I. Las Estructuras*, El Colegio de México. México: Fondo de Cultura Económica.

Pino, Fermín del. (1990) 'Edición de Crónicas de Indias e Historia Intelectual, o la Distancia entre José de Acosta y José Alcina', *Revista de Indias*, Vol. I, Sept–Dec, No. 190: 861–78.

Pinta Llorente, Miguel de la, OSA. (1952) *Actividades Diplomáticas del P. José de Acosta. En Torno a Una Política, y a un Sentimiento Religioso*. Madrid: Consejo de Investigaciones Científicas.

Po-Chia Hsia, Ronnie. (2009) 'The Jesuit Encounter with Buddhism in Ming China', in Üçerler, M. Antoni, SJ (ed.) *Christianity and Cultures. Japan and China in Comparison, 1543–1644*. Institutum Historicum Societatis Iesu: 19–43.

——(2010) *A Jesuit in the Forbidden City. Matteo Ricci 1552–1610*. Oxford: Oxford University Press.

Presta, Ana María. (2008) 'Juan de Matienzo (1520–79)', in Joanne Pillsbury (ed.), *Guide to Documentary Sources for Andean Studies, 1530–1900*, Vol. III, M–Z. USA: University of Oklahoma Press.

Prodi, Paolo. (1987) *The Papal Prince. One Body and Two Souls: The Papal Monarchy in Early Modern Europe*. Cambridge: Cambridge University Press.

Prosperi, Adriano. (1999) *Otras Indias: Missionari della Controriforma tra Contadini e Selvaggi*, in *America e Apocalisse e Altri Saggi*. Rome-Pisa: Istituti Editoriali e Poligrafici Internazionale.

Puett, Michael J. (2002) *To Become a God. Cosmology, Sacrifice, and Self-Divinization in Early China*. USA: Harvard-Yenching Institute monograph series.

Qiong Zhang. (2000) 'Jesuit Scholastic Psychology and the Confucian Discourse', in O'Malley *et al.* (eds) *The Jesuits. Cultures, Sciences, and the Arts, 1540–1773*. Toronto: University of Toronto Press.

Ramada Curto, Diogo. (2005) 'The Jesuits and Cultural Intermediacy in the Early Modern World', *AHSI*, LXXFV, 147: 3–22.

Ramos, Gabriela. (2010) *Death and Conversion in the Andes. Lima and Cuzco (1532–1670)*. Indiana: University of Notredame Press.

Resines Llorente, Luis. (1992) *Catecismos Americanos del Siglo XVI*, Junta de Castilla y León. Spain: Consejería de Cultura y Turismo.

Restall, Matthew. (2004) *Los Siete Mitos de la Conquista Española*. Barcelona: Paidós.

Ricard, Robert. (1995) *La Conquista Espiritual de México. Ensayo sobre el Apostolado y los Métodos Misioneros de las Órdenes Mendicantes en la Nueva España de 1523–1524 a 1572*. México: FCE.

Rienstra, M. Howard. (1986) *Jesuit Letters from China, 1583–84*. Minneapolis: University of Minnesota Press.

Romano, Antonella. (2005) 'Les Jésuites entre Apostolat Missionnaire et Activité Scientifique (XVI–XVIII Siècles)', *AHSI*, Rome, Vol. LXXIV, Fasc. 147, January–June: 213–36.

——(2008) 'Un Espacio Tripolar de las Misiones: Europa, Asia y América', in Corsi, E. (ed.) *Órdenes Religiosas entre América y Asia. Ideas para una Historia Misionera de los Espacios Coloniales*, Centro de Estudios de Asia y África. México: El Colegio de México: 253–77.

——(2011) 'Multiple Identities, Conflicting Duties and Fragmented Pictures: The Case of the Jesuits', in Oy-Marra, E. and Remmert, Volker, *Le Monde est Une Peinture. Jesuitische Identität und die Rolle der Bilder*. Berlin: Akademie Verlag: 45–69.

Rubiés, Joan-Pau. (2005) 'The Concept of Cultural Dialogue and the Jesuit Method of Accommodation: Between Idolatry and Civilization', *AHSI*, Rome, Vol. LXXIV, Fasc. 147: 237–80.

——(2006) 'Theology, Etnography and the Historicization of Idolatry', *Journal of the History of Ideas*, Vol. 67, No. 4: 571–96.

Rule, Paul. (1986) *K'ung-tzu or Confucius? The Jesuit Interpretation of Confucianism*. Australia: Allen and Unwin.

Said, Edward. (1978) *Orientalism*. USA: Routledge and Kegan Paul.

Salomon, Frank. (2001) 'How an Andean "Writing whithout Words" Works', *Current Anthropology*, Vol. 42, No. 1: 1–27.

Sánchez, Sebastián. (2002) 'Demonología en Indias. Idolatría y Mimesis Diabólica en la Obra de José de Acosta', *Revista Complutense de Historia de América*, Vol. 28: 9–34.

Santos Hernández, Angel, SJ. [1999] *Jesuitas y Obispados. La Compañía de Jesús y las Dignidades Eclesiásticas*, Vol. I. Madrid: Comillas.

Saranyana, Josep Ignasi. (2007) 'Teología Sistemática Jesuita en el Virreinato del Perú (1568–1767)', in Marzal, Manuel and Bacigalupo, Luis (eds) *Los Jesuitas y la Modernidad en Iberoamérica, 1549–1773*. Lima: Instituto Francés de Estudios andinos: 33–53.

Schütte, Josef Franz, SJ. (1980) *Valignano's Mission Principles for Japan*, translated by John J. Coyn, Vols I–II. St. Louis, MO: Institute of Jesuit Sources.

Shih, Joseph. (1964) *Le Père Ruggieri et le Problème de l'Evangélisation en Chine*. Rome: Pontificia Universitas Gregoriana.

Spalatin, Christopher A., SJ. (1975) *Matteo Ricci's Use of Epictetus*, excerpts from doctoral dissertation in Facultate Theologiae Pontificae Universitatis Gregorianae.

Spence, Jonathan. (1985) *The Memory Palace of Matteo Ricci*. USA: Penguin.

——(1988) 'Matteo Ricci and the Ascent to Peking', in Ronan, Charles E. and Oh, Bonnie (eds) *East Meets West: The Jesuits in China, 1582–1773*. Chicago: Loyola University Press, 3–18.

Standaert, Nicolas. (1985) 'Note on the Spread of Jesuit Writings in Late Ming China and Early Qing China', *China Mission Studies Bulletin (1550–1800)*, VII.

——(1988) *Yang Tingyun, Confucian and Christian in Late Ming China. His Life and Thought*. Leiden: Brill.

——(1991) 'Inculturation and Chinese Christian Contacts in the Late Ming and Early Qing', *Ching Feng*, December, Vol. 34, No. 4: 1–16.

——(1993) 'Chinese Christian Visits to the Underworld', in Blussé, Leonard and Zurndorfer, Harriet (eds) *Conflict and Accommodation in Early Modern East Asia. Essays in Honour of Erik Zürcher*. Leiden, Brill: 54–70.

——(1994) 'Heaven and Hell in the Seventeenth Century. Exchange between China and the West', in *The Jesuits 1594–1994. Macao and China, East Meets West, Review of Culture*, No. 21 (2nd series), English edition. Macau: Instituto Cultural of Macau.

——(ed.). (2001a) *Handbook of Christianity in China*, Vol. 1: 635–1800. Leiden: Brill.

——(2001b) 'A Case of Cultural Transmission', in Uhalley, J. and Xiaoxin, Wu (eds), *China and Christianity, Burdened Past, Hopeful future*. USA: ME Sharpe: 81–116.

——(2002) *Methodology in View of Contact between Cultures: The China Case in the 17th Century*. Hong Kong: Center for the Study of Religion and Chinese Society (CSRCS).

——(2003) 'The Transmission of Renaissance Culture in Seventeenth Century China', *Renaissance Studies*, Vol. 17, No. 3: 367–91.

——(2008) *The Interweaving of Rituals. Funerals in the Cultural Exchange between China and Europe*. Washington: University of Washington Press,

——(2009) 'Responses and Reflections', in Üçerler, Antoni J. SJ (ed.) *Christianity and Cultures: Japan and China in Comparison 1543–1644*, Bibliotheca Instituti Historici SI 68. Rome: Institutum Historicum Societatis Iesu: 61–64.

Stern, Steve. (1992) 'Paradigms of Conquest: History, Historiography, and Politics', *Journal of Latin American Studies*, Vol. 24, Quincentenary Supplement: The Colonial and Post Colonial Experience. Five Centuries of Spanish and Portuguese America: 1–34.

Struve, Lynn A. (ed.) (2005). *Time, Temporality, and Imperial Transition. East Asia from Ming to Qing*. USA: University of Hawaii Press.

Subramanyan, Sanjay. (1997) 'Connected Histories: Notes toward a Reconfiguration of Early Modern Eurasia', *Modern Asian Studies*, Vol. 31, No. 3: 735–62.

Szeminski, Jan. (1992) 'La Transformación de los Significados en los Andes Centrales (Siglos XVI–XVII)', in Gossen, Gary H. *et al.* (ed.) *De Palabra y Obra en el Nuevo Mundo*. México: Siglo Veintiuno Editores:181–230.

——(2010) '¿Qué Sabemos de Quillqa en Qulla Suyu?', *Estudios Latinoamericanos*, 30: 129–86.

Taylor, Gerald. (1980) 'Supay', *Amerindia* 5, Paris: Association d'Ethnolinguistique Améridienne.

——(2003a) *El Sol, la Luna y las Estrellas No Son Dios … . La Evangelización en Quechua (Siglo XVI)*. Travaux de l'Institut Français d'etudès andines.

——(2003b) *Amarás a Dios sobre Todas las Cosas. Las Confesiones Quechuas, Siglos XVI–XVII*. Perú: Colección Biblioteca Andina de Bolsillo, IFEA No. 25, Lluvia editors.

Üçerler, Antoni, SJ. (2003) Alessandro Valignano: Man, Missionary and Writer, *Renaissance Studies*, Vol. 17, No. 3: 337–66.

Uhalley, J. and Wu, Xiaoxin (eds). (2001) *China and Christianity, Burdened Past, Hopeful Future*. USA: ME Sharpe.

Urbano, Henrique. (1981) *Wiracocha y Ayar. Héroes y Funciones en las Sociedades Andinas*. Cusco: Centro de Estudios Rurales Andinos 'Bartolomé de las Casas'.

Urton, Gary. (1998) 'From Knots to Narratives: Reconstructing the Art of Historical Record Keeping in the Andes from Spanish Transcriptions of Inka Khipus', *Etnohistory*, Summer, 45: 3.

——(2002) 'An Overview of Spanish Colonial Commentary on Andean Knotted-String Records', in Quilter, Jeffrey and Urtonin, Gary (eds) *Narrative Threads. Accounting and Recounting in Andean Khipu*. Texas: University of Texas Press: 3–25.

Van Engen, John. (1986) 'The Christian Middle Ages as an Historiographical Problem', *The American Historical Review*, Vol. 91, June, No. 3: 519–52.

Vargas Ugarte, Ruben, SJ. (1941) *Los Jesuitas del Perú (1568–1767)*. Lima.

——(1953) *Impresos Peruanos (1584–1650)*, Biblioteca Peruana, Vol. VII. Lima.

Varo, Francisco. (1990–92) 'La Edición Crítica del Catecismo Romano', *Scripta Theologica*, 22: 539–94.

Villegas, Juan, SJ. (1975) *Aplicación del Concilio de Trento en Hispanoamérica, 1564–1600. Provincia Eclesiástica del Perú*. Uruguay: Instituto Teológico del Uruguay.

Werner, Michael and Zimmerman, Bénédicte. (2006) 'Beyond Comparison: Histoire Croisée and the Challenge of Reflexivity', *History and Theory 45*: 30–50.

Witek, John, SJ and Sebes, Joseph, SJ (eds). (2002) *Monumenta Sinica*, Vol. I (1546–62). Rome: Institutum Historicum Societatis Iesu.

Yang, C.K. (1961) *Religion in Chinese Society: A Study of Contemporary Social Functions of Religion and Some of Their Historical Factors*. Berkeley: University of California Press.

Zhang Kai. (1997) *Diego de Pantoja y China. Un Estudio sobre la 'Política de Adaptación de la Compañía de Jesús'. Traducción al Español: Tang Baisheng y Kang Xiaolin*. Beijing: Editorial de la Biblioteca de Beijing.

Zhang, Qiong. (2000) 'Jesuit Scholastic Psychology and the Confucian Discourse', in O'Malley *et al.* (eds), *The Jesuits. Cultures, Sciences, and the Arts, 1540–1773*. Toronto: University of Toronto Press.

Zupanov, Ines G. (2001) *Disputed Missions. Jesuit Experiments and Brahmanical Knowledge in Seventeenth Century India*. India: Oxford University Press.

——(2003) 'Twisting a Pagan Tongue. Portuguese and Tamil in Sixteenth Century Jesuit Translations', in Mills, Kenneth and Grafton, Anthony *Conversion: Old Worlds and New*, Studies in Comparative History. Rochester, New York: University of Rochester Press: 109 – 139.

——(2007) 'Correnti e Controcorrenti. La Geopolítica Gesuitica in Asia (XVI Secolo)', in Broggio, P., Cantú, F., Fabre, P.A. and Romano, A. (eds) *I Gesuiti ai Tempi di Claudio Acquaviva, Strategie Politiche, Religiose e Culturali tra Cinque e Seicento*. Brescia, Italia: Morcelliana: 205–18.

Zürcher, Erik. (1993) 'A Complement to Confucianism. Christianity and Orthodoxy in Late Imperial China', in Huang, Chun-Chieh and Zürcher, Erik (eds) *Norms and the State in China*, Sinica Leidensia, Vol. XXVIII. Leiden: Brill: 71–92.

——(1994) 'A Jesuit Accommodation and the Chinese Cultural Imperative', in Mungello, D. (ed.) *The Chinese Rites Controversy: Its History and Meaning*. Nettetal: Monumenta Serica Monograph Series XXXIII: 31–64.

——(1995) 'In the Beginning: 17th-Century Chinese Reactions to Christian Creationism', in Huang, Chun-Chieh and Zürcher, Erik (eds) *Time and Space in Chinese Culture*. Leiden: Brill: 132–66.

——(1997) 'Confucian and Christian Religiosity in Late Ming China', *The Catholic Historical Review*, Vol. 83, No. 4: 614–53.

Index